More Than Friend

Katharine Bronson in Asolo

More Than Friend

The Letters of Robert Browning to
Katharine de Kay Bronson

EDITED, WITH AN INTRODUCTION, BY
MICHAEL MEREDITH

WITH THE EDITORIAL ASSISTANCE OF
RITA S. HUMPHREY

Armstrong Browning Library of Baylor University
and
Wedgestone Press

Published by
Armstrong Browning Library of Baylor University
P.O. Box 6336, Waco, TX 76706
and
Wedgestone Press
P.O. Box 175, Winfield, KS 67156

Distributed by
Wedgestone Press

Library of Congress Cataloging in Publication Data

Browning, Robert, 1812–1889.
  More than friend.
  Bibliography: p.
  Includes Index.
    1. Browning, Robert, 1812–1889—Correspondence.
2. Bronson, Katharine de Kay, 1834–1901.   3. Poets,
English—19th century—Correspondence.   I. Bronson,
Katharine de Kay, 1834–1901.   II. Meredith, Michael
III. Humphrey, Rita S.   IV. Title.
PR4231.A438 1985   821′.8   83–50736
ISBN 0–911459–06–5

Manufactured in the United States of America.

To
CHRIS

Contents

THE LETTERS

Contents

Illustrations

$\mathcal{P}$reface

THE NATURE AND IMPORTANCE of Robert Browning's friendship with Katharine de Kay Bronson has been overlooked by almost all his biographers and critics. Although Mrs. Bronson's two published articles on Browning have been frequently quoted, she is known simply as Browning's American hostess in Venice, the friend to whom he dedicated his last book of poems. Writers who have been given access to Mrs. Bronson's papers have used them to fill in factual detail of the relatively uneventful last decade of Browning's life and have neglected their important biographical significance. In 1952 Betty Miller's stimulating but perverse *Robert Browning: A Portrait* acknowledged that Mrs. Bronson and her daughter were "the major emotional preoccupation" of Browning's final years, but since then no one has attempted to come to terms with the meaning of this remark.

This book is intended to do just that. It publishes for the first time in their entirety all the known letters from Browning and his sister Sarianna to Mrs. Bronson. Mrs. Bronson's side of the correspondence is lost, and was almost certainly destroyed by Browning's daughter-in-law Fannie shortly after her husband's death, but one letter to Browning and eight to Sarianna survive and are printed in their appropriate places in the sequence, where they clearly show Mrs. Bronson's lively graphic style. Mrs. Bronson's articles, "Browning in Asolo" and "Browning in Venice," have been rescued from the magazines in which they first appeared and are reprinted as appendices, as are the unpublished memoirs about Browning in Venice by another American expatriate, D.S. Curtis. The editorial principles and style I have followed are those outlined in Philip Kelley and Ronald Hudson's editorial manual printed in *Browning Institute Studies*, Volume 9, pp. 141–160.

The Introduction relates the letters and reminiscences to Browning's life and poetry, traces the development of Browning's friendship with Mrs. Bronson, explains its growing complexity and assesses its significance for both of them. In putting forward my conclusions I am encouraged by the support I have received from Mrs. Bronson's grand-daughter, Nannina Fossi, who has not only put all the Bronson family papers at my disposal but has welcomed me to her homes in Florence and Asolo. In Asolo I had the pleasure of staying with her at La Mura, the house where

Mrs. Bronson entertained Browning in the autumn of 1889. Marchesa
Fossi's memories of her mother, the former Edith Bronson, remain fresh
and lively and she helped me to understand the many personalities in
Browning's Venetian circle. More important, she corroborated my initial
ideas about the nature of the relationship between her grandmother and
Browning. Without Nannina Fossi's help and enthusiasm this book could
not have been written.

My interest in Mrs. Bronson began in 1978 with a paper I read to the
Ascham Society at Eton College, called "What happened at Asolo?" I
am grateful to my friends in the Ascham Society, and especially to Howard
Moseley and to John Roberts, for their encouragement in urging me to
pursue the subject. Since then I have received generous assistance from
librarians and friends in England and America, including Warner Barnes,
Ashley Brown, John Bury, Herbert Cahoon Jnr., Charles Cox, Helen
Garton, Eleanor Garvey, Mihai Handrea, Gertrude Herbert, John Hitner,
Marni Hodgkin, the late Walter Houghton, Jennie Jennings, Edward R.
Moulton-Barrett, Vivien Noakes, Clifford Press, Vincent Quinn, Christo-
pher Ramsey, Donald H. Reiman, Marion de Kay Rous, Stuart and Sophie
Sperry, Helen Webb, John Wilson, Cary and Peggy Woodward, all of
whom have made my research a very great pleasure. I am also most
grateful to my mother and my brother Tony for reading the proofs and
offering much valuable advice.

I owe a considerable debt of thanks to the staff of the Armstrong
Browning Library at Baylor University, Waco, Texas: to the director,
Dr. Jack W. Herring, for his hospitality and genial, kind interest; to the
librarian, Betty A. Coley, for her indefatigable energy and constant help;
to my assistant, Rita S. Humphrey, who has made a number of valuable
discoveries and performed wonders at the typewriter. In addition to her
patience in reading proofs and many other tasks, I am grateful to Mrs.
Humphrey for editing the D.S. Curtis manuscript in Appendix C. The
Armstrong Browning Library, which owns the letters of Browning to
Mrs. Bronson, has kindly allowed me permission to publish them and to
quote from other unpublished material in its possession. Similar permis-
sion has been granted by the following institutions: the Ashmolean
Museum, Oxford; Balliol College, Oxford; the Fitzwilliam Museum,
Cambridge; the Harry Ransom Humanities Research Center, University
of Texas at Austin; the Houghton Library, Harvard University; the Isabella
Stewart Gardner Museum, Boston, Mass.; the Pierpont Morgan Library,
New York; the Carl H. Pforzheimer Library, New York; Sheffield Univer-
sity Library; Wellesley College Library. John Murray, the owner of the
Browning copyright, has given his permission for publication, as well as
allowing me to consult and quote from the unpublished letters from
Browning to George Smith in his possession.

I received a generous grant from the Busk Fund for travel to Italy in
1981 and to America in 1982, and I much appreciate the personal interest

Sir Douglas and Lady Busk have taken in the book. I have received equal generosity from my former pupil Josh Latner, who has lent me his New York apartment whenever I have needed it, and who has nursed the book along with the kindest attention over the past three years.

Two special debts remain to be acknowledged. Philip Kelley has selflessly put his expertise and vast knowledge of the Brownings at my disposal. His regular letters of advice, encouragement and discovery from across the Atlantic have been a constant source of inspiration, and have cemented a friendship begun many years ago. A three-day working holiday with Philip, Betty Coley and Rita Humphrey in Kansas was the highlight of my research for this book. The fifth member of our party, Chris Davis, has shared much of my travel and been the sternest of critics, best of friends. To our many hours of profitable discussion together I owe most, and to him the book is dedicated.

The Timbralls, Eton College Michael Meredith
23 April 1984

Cue-Titles, Abbreviations & Symbols

ABL	Armstrong Browning Library, Baylor University, Waco, Texas.
Ashmolean	The Ashmolean Museum, Oxford, England.
BAF	*Browning to His American Friends*, ed. Gertrude Reese Hudson, New York, 1965.
Balliol	Balliol College, Oxford, England.
Barclay	"Diary of Miss Evelyn Barclay," *Baylor Browning Interests Series Five*, Waco, Texas, 1932.
BBIS	*Baylor Browning Interests Series*, Waco, Texas, 1927–
BIS	*Browning Institute Studies*, New York, 1973–
BL	The British Library, London.
Browning Collections	*The Browning Collections. Catalogue of Oil Paintings, Drawings & Prints; Autograph Letters and Manuscripts, Books ... the Property of R.W. Barrett Browning, Esq.* London, 1913. Reprinted in Munby, *Sale Catalogues*, VI (1972), 1–192.
"Browning in Asolo"	Katharine Bronson, "Browning in Asolo," *The Century Magazine*, 59 (April, 1900), 920–931. Reprinted as Appendix A.
"Browning in Venice"	Katharine Bronson, "Browning in Venice," *The Century Magazine*, 63 (February, 1902), 572–584. Reprinted as Appendix B.
Browning Memorials	*Browning Memorials: A Catalogue of Books, Drawings, Autograph Letters, and other Relics.* Offered for sale by Bertram Dobell, London, 1913. Reprinted in *BIS*, 2, 77–118.
BT	*Browning's Trumpeter: The Correspondence of Robert Browning and Frederick J. Furnivall*, ed. William S. Peterson, Washington, D.C., 1979.
Charnwood	Dorothea Thorpe, Lady Charnwood, *Call Back Yesterday*, London, 1937.
Checklist	Philip Kelley and Ronald Hudson, *The Brownings' Correspondence: A Checklist*, New York and Winfield, Kansas, 1978.
Curtis	D.S. Curtis' manuscript entitled "Robert Browning." See Appendix C where it is published from the original in the Armstrong Browning Library.
De Vane	William C. De Vane, *A Browning Handbook*, 2nd ed., New York, 1955.

DI	*Dearest Isa: Robert Browning's Letters to Isabella Blagden*, ed. Edward C. McAleer, Austin, Texas, 1951.
Edel	Leon Edel, *The Life of Henry James*, 2 vols., London, 1977.
Fossi	Papers in the possession of Marchesa Nannina Fossi, Asolo and Florence, Italy.
Griffin	W. Hall Griffin, *The Life of Robert Browning*, completed and edited by H.C. Minchin, London, 1910.
Handbook	Mrs. Sutherland Orr, *A Handbook to the Works of Robert Browning*, London, 1885.
Henrey	Mrs. Robert Henrey, *Greenleaves*, London, 1976.
Hewlett	Dorothy Hewlett, *Elizabeth Barrett Browning: A Life*, New York, 1952.
Houghton	Houghton Library, Harvard University, Cambridge, Mass.
Hulton	Zina Hulton, "Fifty Years in Venice." Unpublished manuscript in Ashmolean Museum, Oxford, England.
IGM	Isabella Stewart Gardner Museum, Boston, Mass.
LF	Thomas Westwood, *A Literary Friendship: Letters to Lady Alwyne Compton*, London, 1914.
LL	*Learned Lady: Letters from Robert Browning to Mrs. Thomas FitzGerald*, ed. Edward C. McAleer, Cambridge, Mass., 1966.
LRB	*Letters of Robert Browning*, ed. Thurman L. Hood, New Haven, Conn., 1933.
Mallock	W.H. Mallock, *Memoirs of Life and Literature*, New York, 1920.
Memories	Fannie Barrett Browning, *Some Memories of Robert Browning*, Boston, 1928.
Meredith	Papers in the possession of Michael Meredith, Eton, Windsor, England.
Miller	Betty Miller, *Robert Browning: A Portrait*, London, 1952.
Moore	Clara Bloomfield-Moore, "Robert Browning," *Lippincott's Magazine*, Vol. XLV, No. 46 (May, 1890), 683–691.
Morgan	Pierpont Morgan Library, New York.
Murray	Papers in the possession of John Murray, publisher, London.
N&Q	*Notes and Queries*.
NL	*New Letters of Robert Browning*, ed. William C. De Vane and Kenneth L. Knickerbocker, New Haven, Conn., 1950.
Orr	Mrs. Sutherland Orr, *Life and Letters of Robert Browning*, rev. Frederic G. Kenyon, London, 1908.
Personalia	Edmund Gosse, *Robert Browning: Personalia*, London, 1890.
RB	Robert Browning.
Reconstruction	Philip Kelley and Betty A. Coley, *The Browning Collections: A Reconstruction*, Waco, Texas, New York, London and Winfield, Kansas, 1984.
Rucellai	Papers in the possession of the Rucellai family, Florence, Italy.

RWBB	Robert Weidemann Barrett Browning, son of the poets.
SB	Sarianna Browning, sister of the poet.
SBHC	*Studies in Browning and His Circle*, Waco, Texas, 1973–
Scripps	Browning Collection, The Ella Strong Denison Library, Scripps College, Claremont, California.
Sheffield	Sheffield University, England.
Tennyson Centre	Tennyson Research Centre Collection, Lincoln, England, by courtesy of Lord Tennyson and Lincolnshire Library Service.
Tragi-Comedy	Maisie Ward, *The Tragi-Comedy of Pen Browning*, New York, 1972.
Ward	Maisie Ward, *Robert Browning and His World*. Vol. 1: *The Private Face*, London, 1968. Vol. 2: *Two Robert Brownings?*, London, 1969.
Whiting	Lilian Whiting, *The Brownings: Their Life and Art*, Boston, 1911.
Wilson	Grace Elizabeth Wilson, "Robert Browning's Portraits, Photographs, and Other Likenesses and Their Makers," *Baylor University Browning Interests, Series Fourteen*, Waco, Texas, 1943.
[ ]	Square brackets indicate materials inserted by editors for explanation or clarification.
⟨ ⟩	Angle brackets around a word or part of a word denote an irregularity in the manuscript the nature of which is indicated in a note unless it is damage caused by a seal tear, hole, or physical deterioration of the manuscript. Texts within angle brackets are offered as conjectural readings.
⟨. . .⟩	Angle brackets enclosing ellipsis indicate an actual omission caused by a defect or physical irregularity in the manuscript. Except in the case of text lost through seal tears or holes, the nature of the irregularity is indicated by a note. If this symbol is on a line by itself, the lost text exceeds half a line.
⟨★★★⟩	Angle brackets enclosing triple stars indicate the lack of a beginning or end of a letter.
. . .	Ellipses indicate omissions from quoted material in the introduction or notes, but not from the text of the letters which are reproduced in their entirety.

Introduction

"FOR WE TWO UNDERSTAND each other,—don't we—Dear,—dearest of friends?" wrote Robert Browning in London on 11 March 1884 to Katharine de Kay Bronson in Venice. Six months later in another letter, remembering the holiday he and his sister had spent with Mrs. Bronson the previous year, he reminisced about her gondolier "lighting the way a few footsteps farther to the more than Friend who had come in the rain to take us and keep us."[1]

The warmth and affection of these phrases characterize most of the letters Browning wrote to Mrs. Bronson during the ten years of their friendship. He had had many women friends since his wife's death in 1861; he had been gallant and warm-hearted to most of them, but he seemed to reserve a special place in his affections for Mrs. Bronson—who was "more than Friend" and to whom he happily surrendered himself and his sister "to take us and keep us" for a two-month Venetian holiday. His claim to mutual understanding, which recurs from letter to letter, demanded a response which it seems Mrs. Bronson tried to provide, yet whether she and Browning really ever understood each other is extremely unlikely, as their needs were so different.

Their story is one best suited to the pen of Henry James, who knew them both and who drew portraits of them both in separate books. They themselves, the characters surrounding them, the setting in which they lived, the slow-moving events, the emotional subtleties, are the province of readers familiar with *The Portrait of a Lady* or *The Wings of the Dove*.

Katharine Bronson had all the makings of a Henry James heroine. A wealthy middle-aged American settled in Venice with her daughter, she entertained a cosmopolitan circle of friends in her house on the Grand Canal while her invalid husband retired to Paris to die. James introduced her into "The Aspern Papers" in the small part of Mrs. Prest, an American of fifteen years' standing in Venice, "always interested in the joys and sorrows of her friends."[2] Mrs. Bronson's generosity, her good taste, and the strength that lay beneath the delicate, charming face she presented to the world, are all present in this thumb-nail sketch, which also captures well her tone of voice, her practical conversation with the unexpected French phrase giving a slightly affected nuance to her speech.

xxivIntroduction

Mrs. Bronson's situation—as an attractive woman newly widowed, living with her eligible twenty-year-old daughter Edith in a romantic foreign city—also interested James. He contemplated writing a novel, "Mrs. Max,"[3] in which she would play a leading part, but it was never written and he turned his attention instead to other work, including "The Private Life," his story about Robert Browning.

James had always admired Browning's poetry and had been disillusioned when they met for the first time in London in 1878. Browning was then sixty-six, basking in a newly-found popularity, his greatest works behind him. James, who had been expecting to find something of the young poet who had swept Elizabeth Barrett off her feet more than thirty years before, was disappointed to discover a formally dressed, white-bearded raconteur dominating the dinner conversation. Recoiling from the apparent reality, James described him as "a great chatterer":

> His talk doesn't strike me as very good. It is altogether gossip and personality and is not very beautifully worded. But evidently there are two Brownings—an esoteric and an exoteric. The former never peeps out in society, and the latter has not a ray of suggestion of *Men and Women*.[4]

The more he met Browning, the more this dichotomy fascinated James, until, three years after Browning's death, he wrote "The Private Life" in which he created Clare Vawdrey, "the greatest of our literary glories." Vawdrey, a famous playwright, shares Browning's rich inner and superficial outer life and is actually two people. He possesses a supernatural "double." While the playwright is working alone in his bedroom, the other self is entertaining the company in the drawing-room:

> The world was vulgar and stupid, and the real one would have been a fool to come out for it when he could gossip and dine by deputy.[5]

It is an improbable but neat solution for the difficulties James experienced with Browning's public life, but James was too refined fully to understand Browning, for whom the world could never be vulgar and stupid.

Sadly Henry James was not in Venice in those years Browning stayed with Mrs. Bronson.[6] Indeed it is almost certain that he never met them together. He heard a great deal from her about their friendship and even wrote to her after attending Browning's funeral:

> You must value infinitely now the weeks Browning spent with you in the autumn—which I shall like so much to talk with you about.[7]

This conversation never took place, or if it did James failed to grasp the significance of what she told him, because if anyone had been able to bridge the gap between the two Brownings, to see the whole man, it would have been Mrs. Bronson. Browning revealed to her in his conversation, his letters and his poetry, something more than the distinguished literary figure other people recognized. As his "more than friend" she was given opportunities no other person shared, although she didn't realize the extent of what he was trying to tell her until after his death.

This then was the novel Henry James missed, its leading characters a vigorous elderly English poet and a delicate middle-aged American lady, its plot played out in London, Venice and Asolo between 1880 and 1889, its psychology complex and at times misunderstood by the characters themselves. Luckily, sufficient documents survive for us to substitute fact for fiction, and recreate the events of the decade when Katharine Bronson knew Robert Browning.

KATHARINE DE KAY

Katharine Coleman de Kay was born in 1834, on 14 August, the eldest child of Commodore George de Kay and his fifteen-year-old wife Janet. Her father's family had come to New York from Holland in the seventeenth century and had quickly established themselves as prosperous businessmen, but the sea had always exerted a powerful call to the more restless de Kays of each generation, and in the early nineteenth century it was the turn of Katharine's father to seek excitement as a commander of a brig fighting for Argentina against Brazil in 1827–28. He then travelled the world before settling down to marriage and a quieter life in New York.

Katharine inherited her father's love of romance and adventure. Born on Napoleon's birthday, baptized with water from the River Jordan, held at the font by Fitz-Greene Halleck—the most famous American poet of his day, she led a tomboy existence for the first eight years of her life at Block House Point, on the New Jersey shore of the Hudson, five miles above New York City, where the river is a mile wide. Here her father had bought a fisherman's hut and a strip of land at the foot of the Palisades, perpendicular rocky cliffs half hidden by tall forest trees. Intended originally as a summer home, the hut became the kitchen and dairy of a large stone house which the Commodore built to suit his romantic fancy and his growing family. After a year or two, the de Kays began to live here throughout the year, while the wild river-bank was transformed into a place of great beauty.

To Katharine it was like Versailles. Her mother seemed another Marie Antoinette, as—dressed in a dainty white gown—she moved among the orange and camelia trees, the roses, wax-plants and passion-flowers in the greenhouse. Every day George de Kay would go to New York on business, and, on his return from Manhattan, would hoist a white flag on the far bank of the Hudson and fire a pistol-shot for the boatman to come to row him across the river. He owned a sailing-boat, the *Janet*, and on holidays would take the family upriver for water picnics, with baskets crammed with oyster patties and crab mayonnaise and the best red Chambertin from his cellar.

George de Kay had strong ideas on education: "Let them form their bodies first and then their minds!" So Katharine and her younger brothers learned to ride, row, swim, fence and use bows and arrows before learning arithmetic, reading or writing. They explored the caves, invented games and a secret language, and lived a fantasy life with the few neighbouring children whose parents had built homes on the same stretch of the Hudson. They deceived the local fishermen's children into believing that they were necromancers by burning powders and setting off Catherine Wheels; on one occasion they pretended to change the innocent children into toads by painting their faces green. Animals played an important part in their lives, too, and it was at this time that Katharine began her lifelong attachment to dogs. Her earliest pets were Du-du, a Persian greyhound brought from the East by her father, and two black Newfoundland guard-dogs called Bear and Forbear.

One weekend Katharine and her friends were terrified when three bodies were washed ashore from a river wreck, but living flotsam and jetsam seemed to be continually cast up on the de Kay estate. There was "Old Coon," a hermit for whom the Commodore built a cabin by the river and provided one meal a day, and "Chips," a one-eyed drunken carpenter who had saved the Commodore's life from an enemy sabre stroke in a naval engagement, and who was given a job plus a daily allowance of brandy and tobacco. Chips told the children fabulous stories about sea-serpents and sea-fights in Mexico and South America, and showed them how to tie knots using his 32 double teeth! Mrs. de Kay didn't like him, nor his influence over the children. Above all, she disliked his disreputable appearance, and sent to Europe for a glass eye. Chips was at first delighted by its beauty, but he soon became bored with using it and consigned it to his sea-chest.

Eventually Katharine was given a tutor and started formal schooling at home with some friends of the same age; but she found the teaching dry, and preferred to listen to her mother reading to her from the *Arabian Nights*, *Robinson Crusoe*, Andersen's and Grimms' fairy tales, Miss Edgeworth, and poems by Mrs. Barbauld and by Jane and Ann Taylor. She also enjoyed learning hymns by heart. When she could read, she made a great discovery in the garret: a pile of chocolate-coloured, paper-covered novels, printed in double column, which she devoured—Scott, Dickens, and particularly Bulwer-Lytton. Commenting on this reading in 1890, she wrote:

> I adored Bulwer's sentimentality and revelled in his faultless charac-
> ters which I firmly believed existed *somewhere*, in that world into
> which I should one day be introduced, and make the acquaintance
> of just such beautiful and inestimable men and maidens.[8]

In a way, her whole later life was to be spent in this search, to create an exquisite world in which such people would feel at home.

Immediate plans were less ambitious. George de Kay inherited a large house in New York, built like a French chateau. The family moved there, leaving Block House Point for summer use. It was time, too, for the elder children to be sent to boarding school. Katharine's eldest brother was sent to West Point and she was sent to St. Mary's Hall, Burlington, on the Delaware. This church school belonged to Bishop Doane, one of the first "Ritualists"; the teaching was prejudiced and the atmosphere institutional, and Katharine as the youngest girl in the school felt unwanted. Her one excitement, the discovery of a number of practice pianos, became her greatest disappointment when she tried to play and found that the sounding boards had been removed, to preserve the cloistered silence of the school.

Events abroad soon rescued Katharine from St. Mary's, for in 1847 Ireland suffered the great potato famine. The American government chartered two ships to take relief supplies to the starving Irish, one of which, *The Macedonian*, was put under the command of George de Kay. Katharine, her mother, brothers and sisters all sailed on *The Macedonian*, which was enthusiastically received in Ireland. When the ship was anchored in the Bay of Cork, young Katharine had the great thrill of dancing with the English Admiral Usher, who as a midshipman had been on board the vessel which took Napoleon to St. Helena.

This expedition of mercy had been hastily undertaken; Commodore de Kay had put a very great deal of his own money into the venture, expecting to be reimbursed on his return. The government was dilatory and refused to pay, so George de Kay rented a house in Washington, D.C., to pursue his litigation. He formally applied to Congress:

> The money having been honestly and economically expended in the most honorable service of the country—the country having had the full credit and benefit of the same at home and abroad—the question for Congress to decide is, whether one citizen shall suffer a ruinous fine for faithfully executing its orders, or assume payment of the same.[9]

Congress was still debating the matter when George de Kay died suddenly on 31 January 1849, without receiving a penny for his labours.

Katharine had already started at a new school, the Convent of the Visitation in Georgetown, which she greatly enjoyed, and she remained there until she was a young woman. This was one of the most important periods of her life, because the sobering effect of her father's death sent her all the more willingly to her books, and she was enthusiastically taught by the nuns—delighted to have such an interested and intelligent pupil. Katharine's gift for languages, her interest in scholarship, that seriousness which always tempered the romantic vitality in her disposition, all stemmed from her experiences at the convent.

Soon after leaving school she met Arthur Bronson, ten years her senior, who came from a well-established New York family with large estates in Connecticut. On 11 October 1855 they were married at Grace Church, New York, and left immediately for Europe on an extended honeymoon. One of the first countries they visited was Greece, where Katharine made

up an album which she called "Flowers from Greece," with verses, pressed
flowers and photographs collected on her wedding trip. The range of
quotation used by the young Mrs. Bronson is wide, and pays tribute to
the careful convent teaching she had received: her choice of St. Paul,
Wordsworth, Pope, Milton, Horace, Lucian, Lamartine, and the Greek
tragedians shows a knowledge far beyond that of most women of her age
and social position.

YOUNG KATHARINE BRONSON

Arthur Bronson was to introduce his bride into a rich cosmopolitan
American society, familiar to us today only in the pages of Henry James:
men and women with time on their hands and the intelligence to use it
profitably, in travel, in collecting, and in enjoyment. Europe was their
quarry. It was common to spend a year or more seeing the sights, before
returning—laden with pictures, furniture and other loot—to a fashionable
house in a fashionable American town. Newport, Rhode Island, was one
of these. Here Arthur intended to build a large house on Castle Hill, a
promontory overlooking an inlet, some distance from the centre of the
town. The house would take two years to build, and so he had planned
a two-year honeymoon in Europe. The money for such an expensive
undertaking came from his private income, for there is no evidence to
suggest that Arthur Bronson ever had a job, though he was well educated,
a fine horseman and a lover of the Arts.

After their stay in Greece, the Bronsons spent several months in
Switzerland before moving to Italy. They were much in love. Katharine
confided in her diary:

> It is very pleasant to do anything Arthur likes because he always
> praises me and says I am so good, and as I am fond of demonstrative
> affection it makes me very happy.[10]

and she paints a slightly affected picture of the two of them in Geneva:

> Arthur sits writing French poetry with his hair dishevelled and his
> eye "in a fine frenzy rolling" whilst I sit meekly darning the stockings.

This would be the last time Katharine would describe herself as "meek,"
because she soon emerged as the more intelligent and more adventurous
of the two. In January 1857 the Bronsons joined their friends the Town-
sends to tour Italy as far south as Naples, and it became clear that Arthur
preferred to spend his time in the curiosity shops while the other three
went to see the archaeological sites. They left Arthur behind in Naples
when they climbed Vesuvius ("I could hardly believe it now myself,
going off on an expedition without my darling, as it was the first time
we have been separated since our marriage a year and a half ago.")

Three months in Rome enabled Katharine to form her own opinions
about Italian art. Raphael's *Fornarina* and Guido Reni's *Beatrice Cenci*
she disliked, but she fell in love with Guido's *St. Michael*, which she

thought was one of the finest paintings she had ever seen. The Bronsons visited contemporary artists, and her opinions are no less forthright:

> Drove to Gibson's studio. Saw the pink Venus and the red Cupid and thought both hideous. Mr. Gibson himself is eccentric and conceited. He had some good bas-reliefs, but I only coveted a bust of the young Augustus, *not* by him.

A change comes over Katharine during these two years. To begin with she is "like a child with too many sugar plums" in the Vatican Museum; but by the time she is ready to return to America, she is learning to select, analyse and evaluate works of art, and form far less subjective judgments. Her attitude towards Arthur also changes. The girlish sentimentality of the early part of her diary is replaced by a greater realism. When she goes to Pisa for the second time, on 29 June 1857, she notes:

> We were here last January. Arthur said that he thought it melancholy to revisit a place in travelling; it reminded him so much of the flight of time and the many changes that had taken place. I said, "Oh no, dear, not melancholy; if it is a pleasant place, one is glad to see it again." But I did not tell him how my heart ached when I remembered how happy we were when we were here before—and how in one respect all has changed since then! Poor Arthur. He thought of that when he spoke, I'm sure.

Just what had happened to alter their happiness is not clear. Katharine was ill for six weeks in Florence and it is possible that she may have had a miscarriage, though the type of holiday they were pursuing makes this unlikely. It is more probable that, during Katharine's illness, Arthur indulged in some minor flirtation, which caused him to have the feelings of guilt suggested in the diary entry. Whatever it was, they soon made it up, and rented an apartment in Paris on the Champs Elysées, spending an enjoyable month there before returning to their newly-built property in Newport.

Two extremely happy years followed, during which the Bronsons were accepted into Newport society. In particular, Katharine loved the sailing and the riding on the beach, both of which reminded her of her childhood. Family ties caused them to cross the Atlantic again in 1859 to Dresden, where Janet de Kay and her younger children were now living, and then to Paris, which was becoming Arthur Bronson's favourite city. There Katharine bought a scrap of material from one of Marie Antoinette's gowns. By the time they returned to Newport, Katharine was pregnant, and on 3 July 1861 their daughter Edith was born.

The new baby didn't bring an end to their travels. During the next decade one catches glimpses of them all over Europe: living in Paris in 1866, taking the waters at Schwalbach in Austria in 1867, spied on by Henry James in Venice while they were viewing pictures at the Accademia in 1869, and taking a long excursion to Turkey and Asia Minor in 1870, as far as Balbec. The Bronsons were spending so much time in Europe that they eventually faced a decision whether to stay in America or to join the American expatriate community in a European city. They chose Europe and so in 1875 they left Newport for ever: on 20 October Arthur, Katharine and Edith Bronson, accompanied by their English governess-secretary, Rose Chapman, set sail for Liverpool on the Cunarder *Bothnia*.

It was a tempestuous crossing. For ten days there were gale winds and the boat pitched and tossed. Unruffled, Mrs. Bronson played cards with the novelist Anthony Trollope, who worked on his latest novel every morning whatever the state of the Atlantic, much to the envy of Henry James, another passenger. "The dullest Briton of them all," was Henry James's description of Trollope on the voyage, but young Edith Bronson and her mother were finding the middle-aged novelist far from dull. Hearing that the Bronsons proposed to go to Egypt and the Sudan before finding a permanent home, Trollope pretended to be alarmed by the lack of male company and wrote out the following mock advertisement for Edith:

WANTED

A delicate chested young clergyman of the Church of England, the state of whose health requires the Nile. Religion not indispensable, but no objection. He should wear the sign of the Beast to show his status, and be of unexceptional temper—*but not amatory*. The party will consist of three ladies and a gentleman with whom he must make himself agreeable;—but not more than agreeable to the ladies.

Tuition will be required for a girl of fourteen but the advertisers leave it to the gentleman to select the subject.

N.B. Should the gentleman become really ill he must understand that he will be left on the banks of the river, as the ladies of the party cannot undertake any extra nursing.

As salary is a matter of indifference to the advertisers it is presumed that it will be so equally to the young clergyman.[11]

The *Bothnia* docked at Liverpool. Two weeks later the Bronsons (without their young clergyman) were enjoying the sights of the Nile, as far as the second cataract, with Edith drawing her first sketches from the side of the boat. Their Eastern tour lasted from November 1875 until 30 June 1876, when their boat dropped anchor in Venice. For three months the Bronsons lived in a series of Venetian hotels as they explored the city in the hope of finding a suitable home. On 27 September they discovered the small Palazzo Alvisi on the Grand Canal, which suited their requirements exactly. Negotiations dragged on but were completed on 27 November; on 4 December the Bronsons took possession of the Alvisi at a rent of 325 francs a month.

Enchanted by the new house, Katharine thought it too small to be called a palazzo. Accordingly, she changed its name to the more modest Ca Alvisi, although playfully she sometimes called it her palazzino. Arthur Bronson had the house redecorated and hired a piano, before employing a Madame Milosavich to give the family Italian lessons. Within two

Young Mrs. Bronson, ca. 1860

Ca Alvisi on the Grand Canal, Venice

months the Bronsons had their box at the Fenice Opera House and were
going to Bals Masqués, intent on making Venice their permanent home.

A few more journeys were made from Venice—Spain in 1878 and
Algiers in 1879–80—but Arthur Bronson suddenly developed a severe
mental illness and his personality rapidly deteriorated. Some time in the
middle of 1880 he left Mrs. Bronson for Paris, where he died in 1885.
For the last years of his life, it seems that he was seldom lucid, and
although Mrs. Bronson visited him occasionally, he was not discussed
among her growing circle of friends. Her travelling days were, to all
intents and purposes, over; she and Edith settled down to enjoy life
together at Ca Alvisi and to become part of that cosmopolitan society
which briefly made Venice for the next two decades the expatriate capital
of Europe.

From the first, the Bronsons had been welcomed by the old Venetian
families, the exiled royalty and the artists then living in Venice. Although
there were still pure-bred Venetians like the beautiful fair-haired Contessa
Andriana Marcello, many of the old Venetian aristocratic families had
married foreigners, and so among the leading hostesses were the Austrian
Contessa Maria Mocenego and the Greek Contessas Valmarana and Al-
brizzi. They in turn were joined in Venice by their compatriots like the
Prince and Princess Paul Metternich and Prince Salvador Yturbide, and
the increasing international flavour of the city attracted dethroned royalty
which included the Princess of Montenegro and the pretender Don Carlos
of Spain.

Katharine Bronson also quickly established herself in the small English-
speaking colony, largely dominated by artists and writers. The four
Montalba sisters and their brother welcomed her to their home in the
Campo St. Agnese, while Horatio Brown and his mother entertained her
at their narrow house on the Zattere. She visited the painter Henry Woods
at his studio in the baroque pavilion of the Palazzo Vendramin in the
Carmine. She met Sir Henry Layard, who was still hoping to further his
diplomatic career, but who would soon settle permanently with his wife
Enid in Ca Capello on the Grand Canal. She renewed acquaintance with
Daniel and Ariana Curtis, Americans from Boston, who introduced her
to the Edens and their garden on the Giudecca, which was to become one
of Edith's favourite haunts.

It wasn't long before the Bronsons began to be invited to the glittering
social occasions which enlivened those Venetian winters. Arthur Bronson's departure had little significance, for by 1880 Edith was nineteen,
eligible, accomplished and reserved; Katharine chaperoned her during
her first social engagements, and by her own charm and vivacity ensured
further invitations for herself and her daughter. Acquaintances ripened
into friends, and within a few months of her husband's departure, Mrs.
Bronson was returning hospitality at Ca Alvisi and introducing her new
Venetian circle of friends to visitors from England and America. The
most fruitful and valuable period of her life had begun.

HOSTESS OF CA ALVISI

By Venetian standards Ca Alvisi is neither large nor beautiful. It is a squarish, rather squat building of three storeys, its façade broken by three balconies on the second floor. The large central balcony leads from the main drawing-room, and it was here, shaded by an awning, that Mrs. Bronson and her guests would watch the beauty of the Venetian evening and the activity on the canal, for Ca Alvisi's main attraction was, and is, its position. Directly facing the imposing church of S. Maria della Salute, it stands at the mouth of the Grand Canal not far from St. Mark's Square and the Doge's Palace. Next door there is a break in the line of houses, and behind a pillared portico is a small courtyard, filled with flowering bushes and trees, which belonged to the ancient Palazzo Giustiniani-Recanati, the remaining portion of which stands away from the canal at the back of the courtyard. From 1883 Katharine Bronson rented this adjacent building specially for her guests to give them privacy, and it was here that Henry James, Browning and many others stayed. The courtyard, too, was a welcome addition to the Alvisi, and a wonderful place for alfresco lunches.

Even the largest rooms of the main house seemed compact and familiar, overflowing as they were with furniture brought from Newport and the many works of art the Bronsons had accumulated on their travels. Katharine also admired Venetian art—glass, silver and metalwork—and filled her mother-of-pearl cabinets, her shelves and sideboards, with hundreds of small, delicate objects. It was said that she would have exchanged a Tintoretto for a cabinet of tiny gilded glasses or a dinner-service of the right old silver. The walls were covered with small pictures: a modern water-colour of Venice vying with a framed piece of tapestry or a Greek ikon. To Henry James the interior of Ca Alvisi was theatrical in its display; for him it was "a friendly private box at the constant operatic show, a box at the best point of the best tier, with the cushioned ledge of its front raking the whole scene and with its withdrawing rooms behind for more detailed conversation."[12] The description is apt, for one of the smaller drawing-rooms had been converted into a private theatre for Edith and her friends to act French plays, and the comedies in the Venetian dialect which Katharine wrote and had printed between 1883 and 1894.

Surrounded by her treasures, Katharine would usually entertain her guests from a sofa in the main drawing-room. She enjoyed smoking, and cigarettes in appropriately delicate boxes were on almost every table; she loved small dogs and would always have two or three lying at her feet. Her favourites were pugs and a special miniature breed of Chinese spaniel; their names (Contenta, Trolley, Zizi, Tou Fou, Yahabibi, Moretto, Thisbe and Tubby) were as familiar to the Venetian world as Hardy's dog Wessex to Dorchester or Emily Brontë's Keeper to Haworth. Peppermint chocolates would also be close at hand and a volume of German poetry within

The Drawing Room at Ca Alvisi

Mrs. Bronson's Household Servants at Ca Alvisi, 1887–88
Left to right: Giuseppe (handy-man), Orsola (kitchen-maid),
Luigi Baffo (1st gondolier), Giuseppina (maid), Domenico Damian
(2nd gondolier), Rosalia (cook), Natale Gavagnin (3rd gondolier)

reach. Katharine wasn't physically strong. She suffered frequent headaches and needed plenty of rest. Her health declined during her time at Ca Alvisi, but, by taking regular siestas, she was able to preserve her strength for the important occasion. Like many semi-invalids before her, she converted her disability to her advantage, and gave a style and sense of occasion to her periods of rest.

She maintained a loyal permanent staff of eight, most of whom stayed with her throughout her years in Venice. The middle-aged Giuseppina was the chief maid, looking after Mrs. Bronson and very special guests like the Brownings. She was in charge of Rosalia the cook, Orsola— Edith's maid who also helped in the kitchen—and Giuseppe the odd-job man. Then there were three gondoliers to row Mrs. Bronson and her guests on the lagoon. In a different category altogether was Rose Chapman, a very privileged accountant-housekeeper, greatly loved by the family. "Chappy," as she was called, ordered the rest of the staff around in her broken Italian with its strong English accent, for she had arrived in Venice with the Bronsons and had helped them discover and employ the other servants.[13] When cholera struck Venice in 1886, Katharine removed herself and her staff, including the gondoliers, to Hans Place, London, where she continued to entertain, serving Italian dinners as if life on the Grand Canal hadn't been interrupted.

Entertainment at Ca Alvisi varied with the company. There were few days in the spring and summer when Katharine was not devising some pleasurable evening, whether it was a literary dinner party for no more than six specially chosen guests, or a performance in the little theatre for the Bronsons' Italian friends. Then there might be fifty to entertain to supper, but Katharine was an equally good hostess at home with just her family and a very few close friends. They played games and charades, and improvised scenes. A popular game she invented for her artist friends consisted in drawing a figure on a piece of paper on which five dots, indicating head, hands and feet had been previously marked. She kept the best results, and drawings by Sargent, Story and Chartrain still survive as mementoes of a challenging hour.

Wednesday evenings would be devoted to Edith and her companions, the emphasis on youth and fancy: "Do you think we can get the young people to dress themselves with paper birds?" she wrote to a friend in February 1889 about a St. Valentine's Day party. "I can see in my 'mind's eye' very pretty decorations of birds—pasted on ribbons ... a flight of swallows on white ribbon would be awfully chic. ... Thanks dear for the pains you took for me with the butterflies. You looked so well and the flutterbys were delightful."[14] For the same party she had special postage-stamps printed, depicting red hearts, and also a "Casa Alvisi" cancel stamp with the date 14.2.89, so the young guests could send one another Valentines in a cardboard posting-box at one end of the main drawing-room. The most sumptuous of her entertainments was for Edith's wedding in 1895. To set the seal on the reception, she had hundreds of tiny Cinderella slippers made for the guests to throw after the bridal gondola to give the happy couple good luck for the future.

It is easy, but false, to see life at Ca Alvisi as a round of pleasures and entertainments in a Venetian lotus-land. It is this aspect that Charles de Kay, Katharine's much-loved youngest brother, wittily satirized in a poem he wrote in her birthday book:

> Above the wave of Venice opaline
> Where La Salute charms the wide lagoon
> On poppied wreathes two drowsiheads recline
> And murmur, "Ah, nor loud we call, nor soon!"
> The world's too feverish, hurried, clangorous—
> Wheels, and the vulgar, vex and frighten us!
> And smooth below the gondola's brown keel
> One lotus life two rosy seaworms pass,
> Watching the moon the gold of sunset steal
> And swing to wavings of the briny glass. [15]

But the Tennyson parody neglects two important aspects of Mrs. Bronson's life at Ca Alvisi: her care for the Venetians and her own writings.

Katharine soon discovered some of the wretchedness under the glittering façade Venice presents to the tourist. Many of the gondoliers lived precarious lives; when winter or illness robbed them of their livelihood, their families starved. Mrs. Bronson, who had learned their dialect, gave money to establish charities for out-of-work gondoliers and invited poor Venetian families to live in the upper rooms of Ca Alvisi during the winter months. She also endeared herself to the Venetians by organizing the repair of some of their shrines on the canals, and establishing schools to give a rudimentary education to the young. In this way, she was different from the many other foreigners living in their rich palaces on the Grand Canal; she reached the hearts and understood the minds of the Venetians. They appreciated what she was trying to do, and gave a number of spontaneous demonstrations of affection towards her. There were evenings on which the canal in front of Ca Alvisi was black with gondolas and other boats as she was serenaded. She was not a rich woman by American standards, but in her will she left 20,000 lire to the Venetian poor.

Mrs. Bronson kept a part of every day to herself, so that she could continue to read and develop her mind. Not content with merely reading the latest German and French authors, she translated many of their poems, as well as writing a number herself. She had no pretensions as to the quality of her work, and, although she had poems she had written on her visit to Algiers privately printed, it was more as a travel diary for her friends than anything else. She sent a number of copies to friends in America, including one to the writer and critic T.G. Appleton, who dashed any secret hopes of publication she may have had by his reply:

> A friend of mine read them out loud to us the other night, and we
> all agreed upon their beauty, their harmony, their natural and easy

> movement. I think a journal in verse is the legitimate use of amateur
> poetry. It is only vulgarised by the touch of the public; and that's
> why I don't write an article upon it. . . . I think a sweet poet displaying
> his heart-fibres to the world is like one of those Pont-Neuf mendicants
> showing his sores.[16]

Katharine later showed some of her poems to Browning, who corrected
metrical clumsinesses and suggested improvements; he was much more
encouraging than Appleton, but, reading Mrs. Bronson's poetry today,
one is only too aware that she possessed a very minor muse.

Her scholarship is another matter. Katharine Bronson had strong intellectual interests. Although she published little, she left behind her a rich
store of manuscripts. Most of her research was accomplished in the years
between 1880 and 1890, when she began a close study of Venetian history.
She published an article on Burano lace[17] and prepared rough drafts on
subjects such as "The Lost Islands of the Lagoon," "Ancient Venetian
Maps" and "The Arsenal"; but her *magnum opus*, on which she must
have spent several years and employed a number of artists as copyists in
the State Archives, is a large book on Venetian naval architecture running
to hundreds of pages.[18] It is a definitive work, beautifully illustrated,
and one cannot understand why it wasn't published. It traces the history
of Venetian craft of all types, from the humblest rowing-boat to the
state-barges of La Serenissima and the nineteenth-century man-of-war,
and one can only assume that Mrs. Bronson wrote it as a labour of love,
rather than for money or academic reputation. Her generosity in such
matters can be seen in the contribution she made to her friend Emily
Lawless's book on Ireland,[19] in which she placed her first-hand knowledge
of the events of 1847 and other information freely at the author's disposal.
Of her own published work, there remain only her two articles on Browning, one of which was printed in her lifetime, and the other published
posthumously. In another age and in other circumstances, Mrs. Bronson
might have made writing her career, but her fortune was to befriend
scholars, artists and writers, and her easy scholarship served merely to
enable her to converse intelligently and on equal terms with some of the
liveliest minds of her generation.

BROWNING AND VENICE

Among the many writers who were entertained and befriended by
Katharine Bronson in Venice, Robert Browning had a special place in
her affections from their first meeting. It was clear to those who knew
them both that they possessed an instinctive understanding for each other.
"Their friendship was real harmony," wrote Zina Hulton, a young Anglo-
Italian acquaintance, and she described a dinner party Browning attended
at Ca Alvisi as "a delightful evening, for he was at his best, as he always
was in Mrs. Bronson's company."[20]

The two met for the first time in October 1880 and were probably introduced by their mutual friend, the American sculptor William Wetmore Story, though Browning is also thought to have received from Anthony Trollope a letter of introduction to Mrs. Bronson.[21] Browning was on holiday with his sister Sarianna, staying at a spartan hotel on the Grand Canal, as he had done for the two previous years. Venice was familiar territory for him, yet he could hardly have expected that this chance meeting with Mrs. Bronson in Venice when he was in his sixty-ninth year would have as great an impact on him as his introduction to the city over forty years before. That it did was not entirely fortuitous, because Venice and the inland Veneto had from the first provoked an unique response in Browning and had affected his sensibilities more dramatically than any other place.

Venice had been Browning's first stop in Italy when in June 1838, frustrated at his inability to complete *Sordello*, he had left England in search of some local colour for his poem set in twelfth-century Italy. The full force of Italy, its hitherto unknown and exciting way of life, overwhelmed Browning in Venice; he fell under its spell and spent two full weeks roaming the city before setting out on his walking tour of the Veneto. His discoveries at Bassano, Asolo and Possagno had more to do with the atmosphere and the quality of life than with the background to *Sordello*, although he did visit many of the places connected with the poem.

Memories of this first visit to Italy never left him. The sights and sounds of Venice and the Veneto emerge fresh and vivid in the letters and poems of the next twenty years. A kaleidoscope of colourful men and women tumble onto the page: peasant girls unloading fruit and flowers from Venetian barges, guests dancing at midnight at a rich ball in the Pucci Palace, a timid woman from Possagno superstitiously lighting a candle every time the thunder rumbled, only to blow it out again quickly to save the wax, ice-cream eaters running for cover when the *bora* struck in Trieste, lovers gliding across the lagoon in a gondola. Even the tune the children sang in Venice "arm over neck" remained in his mind. He jotted it down for Fanny Haworth on his return, only to resurrect it sixteen years later in "A Toccata of Galuppi's."[22]

Browning returned to Venice in 1851 with his wife. They spent four weeks in May and June exploring the canals together and sitting every evening in St. Mark's Square, listening to the music outside Quadri's and Florian's, going to the opera, "swimming" in gondolas and behaving like enthusiastic tourists. Elizabeth enjoyed herself so much that she "longed to live and die there—never to go away,"[23] but Browning was ill. It seems that on this occasion Venice was too much for him.[24] Perhaps Elizabeth's enthusiasm aroused dormant feelings, which he wasn't able to communicate to her, because Browning's attraction to Venice was more than simply its beauty, past history or the life of its inhabitants.

There was a decadent luxury about the crumbling buildings which he enjoyed and to which one part of him succumbed. What could be better, he wrote to G.W. Curtis in 1847, than "getting to be as rich as Rothschild, buying all Venice, turning out everybody, and ensconcing one's self in the Doge's Palace, among the dropping gold ornaments and flakes of what was lustrous colour in Titian's or Tintoret's time, [and] waiting for the proper consummation of all things and the sea's advent?"[25]

This luxury also had strong sexual overtones, which are revealed in Browning's Venetian poems. In *Sordello*, the narrator's eye is taken by the beauty of the girls from the Veneto:

> Ah, beneath
> The cool arch stoops she, brownest cheek!
> Nay, that Paduan girl
> Splashes with barer legs[26]
> (III, ll. 687–688, 691–692)

In "A Toccata of Galuppi's" the reader is reminded of "the breast's superb abundance where a man might base his head," while the lovers in "In a Gondola" during their sensual journey experiment with the moth's kiss and the bee's kiss before a consummating embrace:

> Heart to heart
> And lips to lips! Yet once more, ere we part,
> Clasp me and make me thine, as mine thou art![27]
> (ll. 223–225)

during which he is murdered.

In these last two poems, in which the Venetian setting is strongly emphasized, the intensity of physical love is allied to a self-consuming destructiveness. Somewhere bound up with the decaying beauty of Venice and its people, there was for Browning a sensual enjoyment to which he could not but respond, though at the same time he was aware of his self-indulgence, which gave an uneasiness to his moral viewpoint.[28]

From his first visit he noticed the sharp contrasts that existed in Venice, between rich palaces and back canals choked with refuse, between the grandeur of the buildings in St. Mark's Square and the slippery stones underfoot which necessitated careful walking. The contrast between rich and poor, weak and powerful, were accentuated in Venice, yet he felt that here they co-existed as part of an organic whole, as in nowhere else he had been. Browning put these ideas into *Sordello*:

> Venice seems a type
> Of Life—'twixt blue and blue extends, a stripe,
> As Life, the somewhat, hangs 'twixt nought and nought:
> 'Tis Venice, and 'tis Life—
> (III, ll. 723–726)

This idea he held to and repeated in a slightly different form in *Fifine at the Fair*, when he makes Don Juan say:

> There went
> Conviction to my soul, that what I took of late
> For Venice was the world; its Carnival—the state
> Of Mankind, masquerade in life-long permanence
> For all time, and no one particular feast-day.
>
> (ll. 1856–60)

This was written in 1872, long after Venice had lost its sensuous appeal, yet it is interesting how in this poem dealing with attitudes to physical love, with a philandering Don Juan unfaithful to his spiritual wife Elvire and yearning for the gypsy Fifine, Browning should turn again to the inspiration of Venice for an important section of the poem.

The use of Venice as a cosmic symbol, therefore, suggests the importance the city had held for Browning in the past, but there is nothing to suggest when he introduced Sarianna to the city in 1878 and returned in 1879 that it cast its old spell over him or provided him with anything more than it does to most visitors. They saw almost no one and they lived a simple life in a particularly plain and uncomfortable hotel.

The meeting with Mrs. Bronson changed all that. For a second time Browning's love for Venice was kindled. For a second time the effects were spontaneous. "You have given Venice an association which will live in my mind with every delight of that dearest place in the world,"[29] he wrote to Mrs. Bronson from London within a few weeks of their first meeting. In the coming years Venice would resume its importance in his life.

VENETIAN AUTUMNS

Little is known about the first meeting between Browning and Katharine Bronson in 1880, or how many times they saw each other during the month he was in Venice. It is likely that Browning visited Ca Alvisi on 13 October, because on the following day he wrote an important impromptu poem in Edith's autograph book.

The second series of *Dramatic Idyls* had been published earlier in the year and its epilogue had aroused controversy. In this poem Browning contrasted two types of poet, the sensitive romantic and the less fashionable grafter of verse. While the first received immediate recognition, Browning maintained that the second was deeper-rooted and would eventually be recognized as "a nation's heritage":

> "Touch him ne'er so lightly, into song he broke:
> Soil so quick-receptive,—not one feather-seed,
> Not one flower-dust fell but straight its fall awoke
> Vitalizing virtue: song would song succeed
> Sudden as spontaneous—prove a poet-soul!"
>
> Indeed?
> Rock's the song-soil rather, surface hard and bare:
> Sun and dew their mildness, storm and frost their rage
> Vainly both expend,—few flowers awaken there:
> Quiet in its cleft broods—what the after age
> Knows and names a pine, a nation's heritage.

Several critics thought that Browning was writing autobiographically and intended the second type of poet to include himself. Presumably the same question was asked him at Ca Alvisi and, to put an end to the matter, he claimed that he was thinking of Dante and that there was no personal reference at all. When Edith offered him her book, he took it back to his hotel, and next morning wrote:

> Thus I wrote in London, musing on my betters,
> Poets dead and gone: and lo, the critics cried,
> "Out on such a boast!"—as if I dreamed that fetters
> Binding Dante, bind up—me! as if true pride
> Were not also humble!
>   So I smiled and sighed
> As I oped your book in Venice this bright morning,
> Sweet new friend of mine! and felt the clay or sand
> —Whatsoe'er my soil be,—break—for praise or scorning—
> Out in grateful fancies—weeds, but weeds expand
> Almost into flowers—held by such a kindly hand![30]

The charm of these verses, the witty self-deprecation Browning uses as he parallels and echoes the original poem, could not fail to have delighted Edith and her mother. The compliment to Edith was genuine: soon after their first meeting the Brownings had accepted the Bronsons as friends.

Encouraged by such a positive response, Katharine Bronson was quick to take the initiative the following year. Soon after the Brownings' arrival in Venice on 21 September 1881 she sent a bouquet of flowers round to their hotel and invited them to dinner to introduce them to American friends then visiting Venice, the first of several such occasions that September and October. Browning also enjoyed rides on the lagoon in Mrs. Bronson's gondola, even though Mrs. Bronson herself was sometimes prevented by illness from going. There were times, too, for quiet conversations at Ca Alvisi, and Katharine showed Browning some of her poems. He delayed his departure a week and finally left Venice on 1 November, the day of a gondola strike, carrying an early Christmas present—an album of photographs of the city in which Mrs. Bronson had written a dedicatory poem:

> Prince of word painters, I dare offer thee
> Venetian shadows, colourless and drear—
> Since the fair dial of thy memory
> Has only marked the sunshine of the year
> And can recall with a magician's skill
> Its own dear Venice, at its own dear will.[31]

The charm, the open flattery, of these lines was not lost on Browning. Back in London, he looked at the photographs constantly in the next few months and remembered his happy vacation: "You remain for me a dearest of friends ... In Venice ... should you be there next autumn, it will go hard with me if I do not meet you again."[32] He and Katharine Bronson began writing to each other regularly every two or three weeks, and she sent him ideas for new poems, as well as evening studs and cuff links to complement some she had given him in Venice for day use. Browning wasn't embarrassed by this generosity, probably because he realized that it was merely part of Mrs. Bronson's free and impulsive nature to give presents, and in his turn he pleased her by running errands for her. One of these was to return a seventeenth-century book she had found in Venice to its former home, the library of Woburn Abbey, home of the Dukes of Bedford. He also took out a subscription in her name to the Browning Society, while Sarianna sent her some of the latest photographs of her brother.

It is easy to misunderstand the beginnings of their friendship and see it merely as an elderly poet succumbing to the enthusiastic adoration of an admirer twenty-two years younger than he. Adoration there may have been, but there was also a sensitivity and a warmth about Katharine Bronson's personality which instantly attracted Browning and which he wished to reciprocate. "The best thing the Old Year gave me," he wrote on New Year's Day 1882, "was the confirmation of your friendship for me, which I dared hardly be sure of when we first met,"[33] and earlier he told her that he couldn't write a long letter to thank her for a present because that would need "a quieter pulse than your gift, of this morning, sets in motion."[34]

Already he had anticipated a return to Venice the next autumn, when word reached him that the Albergo Universo had run into financial difficulties, sold its furniture and closed down. In telling Mrs. Bronson this bad news, Browning explained that the Europa Hotel, close to her house, was too noisy for his taste but that he hoped Sarianna and he would be able to rent an apartment elsewhere—a transparent opening for an invitation to stay at Ca Alvisi. Mrs. Bronson was quick to respond; she wouldn't herself be in Venice that autumn, she told him, but he and his sister were welcome to use her house. Browning was firm and spirited in his reply: "As for occupying Cà Alvisi with all the Cà Alvisi-ishness out of it,—any other place in the Universe—even the *Universo*!"[35] He would have to make do with seeing her in London in the spring.

And so in May 1882 Mrs. Bronson arrived in London and visited Browning at Warwick Crescent—where, on the 20th, Browning gave her a copy of his photograph, taken appropriately "At Home" by Samuel Walker, in which he is pictured relaxed and cross-legged in his desk-chair. She made him promise to sit to Henrietta Montalba for a terra-cotta bust which she had commissioned, and she also brought him two brass salvers he had ordered the previous year in Venice. They talked about two topics then uppermost in Browning's mind: his notice to leave Warwick Crescent so that the house could be pulled down to make way for a new railway, and the activities of yet another publisher prying into Elizabeth Barrett Browning's life for information to include in a new series about famous women of the century.

Whether or not it was this stay in London and her realization that Browning's private life could be easily flustered and disturbed that made

Robert Browning. May 20ᵗʰ 83.

SAMUEL A. WALKER.   230, REGENT STREET, W.

Katharine Bronson, 1881

Mrs. Bronson change her mind about the autumn is not clear, but change her plans she did, and made arrangements to be back in Venice by October. Browning and Sarianna—who had already been invited by Reginald Cholmondeley to spend part of the autumn in Ischia—decided, therefore, to visit Venice for a quiet holiday en route for Naples, and stay, not at Ca Alvisi, but in rooms secured for them by Mrs. Curtis.

They left London on 1 August and spent nearly six weeks in the French Alps, at St. Pierre de Chartreuse. There they learned of the accidental death in Ischia of one of Mr. Cholmondeley's young house guests, who had fallen from a precipice while sketching. This incident prevented the Brownings from proceeding further south than Venice. Accordingly, they set their steps towards Mrs. Bronson, only to be halted first at Milan and then, tantalizingly close, at Bologna, by torrential rain. After twelve days' wait and with Browning now afflicted by a liver complaint, which he thought was rheumatism, they gave up the unequal struggle and returned to London.

Although he still continued to write, Browning's letters to Venice for the rest of the year lost much of their sparkle, and he was in danger of allowing the friendship to cool. Then, the news of Richard Wagner's death in Venice in February 1883 reminded him that he hadn't heard from Mrs. Bronson for a long while. In reply to his inquiry, Mrs. Bronson wrote by return and alarmed Browning with news of a studio-house she had been negotiating for him in Venice to replace Warwick Crescent. She had misunderstood a chance remark he had made and thought he would consider making Venice a permanent home, and had discovered that the small building next to the Ca Alvisi was vacant. Browning wrote back quickly to put matters straight and explained that he could never leave London; he went on to claim that she would find him a troublesome tease as a neighbour, continually nagging her to look after her health, but he and Sarianna would happily accept her invitation to spend the autumn with her in Venice.

On 4 October 1883 her gondoliers were waiting outside the Venice railway station to row the Brownings down the Grand Canal to the apartment Katharine had just rented in the Palazzo Giustiniani-Recanati, next door to Ca Alvisi. In that long, hot autumn she persuaded Browning to extend his holiday from a month to six weeks and then to over two months. "It is hard to extricate oneself from the all-embracing kindness of our Hostess here,"[36] he wrote, enjoying the attention he was receiving where every night there were fresh guests to entertain and be entertained by. If there were fewer English compatriots than usual because of a cholera scare, there were instead a superfluity of foreign royalty and nobility gracing Mrs. Bronson's drawing-room; Browning enjoyed conversations with Don Carlos, Pretender to the thrones of France and Spain, about the identity of the Man in the Iron Mask and the fate of the young Dauphin in the Tuileries.

Browning walked a lot, enjoyed the gondola rides, and eagerly fell in with Mrs. Bronson's impulsive suggestion that they take a boat down the

Adriatic to Brindisi and from there make their way by water to Athens. It proved a madcap scheme and Browning realized that the short time they would be able to spend in Athens wouldn't compensate for the long, tiring journey, particularly as Mrs. Bronson's health was too frail for a rushed excursion. But, he said confidently, the "cherry" vainly "bobbed at" this year might be bitten and swallowed next time.[37]

Mrs. Bronson and Browning were now close friends. She was writing playlets in the Venetian dialect with his encouragement, while he corrected translations of German poems she had made. She didn't smother him with attention, because she realized that he needed time to himself. It was the understanding way in which she tended to his needs, allowing him an independence to think and write, that pleased Browning. He had arrived at the Giustiniani-Recanati with much of the early part of *Ferishtah's Fancies* in his suitcase, and he was able in the warm November and December Venetian mornings to continue this work with a cool breeze blowing through his open window. Some of the mellow optimism in *Ferishtah* reflects the personal happiness he experienced while writing it, first in the Italian Alps and then at Venice. Two minor works were also accomplished at this time: the Goldoni sonnet and the witty sonnet to Rawdon Brown, the English expatriate who simply couldn't leave his pretty house on the Grand Canal to return home. Browning experienced similar difficulty, but eventually on 8 December he left Venice, met bad weather on the other side of the Alps, endured an extremely rough Channel crossing and found himself in London without a house to go to—Warwick Crescent being temporarily barred to him because of the death of one of his servants from diphtheria. No wonder that Sarianna on New Year's Day wrote to Katharine Bronson:

> You cannot think how incessantly we dwell on the memories of the pleasant past. We are in Casa Alvisi in spirit daily, and I picture to myself all that is going on in the well-loved rooms.[38]

Browning's thanks were more personal, if less direct:

> My own dearest Friend ... You well know how happy I was, those two full months, in the enjoyment of your presence ... and [I] feel sure that so long as you and I are on earth there will only be so much more or less earth and sea between us: and, for my part, be you as sure that whenever I can overpass these, in the body and not merely the soul, I will once—and if God please—many times again be with you.[39]

Katharine was openly sentimental in the letter she sent to London:

> I suppose I will one day get used to your absence, but the time has not come yet, & I look with the same sadness across the lonely court every morning & evening.[40]

and she kept among her papers some lines Browning had written for her during the holiday:

K. DE K. BRONSON
Pray, do I write your name the proper way?
Dear Friend, I think so: and yet, sooth to say,
I see one striking error: come what may,
My love for you admits of no D.K.!⁴¹ [41]

LYRIC INTERLUDE

Browning spent January 1884 completing *Ferishtah's Fancies*, which
was published later that year. It is a closely structured book of twelve
blank-verse poems, each of which poses a question of faith, belief or
moral conduct—which is then answered by an imaginary Persian sage,
Ferishtah, who to all intents and purposes is Browning himself. After
each blank-verse poem there is a short love lyric, attached to and relevant
to the main poem. In this way, love and reason are closely paralleled, as
Browning's intention is to persuade his readers that love can prove or
justify issues as well as—or better than—cold reason.

The value of the book lies in the freshness and boldness of the twelve
love lyrics. Taken together they demonstrate a wide variety of tone and
feeling in their depiction of moments of stress, difficulty or happiness in
a relationship between a man and a woman. They do not explore a situation
psychologically, as earlier lyrics do; they are considered statements about
aspects of love, spoken with a quiet but firm assurance. While most are
meditative, a few confidently proclaim the value of physical love.

The poems owe a great deal to Browning's stay with Katharine Bronson
the previous autumn; his growing affection for her colours many of the
lyrics. Just as in the main body of the book Ferishtah is a thin disguise
for Browning, and the conclusions he reaches are a summary of Browning's own ideas, so in the love lyrics the ideas and emotions are the
poet's, many of them recently resurrected by his friendship with Mrs.
Bronson.

Katharine's influence varies from poem to poem. Some have little or
no connection with her and Venice, but the majority do. Her physical
frailty, for instance, provides a starting-point for one poem:

So, the head aches and the limbs are faint!
Flesh is a burthen—even to you!
Can I force a smile with a fancy quaint?
Why are my ailments none or few?

The contrast between Katharine's weakness and the older Browning's
robustness provokes speculation about mental and physical strength,
which soon leaves the original poetic stimulus behind. Similarly, Mrs.
Bronson's extreme concern for Browning's welfare, which was later to
develop into a worship of him, evokes the half-humorous response:

Man I am and man would be, Love—merest man and nothing
                                       more.
Bid me seem no other! Eagles boast of pinions—let them
                                       soar!
I may put forth angel's plumage, once unmanned, but not
                                       before.

It would be wrong to call these poems autobiographical, but the speaker
in many of them is Browning rather than a *persona*, and there is an
emotional truth in them which springs from his recent experience in
Venice. Take, for example, the lyric:

Ask not one least word of praise!
    Words declare your eyes are bright?
What then meant that summer day's
Silence spent in one long gaze?
    Was my silence wrong or right?

Words of praise were all to seek!
    Face of you and form of you,
Did they find the praise so weak
When my lips just touched your cheek—
    Touch which let my soul come through?

The lightest of kisses, the poet suggests, expresses more than words can
ever do. The genesis of the poem lies in Browning's growing attraction
for Katharine Bronson and the difficulty he finds in articulating his feelings
towards her. Words, whether written in a poem or spoken in the drawing-
room at Ca Alvisi, lack the subtlety he requires, and so he fails to speak,
and instead allows the gentlest of formal kisses to speak for him. At the
very time he was writing the poem, he expressed the same idea in a letter
to Mrs. Bronson: "[Give] my love to Edith—as if the words had never
gone stiff into *formula*."[42] The poem as printed in *Ferishtah's Fancies*
does not identify Mrs. Bronson and Ca Alvisi; instead, it generalizes a
specific situation Browning experienced. This is the technique he uses in
other lyrics in the book, such as "Wish no word unspoken," "Once I saw
a chemist" and "Verse-making was least of my virtues."

The awakening of feeling shown in the lyrics was complicated by
memories of his dead wife, which began to recur strongly at this time,
and which Browning had to come to terms with. In the poem "Not with
my Soul, Love!" the speaker is struggling to find a release from sexual
restraint:

Not with my Soul, Love!—bid no Soul like mine
    Lap thee around nor leave the poor Sense room!
Soul,—travel-worn, toil-weary,—would confine
    Along with Soul, Soul's gains from glow and gloom,
Captures from soarings high and divings deep.
Spoil-laden Soul, how should such memories sleep?
Take Sense, too—let me love entire and whole—
    Not with my Soul!

Eyes shall meet eyes and find no eyes between,
  Lips feed on lips, no other lips to fear!
No past, no future—so thine arms but screen
  The present from surprise! not there, 'tis here—
Not then, 'tis now:—back, memories that intrude!
Make, Love, the universe our solitude,
And, over all the rest, oblivion roll–
      Sense quenching Soul!

The man pleads for a full physical relationship with the woman who has asked him for a spiritual love. He tells her that a total commitment, "entire and whole," is necessary, or memories of a more sacred love will intrude, and he and the woman will find a phantom standing between them. The poem cries out for a biographical interpretation, and almost all critics have seen the speaker with the spoil-laden soul as Browning, and the memories that will not sleep those of Elizabeth Barrett. This supposition is in keeping with Browning's earlier practice (he had, for example, used Elizabeth in the 1872 poems "Amphibian" and "The Householder"), and, in the context of *Ferishtah's Fancies*, is most probable.[43]

It is not clear to whom the poem is addressed. The choice of the American millionairess Clara Bloomfield-Moore, first proposed by herself and then adopted by some later biographers, is incongruous and unlikely.[44] There is nothing specific to identify the woman with Mrs. Bronson either; and it may be that, as in so many poems in the book, the strong emotions have become generalized. Browning is contemplating, not for the first time, the problem posed by a reawakening of joyful love, a love he had formerly felt for his dead wife, and which he felt was a disloyalty to her memory.

It was at about this time that Browning began to relate Elizabeth to Katharine Bronson. When Katharine gave him an 1848 coin issued by the Venice Republic, he attached it to his watch chain, where he had for twenty years kept Elizabeth's wedding ring. Both were "tokens of love" he told her, and he would be reminded of her (and presumably Elizabeth too) every five minutes by the ticking of his watch.[45] Even more significant was his decision to add the name of the Palazzo Giustiniani-Recanati to the Epilogue to *Ferishtah's Fancies*. This he did at the proof stage; and, in asking Katharine Bronson's permission, he wrote, "the last [poem] seemed to belong to the beloved place where it was penned,—as I wanted to remember—or be remembered rather."[46] This poem, written in Venice and completed on 1 December 1883 is clearly addressed to the spirit of Elizabeth Barrett.

The Epilogue concerns Browning's view of the world, whether it is "a cry of just weariness and woe" or "perfection, nothing less." When the moon pierces through the gloom, "the world displays its worth" and Browning thinks he sees meaning and order in life. Then suddenly he questions his optimistic viewpoint. What if he be deluding himself on account of the happiness he has received in life from human love? More specifically, could his love for Elizabeth have impaired his judgment?

EPILOGUE

Oh, Love—no, Love! All the noise below,
     Love,
     Groanings all and moanings—none of Life I
     lose!
All of Life's a cry just of weariness and woe,
     Love—
     "Hear at least, thou happy one!" How can
     I, Love, but choose?

Only, when I do hear, sudden circle round me
     —Much as when the moon's might frees a
     space from cloud—
Iridescent splendours: gloom—would else con-
     found me—
     Barriered off and banished far—bright-edged
     the blackest shroud!

Thronging through the cloud-rift, whose are
     they, the faces
     Faint revealed yet sure divined, the famous
     ones of old?
"What"—they smile—"our names, our deeds
     so soon erases
     Time upon his tablet where Life's glory lies
     enrolled?

"Was it for mere fool's-play, make-believe and
     mumming,
     So we battled it like men, not boylike sulked
     or whined?
Each of us heard clang God's 'Come!' and each
     was coming:
     Soldiers all, to forward-face, not sneaks to lag
     behind!

"How of the field's fortune? That concerned
     our Leader!
     Led, we struck our stroke nor cared for doings
     left and right:
Each as on his sole head, failer or succeeder,
     Lay the blame or lit the praise: no care for
     cowards: fight!"

Then the cloud-rift broadens, spanning earth
     that's under,
     Wide our world displays its worth, man's strife
     and strife's success:
All the good and beauty, wonder crowning
     wonder,
     Till my heart and soul applaud perfection,
     nothing less.

Only, at heart's utmost joy and triumph, terror
     Sudden turns the blood to ice: a chill wind
     disencharms

All the late enchantment! What if all be error—
If the halo irised round my head were, Love,
    thine arms?
Palazzo Giustinian-Recanati, Venice:
    December 1, 1883.

The last verse tempers Browning's optimism, but does not destroy it. Love need not delude, but may just as easily confirm. The question is open-ended, and the positive values expressed throughout *Ferishtah's Fancies* are seen more realistically by the self-questioning.

"Epilogue," then, was the poem that "seemed to belong to the beloved place where it was penned," the poem "as I wanted to remember—or be remembered," the first acknowledged poem which was to relate Browning to Mrs. Bronson, and to relate Mrs. Bronson to Elizabeth Barrett. The inference from the poem and from Browning's comments in his letter is clear.

Elizabeth had made Browning supremely happy in the past and helped him form his positive view of the world. Her memory had provided him with a love sufficient to colour his attitude towards life, but this love was now being reinforced, if not replaced, by a living love for Mrs. Bronson. Browning's temporary fear is that the optimism of *Ferishtah's Fancies*, partly written in such happy and propitious circumstances in Venice, may be too subjective owing to the benefit he has received from the love shown him by Mrs. Bronson. The arms that form the halo irised round his head are now both Elizabeth's and Katharine's.

It is not surprising that Browning should link the two women together in this way, because Mrs. Bronson had much of the same appeal to him that Elizabeth had had those many years before in Wimpole Street. She was frail, intelligent and modern in her ideas. In his world, men were physically strong, but relied on women for comfort and moral support. Katharine, like Elizabeth, gave both, and seemed to possess an instinctive understanding of his wants and needs. She shared many of his ideas, she had a good sense of humour, and she admired him. It is easy to understand why Browning should become strongly attracted to her and why she should influence the poems he was writing.

OTHER MATTERS

By the autumn of 1884 Browning's feelings for Mrs. Bronson were stronger than perhaps it was wise to show. Although her marriage had broken down, she was still a married woman, and the sick Arthur Bronson was a convenient obstacle to prevent Browning from being more open with his affections. His letters to Katharine during the year are full of witty, extravagant compliments, almost as if he is playing an elaborate game, or donning a mask behind which he can disguise his true feelings:

Oh the dear, dear Friend,—will she not be glad to think how glad *I* am, who can tell her that my precious "Case" arrived, and all its

precious packages came safely as safely could be,—so that my heart
is no more broken than are her gifts.[47]
   Would I could fly to a home of mine and a housemate beyond the
sea—"Wenn ich ein voglein wäre!" But I must remain here, wingless
except in fancy-flights to my own friend of whom I am the own friend
while this machine is to him.[48]

Browning had always found it difficult to commit himself emotionally.
His gaucheness had caused problems in the past; in the new situation in
which he now was, he used the presence of Sarianna and Edith to make
himself less vulnerable. He was genuinely fond of Edith; Sarianna was
genuinely fond of Katharine. The four of them enjoyed one another's
company; and, with Arthur Bronson ill in Paris, Browning could feel
sufficiently protected to enjoy the attention he was receiving and indulge
himself in harmless flights of fancy about Katharine Bronson.
   The artificial nature of the relationship was forced into realistic perspective by the death of Arthur Bronson in March of the following year. Mrs.
Bronson was with him when he died, and made arrangements for a
monument to be erected over his grave in the cemetery of St. Germain-en-
Laye. She waited in Paris to tidy up financial matters before returning to
Venice and from there to a spa to recuperate.
   Browning had planned to spend a sixth autumn in Venice in 1885,
during which he wanted to introduce his son Pen to the city. At the last
minute, however, Katharine Bronson decided she might stay at Trentino
in the Austrian Tyrol, where she was convalescing, and, therefore, might
be unable to entertain him and Sarianna in Venice. Browning wrote
hurriedly, in not wholly appropriate language for the present situation,
but in his former vein:

> It will be heart-breaking if you are not in Venice ... but for Pen's
> mortification if we do not keep tryst with him, we should turn away
> our heads from the vacant shrine and departed glory—fine words but
> happening to be true.[49]

Mrs. Bronson changed her mind and the Brownings stayed at the Palazzo
Giustiniani-Recanati as usual, but their visit was not a success, and, for
the only time in his ten-year friendship with Katharine Bronson, Browning
longed to return home before his holiday was over. There were a number
of reasons for this. Autumn 1885 was intolerably wet; it rained almost
incessantly in Venice, so Browning was prevented from going on his
favourite walks and Sarianna caught a bad cold. There was less entertainment than usual, as Mrs. Bronson was still in mourning for her husband,
and there was the added complication of Pen.
   Pen Browning had arrived in Venice with a friend a few weeks before
his father, but he became a frequent visitor to Ca Alvisi after Browning's
arrival. He had fallen in love with the city, so Browning began negotiations
to purchase the Palazzo Manzoni as a second home, a place where Pen

Arthur Bronson, 1878

Robert Browning, 1883

could live, continue his career and become part of the artists' colony then in Venice. There are also indications that Browning hoped the yet unmarried Pen might fall in love with the attractive Edith Bronson and further link the two families. Neither idea materialized. The purchase of the palazzo proved more difficult than Browning imagined, owing to legal difficulties, and Edith Bronson was in no way attracted to the balding 36-year-old Pen. One suspects that there were a number of tensions at Ca Alvisi during that October and November. Browning was never subtle in matters requiring tact or finesse, and Mrs. Bronson was not in good enough health to be able to smooth his way. The continual rain only made matters worse. By 9 November Browning was writing to England, "I stay here for a little matter of business, and not pleasure."[50]

Certainly the wretched autumn of 1885 seems to have dampened Browning's friendship with Katharine Bronson. Although he saw her in London the following year and invited her and Edith to Oxford parties to mark the end of Benjamin Jowett's vice-chancellorship, he wrote less frequently. Only two letters survive from 1886, three from 1887; and there is a gap in their correspondence from June 1887 to May 1888.[51] Even the tone of the few letters that exist is slightly more formal than the playful banter of earlier years, though he is always friendly.

Browning turned his mind to other matters: to writing a new book, *Parleyings with Certain People of Importance in Their Day*, and to the impending upheaval of a house-move in London from Warwick Crescent to De Vere Gardens. Holidays were spent with Sarianna in Wales and Switzerland; and in 1887 Pen was at last married, to a friend of former years, the American Fannie Coddington. Marriage revived Pen's hopes of a Venetian home and he explored the possibility of buying the imposing Palazzo Rezzonico on the Grand Canal, which was later purchased with Fannie's money. Browning, too, found his interest in Venice and Mrs. Bronson suddenly reviving.

The prelude to the second and more important stage in their friendship started quietly with Browning's exhaustion after a busy social season and the dislocation of his life during the house removal. Plagued by importunate nobodies intent on his opinion of this and that, he wrote to Mrs. Bronson on 8 August 1888, asking if he and Sarianna could come to her in Venice "for a short stay" after spending a month with Pen and Fannie at Primiero in the Tyrol:

> But if I am to get any good out of my visit I must lead the quietest of lives, and be lulled by the cigarette-smoke of just my friend—not the *chiacchere* of new acquaintance.[52]

The return to Mrs. Bronson, then, was for peace and quiet, for an understanding and familiar friend to soothe him. Browning had aged considerably in the two years since he had last seen her; he was finding the London winters with their smoke and fog increasingly more difficult to endure, and he was tired physically and mentally.[53]

By the time he reached Venice on 12 September, Browning had recovered some of his spirits. The fresh, clean air of Primiero and the attentions of Pen and Fannie had helped his recuperation, and he was looking forward to his short stay with Mrs. Bronson:

> My stay will be short—but *sweet* in every sense of the word, if I find her in good health, and, in all other respects, just as I left her.[54]

His letters from Primiero are full of expectancy, and show a return of the half-comic banter of three years before:

> Hear a conundrum to the point. "What is Freezing-point?—32°. What is Squeezing-point? Two in the shade:" and this is the shade, and here are you and I,—and the squeezed writing follows of necessity— and desists through discretion.[55]

A week later, on 30 August, he sent her a box of love-in-the-mist flowers with the manuscript of a new poem, "White Witchcraft," which is as playful in its tone as the former letter. Addressed presumably to Katharine, the poem imagines the two of them transformed by white magic into animals. She becomes a fox, while Browning portrays himself as a toad, looking at her with eyes of adoration. There might even be a pearl (her favourite jewel), he suggests, "beneath his puckered brow," if she cared to look:

> If you & I could turn to beasts what beast should either be?
> Shall you and I play Jove for once? Turn fox, then—I decree;
> Shy wild sweet stealer of my grapes! Now do your worst for me[!]
>
> And thus you think to spite your friend—turned loathsome:
> what, a toad?
> So, all men shrink & shun me? dear men, pursue your road!
> Leave but my crevice in the stone, a reptile's fit abode!
>
> Now say your worst, Canidia! "He's loathsome, I allow:
> There may or may not lurk a pearl beneath that puckered brow:
> But then the eyes which follow mine—love lasts there, anyhow."

The implications are self-evident; Browning intended to enjoy his visit to Venice, and show his devotion.

In fact the Venetian holiday exceeded his expectations, and the short stay became three glorious months. He was made "perfectly happy" by Mrs. Bronson, who had prepared rooms for the Brownings in Ca Alvisi itself rather than in the Giustiniani-Recanati. His days were spent simply. A morning walk with Sarianna in the public gardens, looking at the animals in the open-air zoo, was always followed by a gondola ride with Mrs. Bronson in the afternoon, often to the Lido. Browning, sometimes with Edith as a guide, used to explore the canals, stop at the antique shops, or rest outside the church of Santi Giovanni e Paulo in his favourite square and gaze on the Colleoni statue. "The weather here is wonderful," he wrote to his publisher George Smith, "such a succession of summer

days, with the addition of a bracing autumn-wind, I never experienced
before. I have recovered so much health and strength that it seems suicidal
in some measure to return at once to London and the fogs."[56] To an artist
friend he described another glorious day: "A sun floods the room from
the open window, while an autumnal freshness makes it more than
enjoyable, almost intoxicating."[57] Browning had time to do some writing,
and by now he planned to dedicate his next book to Mrs. Bronson. During
the autumn his feelings towards her deepened and returned to what they
had been in 1884. His letters to her on his return to London are full of
gratitude:

> Dearest friend,—I may just say *that*, and no more: for what can I
> say? I shall never have your kindness out of my thoughts,—and you
> will never forget me, I know.[58]

Mrs. Bronson was missing him, too, and in her Diary-Calendar, designed
and decorated for her by Edith, in which she had carefully recorded the
dates of the Brownings' arrival and departure, she wrote the following
poem:

> We each and all hold fast
> An ever-living treasure,
> Since memory of past
> Is surely present pleasure,
> So when you're far away
> And cruel seas divide us,
> We both may truly say—
> This joy is not denied us.[59]

A fortnight later Browning wrote:

> Yes, dearest friend, I can well believe you think of me sometimes,
> even oft times, for in what place, or what hour, of the house or the
> day, can you fail to be reminded of some piece of kindness done by
> you and received by me during those memorable three months when
> you cared for me and my sister constantly, and were so successful
> in your endeavour to make us perfectly happy? Depend on it, neither
> I nor she ... forget you for a moment—nor are we without your
> names on our lips much longer, when we sit quietly at home of an
> evening and talk over the pleasantest of pleasant days ... so, simply,
> God bless you, my beloveds![60]

Browning was always enthusiastic and generous, yet these remarks surpass
the gallantries he wrote to other women. Edith and Sarianna are still both
included in his thanks and gratitude, but the autumn of 1888 marked a
significant shift in his feeling for Mrs. Bronson. For the last time in his
life he was beginning to fall in love, a love he was to try to express to
her the following autumn when they were together in Asolo.

INDIAN SUMMER AT ASOLO

Browning first mentions the small walled hill-city of Asolo, situated
between Bassano and Treviso in the foothills of the Alps, in his poem

Sordello. He draws an optimistic, idyllic picture of an Asolan boy singing
Sordello's lay as he climbs the hills:

> Lo, On a heathy brown and nameless hill
> By sparkling Asolo, in mist and chill,
> Morning just up, higher and higher runs
> A child barefoot and rosy. See! the sun's
> On the square castle's inner-court's low wall
> Like the chine of some extinct animal
> Half turned to earth and flowers; and through the haze
> (Save where some slender patches of grey maize
> Are to be overleaped) that boy has crossed
> The whole hill-side ... singing all the while.
>
> (VI, ll. 853–864)

He had visited Asolo in 1838 on his first journey to Italy and it had
enchanted him. Its arcaded streets, the frescoed houses, the extraordinarily
beautiful views of the neighbouring countryside, whether across the plain
to Venice or to the Alps in the north, all fascinated Browning. But, above
all, its atmosphere and its history gave it a particular charm. There was,
and still is, a timelessness about Asolo, a sense that great events have
passed, and left not only their ruins behind, but something of their spirit.
Once, in the late fifteenth and early sixteenth centuries, the kingdom of
the exiled Queen Catherine Cornaro of Cyprus, it has within its walls a
feeling of the completeness of an independent whole, where past and
present have been inextricably bound together. Where better for Sordello's
lay to be perpetuated than in this city? And that is why Browning chose
an Asolan boy to sing the song at the conclusion of the poem.

Back in England, Browning could not rid himself of the influence of
Asolo. It became the setting for his next work, the poem-play *Pippa
Passes*, in which the innocence and faith of young Pippa, a silk-weaver
from Asolo, is contrasted with the evil and cruelty of the people around
her. Here for just twenty-four hours Asolo becomes a microcosm, and
man's lusts, ambitions, idealism and cruelty are shown up for what they
really are. Repentance and hope, renewed hope, is the keynote and the
conclusion of the poem, for it is in Asolo that God's in his heaven and
all's right with the world.

Browning was not to see Asolo again for forty years. Something stopped
him from returning. He had a recurrent dream that he saw Asolo in the
distance, but that he was held back and frustrated from reaching it:

> I am traveling with a friend, sometimes with one person, sometimes
> with another, oftenest with one I do not recognize. Suddenly I see
> the town I love sparkling in the sun on the hillside. I cry to my
> companion, "Look! look! there is Asolo! Oh, do let us go there!"
> The friend invariably answers, "Impossible; we cannot stop." "Pray,
> pray let us go there!" I entreat. "No," persists the friend, "we cannot;
> we must go on and leave Asolo for another day," and so I am hurried
> away, and wake to know that I have been dreaming it all, both
> pleasure and disappointment.[61]

View of Asolo, Showing La Rocca and the Cathedral

La Mura

Eventually the dreams ended when in 1878 Browning and Sarianna spent a week there on their way to Venice, and he felt that much of the mystery had departed. Although they both had a pleasant holiday, Asolo was "more ordinary-life-like."[62]

It was, therefore, something of a surprise for Browning to learn in June 1889 that Mrs. Bronson had visited Asolo, had herself been captivated and intended to return. He had told her about it, mentioning its delights the previous year as he reminisced about the old days; and presumably she had read his poems. However, on discovering that she now shared all his initial enthusiasms, he was cautious in his comments:

> I ... am apprehensive that, if you return for July and August the heat may be as overpowering as S. and I found ... Why not try Primiero—a delightful retreat, quite as near Venice, and much more likely to invigorate you than Asolo—besides being as lovely in its way.[63]

Mrs. Bronson chose to disregard him, returned to Asolo the following month, and purchased a small house, La Mura, set in the walls of the city next to one of the gates, with a wild, attractive stretch of the hillside as a garden. Browning became immediately more interested:

> Go there and get all the good out of the beautiful place I used to dream about so often in the old days—till at last I saw it again, and the dreams stopped—to begin again, I trust, with a figure there never associated with Asolo before. Shall I ever see you there in no dream?[64]

One suspects that this may have been one of Mrs. Bronson's intentions in buying La Mura, although the house was too small to entertain comfortably both Robert and Sarianna. When, therefore, Browning eventually decided in August that he would cross the Channel again and visit Italy once more, she made arrangements for brother and sister to stay in a house owned by Signora Nina Tabacchi, almost opposite La Mura in the main street. Arriving there in September, Browning and Sarianna lingered week after happy week until cold weather in early November brought their holiday to an end, and they returned reluctantly to Venice and Pen and Fannie in the Palazzo Rezzonico.

From the beginning Browning enjoyed his stay in Asolo and was surprised by the warmth of the reception given to him and Sarianna. Mrs. Bronson had "out-Bronsoned herself"[65] in her care for their comfort:

> [She] has simply outdone herself in kind forethought for us—far too kind. For she has fitted up rooms for us in a house just opposite her own,—whitewashed, painted and adorned merely for our sake, and abundantly furnished with bran-new *mobili* which, I hope, may be turned to account in her own dwelling: the linen,—every article in abundance—so as properly to instruct the natives, for there is an arrangement which makes me a capital bath-room. The woman of the house is well-known to Mrs. B. and the service is perfect. We breakfast and lunch here, then take tea, go out, and dine over the way. The place quite justifies my early impression of it as extremely beautiful.[66]

It is not surprising that he inscribed the latest photograph of himself, which he had brought for her: "Robert Browning, Sept 5 Asolo 1889, written in great joy at finding himself there."

Mrs. Bronson proved to be as useful and generous a hostess in Asolo as she had been in Venice. She arranged carriage drives every afternoon and allowed Browning to choose the routes. They went everywhere: Bassano, Possagno, Castelfranco—and to La Barca della Regina, the ruined pleasure-gardens of Queen Caterina Cornaro, converted into a slovenly farmhouse adorned with the fading coats-of-arms and frescoes of a bygone magnificence. Pigs were styed where peacocks once walked in the water-gardens. Returning from one such expedition, Browning was uncharacteristically silent. Mrs. Bronson asked if anything was the matter, only to learn that he had been composing a poem in his head and had completed it on the journey.

Systematically they explored all the scenes of his past visits, noting the changes of fifty years. With an almost obstinate determination Browning checked and rechecked to see if his memory had played him false. At neighbouring San Zenone, for example, a single tower remained of the twelfth-century tyrant Alberic's castle, pulled down by the local townsfolk in horror at his family's brutality. Browning had visited it in 1838 on foot and recorded his visit in *Sordello*:

> Wild o'er his castle on the pleasant knoll,
> You hear its one tower left, a belfry, toll–
> The earthquake spared it last year, laying flat
> The modern church beneath, no harm in that!
> Chirrups the contumacious grasshopper,
> Rustles the lizard and the cushats chirre
> Above the ravage: there, at deep of day
> A week since, heard I the old Canon say
> He saw with his own eyes a barrow burst
> And Alberic's huge skeleton unhearsed
> Only five years ago.
>
> (VI, ll. 783–793)

The canon was long since dead, but the tower still stood and Browning went to visit it, telling his friends the story as they approached San Zenone. They reached the tower as Mrs. Bronson describes:

> As the author of "Sordello" looked thence upon the wild land at the foot of the eminence, he said: "Just think of Alberico tied to the heels of his horse, dragged to death over those sharp rocks and stones!"
>
> Vainly we tried to persuade him not to climb the insecure wooden staircase within the tower. It seemed a dark and perilous place, I thought. My mind was filled with dreadful memories of the past, so much so as to make me doubt the honest intent of the poor and surely innocent custodian who accompanied us. It was evident that the poet had set his mind upon looking out from the very top of the tower, and entreaties to the contrary were useless. I well remember waiting

in terror for his return, and that my excited imagination played me
cruel tricks on the occasion. From the top he could scan the whole
Venetian plain from north to south in its bright autumn tints under
a declining sun. He remained there some time in contemplation; what
were his thoughts, who can say? We can be sure they were great and
far-reaching ones.[67]

Browning safely descended and at the foot of the tower bought some
arrow-heads a peasant brought him from the neighbouring fields—and
then fast home to La Mura in the carriage. For him the centuries of past
history that Asolo had seen, the feuding Guelfs and Ghibellines, the
cultured court of Queen Caterina, the cradle and grave of the sculptor
Canova, lived again as he examined building, fresco and statue. Yet he
was doing something more than careful sightseeing, for he himself was
part of the history of Asolo. Fifty years previously he had experienced a
revelation there. "I was right to fall in love with this place fifty years
ago, was I not?" he now anxiously asked Mrs. Bronson. "We outlive
some places, people and things that charmed us in our youth, but the
loveliness of this is no disappointment; it is even more beautiful to me
now than then."[68]

But things had changed. The echo in the Rocca was missing, and he,
too, hadn't he changed? The historical Browning of 1838 and the living,
breathing Browning of 1889 inhabited the same body, but what exactly
was the connection between them? Fancy and fact: how to distinguish
the two? What was fact? What fancy? These were the questions he tried
to answer each morning in his lodging as he put pen to paper. "To think
that I should be here again!" he kept saying to himself, as if he felt himself
in the power of something supernatural. He worked hard. The manuscript
of his book of poems began to take a new shape under the influence of
his recent experiences in Asolo. This Browning acknowledged when he
decided to call it *Asolando*, in honour of the city and its most distinguished
intellectual, Pietro Bembo. He spent as much time rearranging and revising
the poems he had brought with him as in writing new ones; and the
sub-title of the volume, *Fancies and Facts*, showed the fresh theme the
book was to explore.

In this happy mood Browning's poor health, already improving before
he reached Asolo, left him. After a few weeks his coughing stopped and
his short breath eased. He felt much younger: although the realist in him
knew he hadn't long to live, he told Katharine he was good enough for
another ten years yet. He made plans to buy some land facing hers across
the valley to build a house, for he now saw their two lives drawing closer
and closer to each other. After all, he would never have returned to Asolo
if she hadn't encouraged him; she was now sharing with him the rediscovery of his past and all that it meant to him, and she seemed to understand
what he was experiencing. Certainly he hadn't met a woman of such
sympathy since Elizabeth died. His feelings, already engaged the previous
year in Venice, now matured from warm friendship into love.

September passed and the first two weeks of October. Mrs. Bronson had intended to return to Venice for the autumn season long before this, but she stayed in Asolo with the Brownings. By the 15th the manuscript of *Asolando* was ready to send to the publishers; several new poems had been written, and all the rest had been revised. The order, too, had been carefully chosen. As a final touch, Browning wrote two paragraphs of dedication, the longest dedication in any of his books. Addressed to Mrs. Arthur Bronson, it started:

> To whom but you, dear Friend, should I dedicate verses—some few written, all of them supervised, in the comfort of your presence, and with yet another experience of the gracious hospitality now bestowed on me since so many a year,—adding a charm even to my residences at Venice, and leaving me little regret for the surprise and delight at my visits to Asolo in bygone days?

On looking more closely at this sentence, one appreciates that "Friend" is capitalized, which is not strictly necessary and which gives emphasis to the relationship. Browning then says that Katharine Bronson made the charming city of Venice appear even more charming by her presence, and that she makes up for the surprise and delight he once found at Asolo, but which he has now lost with old age. Mrs. Bronson herself therefore is the new delight, the new pleasure. She was not to read these words until she was given a set of proofs of *Asolando* in Venice just before Browning's death. Unaware of Browning's growing love, she accompanied him and Sarianna to the delightful eighteenth-century theatre built within the ruined walls of Queen Caterina's castle to watch a touring company twelve times in as many days. She listened to Browning play the spinet at La Mura and read aloud from the poets. There were occasional visitors, but for the most part Browning was thrown more and more into Mrs. Bronson's company, while Sarianna sat quietly with her tatting on the sofa. He was 77 and Katharine was 54; she honoured and flattered to be hostess to one of the world's greatest poets, he requiring something deeper and more realistic in their relationship. How could he tell her what he felt? Rather than risk a scene which might spoil the Asolan idyll, Browning expressed his feelings in his poetry.

ASOLANDO

Asolando consists of thirty miscellaneous poems, ranging in length from 8 to 352 lines. They are in different forms—blank verse, couplets and stanzas—and different genres. There are narrative poems, dialogues, lyrics, a dramatic monologue, and speculative poems in which Browning explores ideas in his own person. An autobiographical prologue and epilogue begin and end the volume.

The revision and regrouping Browning had done in Asolo gives the book a loose but meaningful structure. The diverse poems in their contrasting styles complement and develop one another as they explore the relationship between fact and fancy, first in love, then in the characters

The Old Theatre, Asolo, ca. 1890

Perhaps but a memory, after all!
— Of what came once when a woman leant
To feel for my brow where her kiss might fall.
  Truth ever, truth only the excellent!

Now.

(new Page. 7.

Out of your whole life give but a moment!
All of your life that has gone before,
All to come after it, — so you ignore
So you make perfect the present, condense,
In a rapture of rage, for perfection's endowment,
Thought and feeling and soul and sense —
Merged in a moment which gives me at last
For once you around me, beneath me, above me —
Me — sure that despite of time future, time past, —
This tick of our life-time's one moment you love me!
How long such suspension may linger? Ah, Sweet —
The moment eternal — just that and no more —
When ecstasy's utmost we clutch at the core
While cheeks burn, arms open, eyes shut and lips meet!

Manuscript of "Now" from *Asolando*

of men and women, and finally in religious belief. While some of the poems have specific reference to Browning, many are historical and anecdotal. Familiar subjects from former books recur, such as a monologue spoken by a pagan in Rome at the advent of Christianity, or the relationship of a second-rate painter to his wife. Among this miscellany there are three poems with strong autobiographical content—"Inapprehensiveness," "Development" and "Epilogue," each of which concludes one of the three major groups of poems in the book. These poems specifically relate the three topics of love, people and religion to Browning and to 1889.[69]

Asolando is Browning's last book in more ways than one. Ever since *Ferishtah's Fancies*, he had been recapitulating and redefining his ideas. In *Parleyings* he addressed the spirits of seven men whose work he had known from boyhood and who had influenced his life in the spheres of philosophy, history, poetry, politics, painting, Greek and music.[70] *Asolando* saw a further recapitulation, as an old man looked back on life in a more personal way than in his two previous books. His arrival in Asolo had provided Browning with the stimulus for a reappraisal, not only because of his previous visit there as a young man, but because Browning soon discovered within its walls a scenario which recalled so much of his earlier life. Where else could he have found so intimately huddled together a medieval castle, a Renaissance palace, a cathedral, a monastery and an eighteenth-century theatre? There were religion, history, art and music in Asolo, as well as the Italian landscape and the Italian people. The more Browning stayed, the more Asolo took hold of his subconscious. Mrs. Bronson's presence in the city, her evident affection, and his own love towards her not merely existed as a reality in the present but recalled other love he had experienced as a younger man. The more he stayed with her, the more she unconsciously fulfilled both roles. *Asolando*, therefore, became Browning's final statement about life, both the accumulated wisdom of his years and also life as he saw it in the present, in old age. Mrs. Bronson gave the impetus for his thoughts and feelings about love, just as she provided, as an affectionate human being, a fresh meaning for him in the present at La Mura.

The love lyrics in *Asolando* explore means of achieving the essential truth which lies at the centre of love. A number show lovers failing in the quest, usually because they blur fact and fancy; but the most startling are those of strong physical passion in which the truth is sought in the intensity of the factual present:

NOW

Out of your whole life give but a moment!
All of your life that has gone before,
All to come after it,—so you ignore
So you make perfect the present,—condense,
In a rapture of rage, for perfection's endowment,
Thought and feeling and soul and sense—

> Merged in a moment which gives me at last
> You around me for once, you beneath me, above me—
> Me—sure that despite of time future, time past,—
> This tick of our life-time's one moment you love me!
> How long such suspension may linger? Ah, Sweet—
> The moment eternal—just that and no more—
> When ecstasy's utmost we clutch at the core
> While cheeks burn, arms open, eyes shut and lips meet!

The strength of feeling in this lyric has surprised and even embarrassed critics. Written a year previously and revised in Asolo, it captures the resurgence of love Browning was experiencing at the time and also his optimism that "the good minute" may be found and be made permanent. After the initial exclamation, the ideas tumble out in a torrent of excited phrases, until eventually, after nine lines, one is forced to pause for breath and ask the inevitable question: "Can this last?" The confident, idealistic lover asserts that the strength and commitment of their love will eternalize it, and the poem finishes with a series of highly physical images. In the context of Browning's situation when he revised the poem, the physicality is understandable, and it is possible that he intended the reader to take the optimism at face value. There is, however, a strident tone to the poem, an over-assertiveness, a sense of strain, as the lover describes to his girl how they will achieve the sublime. The more one examines the diction, the less convincing it appears: "rage," "clutch," "burn," are negative concepts; the constant use of the first person singular gives a feeling of desperation to the lover's declaration, and makes the girl an extremely passive figure. There would seem, therefore, to be little real communion between them, in spite of the lover's assertion to the contrary.

Other poems in *Asolando* show the same physicality, especially the autobiographical "Inapprehensiveness," which describes Browning's feelings for Mrs. Bronson. There is in this poem a similar lack of fulfillment, but the feeling is definitely one of frustration, one of lost opportunity. At the beginning of the poem Browning pictures himself with Mrs. Bronson in the loggia at La Mura looking up at the ruins of Queen Caterina Cornaro's castle. The identification is clear to anyone in command of the biographical and topographical facts,[71] but for the general reader Browning portrays an old man standing with a younger woman looking across a valley in Asolo at a ruin:

> We two stood simply friend-like side by side,
> Viewing a twilight country far and wide,
> Till she at length broke silence. "How it towers
> Yonder, the ruin o'er this vale of ours!
> The West's faint flare behind it so relieves
> Its rugged outline—sight perhaps deceives,
> Or I could almost fancy that I see
> A branch wave plain—belike some wind-sown tree

Chance-rooted where a missing turret was.
What would I give for the perspective glass
At home, to make out if 'tis really so!
Has Ruskin noticed here at Asolo
That certain weed-growths on the ravaged wall
Seem" ...

There is a deceptive air of calm peacefulness in the situation. The evening landscape in a twilight country with the faint flare of the setting sun, the ruin with its missing turret and its ravaged wall, would seem to reflect the serene old age of the speaker as he stands "simply friend-like" with the younger woman beside him. Her leisured musing with its domestic and literary detail is completely bound up with the scene in front of her, and she pays little attention to her companion:

That certain weed-growths on the ravaged wall
Seem" ... something that I could not say at all,
My thought being rather—as absorbed she sent
Look onward after look from eyes distent
With longing to reach Heaven's gate left ajar—
"Oh, fancies that might be, oh, facts that are!
What of a wilding? By you stands, and may
So stand unnoticed till the Judgment Day,
One who, if once aware that your regard
Claimed what his heart holds,—woke, as from its sward
The flower, the dormant passion, so to speak—
Then what a rush of life would startling wreak
Revenge on your inapprehensive stare
While, from the ruin and the West's faint flare,
You let your eyes meet mine, touch what you term
Quietude—that's an universe in germ—
The dormant passion needing but a look
To burst into immense life!"

The shift of tone as we enter the speaker's mind is dramatic. The fragmented syntax, as the strength of feeling propels the thought forward, is in sharp contrast to the measured periods of the woman's speech. The tension and frustration he is experiencing is clearly shown in the incomplete phrases and the linguistic extravagance, as he allows his "wilding" of an idea free rein to develop itself. Twice he uses the phrase "dormant passion," returning to it for an explosive conclusion:

Then what a rush of life would startling wreak
Revenge on your inapprehensive stare.

Unlike his companion, the speaker won't accept the twilight country of old age with its ruin and faint flare. For him the view is picturesque, not emblematic, and his feelings are youthful—like the wind-sown tree which has rooted itself in the wall of the ruin. He has the fancy that, even now, these feelings could be reciprocated, if only the woman would understand:

> The dormant passion needing but a look
> To burst into immense life!

But she is unaware of his feelings, and the poem ends:

> "No, the book
> Which noticed how the wall-growths wave" said she
> "Was not by Ruskin."
> I said "Vernon Lee?"

The anti-climax in which the speaker capitulates and appears to accept the woman on her own terms, makes it clear that fact conquers fancy. He will never tell her about his love for her, because she would never understand, and so he keeps his secret and the good minute goes.

"Inapprehensiveness" reflects accurately Browning's feelings for Mrs. Bronson in Asolo, but the conclusion is less resigned than at first appears. Mrs. Bronson's comments about Ruskin, which place their relationship on an aesthetic-literary plane, is countered by Browning's reference to Vernon Lee. In reluctantly accepting Mrs. Bronson's inapprehensiveness, Browning is at the same time challenging her. Vernon Lee was the pen name of Violet Paget, a precocious writer, only 33 in 1889 with three or four books already published, including one in which she criticized Ruskin's ideas on art. Mrs. Bronson's thoughts, therefore are on old men, Ruskin (and Browning), while Browning's are centred on modern, younger women.[72] There is no quietude in his old age if only Mrs. Bronson would encourage him.

The reason for Mrs. Bronson's lack of awareness of Browning's feelings is made clear in another autobiographical poem, the epilogue to *Asolando*, which not merely concludes the book, but more specifically completes the section in *Asolando* dealing with religious belief. It is the religious aspect of the poem which has made it famous, as Browning's final assessment of his attitude to life and death:

> At the midnight in the silence of the sleep-time,
>   When you set your fancies free,
> Will they pass to where—by death, fools think, imprisoned—
> Low he lies who once so loved you, whom you loved so,
>   —Pity me?
>
> Oh to love so, be so loved, yet so mistaken!
>   What had I on earth to do
> With the slothful, with the mawkish, the unmanly?
> Like the aimless, helpless, hopeless, did I drivel
>   —Being—who?
>
> One who never turned his back but marched breast forward,
>   Never doubted clouds would break,
> Never dreamed, though right were worsted, wrong would triumph,
> Held we fall to rise, are baffled to fight better,
>   Sleep to wake.
>
> No, at noonday in the bustle of man's work-time
>   Greet the unseen with a cheer!

Bid him forward, breast and back as either should be,
"Strive and thrive!" cry "Speed,—fight on, fare ever
There as here!"

The poem is addressed by a dead man to a living woman. Browning acknowledged that he was the man, and for this reason Sarianna hated to hear him read the poem aloud, because she felt it so full of foreboding. The identification of the woman as Mrs. Bronson is logical, not merely because *Asolando* is dedicated to her and she is mentioned as the friend with the optic glass in the Prologue, but because without her presence in the poem, the first two verses make very little sense.[73] These deal with Browning's love for her and the limitations of that love. To begin with he acknowledges their mutual affection ("who once so loved you, whom you loved so") before acknowledging a flaw:

Oh to love so, be so loved, yet so mistaken.

He is saying that both he and Mrs. Bronson were in love with one another but in different ways. While he loved her physically as a woman, as is clear from "Inapprehensiveness," her love for him was one of adoration. To Katharine Bronson he was always "the author of *Sordello*," "the great poet." "If I try to recall Robert Browning's words," she once said, "it is as though I had talked to a being apart from other men. My feeling may seem exaggerated, but it was only natural when one considers my vivid sense of his moral and intellectual superiority, and connects that with his kindness to me and mine."[74] In a suppressed passage from her article "Browning in Venice," she developed this idea:

When I had the happiness of seeing him constantly I could not hold a clear or critical opinion of him. I only felt a vague sense of wonder that I, so insignificant a person in comparison with this exalted human-being, should be permitted to know him, to hear him converse, to watch the ever-changing expressions of his wonderful, mobile face, to see the genial sympathetic smile, to receive now and again words of affectionate interest in me and mine from his eloquent lips. . . .
    Do not think I exaggerate when I assure you that from the first day I knew him until the last[,] I was always under an impression, never inspired by any other great personage, I am with one of God's interpretors, one part is undoubtedly human, but the divine spark which we all carry about with us, is in this man a great flame; he is above and beyond all other mortals, he has been instructed with the secrets of Heaven, he has looked with divinely-given second sight into the world to come. The sentiment with which he inspired me was not what men call love, but was a reverence.[75]

Mrs. Bronson was also writing poetry during the summer and autumn of 1889, including a series called "Garden Fancies" (a title she had borrowed from Browning). One poem, written just before Browning arrived in Asolo, is addressed to him:

> Now the shadows darken,
> Now the stars are bright,
> Ah what tender yearning—
> Wanders through the night.
>
> Through the seas of dreamland
> Finding peace nor rest,
> Glides my soul in longing
> To thy faithful breast.
>
> Take its deep devotion!
> All belongs to thee,
> Well thou knowest it never
> May return to me.[76]

Try as he might, Browning was unable to change this attitude. He deliberately spoke to her of ordinary things, and she found him "tenderly sympathetic." Did she also find him attractive? The following description suggests that she did:

> He had no personal vanity: it never occured to him to admire himself in any way, to call attention to the beauty of his hand, which in old age was the hand of youth, nor did he seem to be aware of the perfect outline of his head, the colour and brightness of his eyes, or the fairness of his skin, which, with his snow-white hair, made him look as if carved in old Greek marble.[77]

It is a sympathetic portrait; but, physical though it may be, the aesthetic sense dominates.

Sadly, Mrs. Bronson did not understand Browning's feelings for her, but instead cosseted the poet, wrapping him up warmly against the autumnal air, putting extra rugs round his knees when they went out in the carriage until he protested loudly. He wasn't mawkish, unmanly, hopeless, helpless. Far from slothful, he was active, regularly walking up the steep path to the ruins of the castle on the Rocca above Asolo. He didn't drivel, but had clear aims. She was loving him in the wrong way; she was mistaking him.

Browning was realistic enough to accept that the way of physical love was closed to him, and that Mrs. Bronson would never be able to respond. He, therefore, turned to the afterlife and in the Epilogue looked forward to life after death.

Although he had gaily told Mrs. Bronson he had another ten years to live, Browning was deceiving himself with another fancy. His health had further deteriorated during 1889 and people were beginning to notice his frailty. Earlier in the year in Cambridge, Edmund Gosse was surprised to find Browning so mentally active because "his life ... [was] so manifestly waning in essential vigour ... Cold upon cold left [him] weaker; the recuperative power was rapidly and continuously on the decrease."[78] Browning was beginning to talk about his death and qualify many statements with the words "If I live ..." His photographs clearly show the decline, and his manservant, W.H. Grove, claimed that:

[A] very interesting thing happened when I took the last photograph
of him before he went to Venice for the last time. After the sitting
was over he placed his hand on my shoulder and said, "Now, William,
this is the last photograph I shall ever have taken and I hope it will
be of some use to you."[79]

The stay in Asolo improved his health almost miraculously, but even
there, when saying goodbye to his friends the Storys who had been visiting
La Mura, he put an extra warmth into his handshake and an extra emphasis
on the meaning of their friendship, as if he wouldn't see them again.

It is not, therefore, surprising that Browning should have ended
Asolando with a poem in which he asked Mrs. Bronson to consider him
after his death. When I die, he asks her, will you be sorry, thinking that
I am imprisoned in the grave? If so, you will be wrong, because the
afterlife is merely a continuation of life on earth; therefore, acknowledge
me and encourage me as I live the same type of life elsewhere that I lived
on earth:

> No, at noonday in the bustle of man's work-time
>   Greet the unseen with a cheer!
> Bid him forward, breast and back as either should be,
> "Strive and thrive!" cry "Speed,—fight on, fare ever
>   There as here!"

These sentiments support ideas about death that Browning had been
expressing for a number of years. William Sharp records these most
graphically when he remembers Browning saying:

> Death, death! It is this harping on death I despise so much . . . this
> idle and often cowardly as well as ignorant harping! Why should we
> not change like everything else? . . . Why, *amico mio*, you know as
> well as I that death is life, just as our daily, our momentarily dying
> body is none the less alive and ever recruiting new forces of existence.
> Without death, which is our crapelike churchyardy word for change,
> for growth, there could be no prolongation of that which we call life.
> Pshaw! it is foolish to argue upon such a thing even. For myself, I
> deny death as an end of everything. Never say of me that I am dead![80]

DEATH IN VENICE

On 31 October the Brownings left Asolo for Venice and the Palazzo
Rezzonico, where Pen and Fannie were waiting to welcome them for the
first time to their new home. Mrs. Bronson followed them to Venice a
week later, and they were all soon exchanging visits between the Rezzonico and Ca Alvisi. For the following three weeks they met almost
every day, for tea, at the theatre and at social gatherings, such as the
occasion when Browning declaimed poems from *Asolando* for two hours
in the Palazzo Barbaro at the request of the Curtises. Browning's life-style
in Venice at this time was foolhardy for a man of his age; he used every
minute of the day and sampled all kinds of entertainment. He quickly
established a regular routine. Rising at 6:00 A.M., he read for two hours

before breakfast at 8:30. At 10:30 he went to the Lido with the Curtises for a long walk, irrespective of the weather, which was damp and windy by the end of November. The afternoons were spent with Mrs. Bronson, and every evening there was a dinner-party of some sort before he retired to bed at 10:30. He found the restored Rezzonico most appealing and attractive, and spent a great deal of time in the "Pope's room," a small sitting-room on the mezzanine, which was more intimate than the grandiose state rooms. Here he enjoyed feeding the tame parrot, Jacko, one of Pen's many pets. To the last Venice lived up to his expectations. "No place, I think, ever suited my needs, bodily and intellectual, so well," he wrote on 9 November. [81]

News of his arrival in Venice brought a crowd of friends to the Rezzonico; Browning saw them all and was frequently prevailed upon to read from the page proofs of *Asolando*. His courtesy and generosity seemed inexhaustible. He spent every hour of the day in some useful activity, giving himself almost no rest in spite of increasing breathlessness, which was clearly affected by the steep stairs of the Rezzonico. Eventually, his weak heart and the bronchitis he contracted in the damp atmosphere got the better of him. He coughed more and more, and on 1 December was persuaded to take to his bed. Doctors were summoned, and for twelve days Browning sank deeper into a final slumber which finally overcame him on 12 December.

A few days before his death a parcel arrived containing an advance copy of *Asolando*; on the morning of the 12th, Fannie—with Dr. Cini's permission—gave it to Browning, who unwrapped it and commented on the pretty colour of the binding. Fannie described the scene:

> He was very weak and impulsively seizing the book, which was upside down, turned it very quickly,—as if afraid his strength would fail him,—looked for two different things he wanted to see, found them, and then throwing the book to the bottom of the bed, turned to Dr. Cini and said:—"That's a little of the work I've done in my lifetime!" A few minutes later he called me ... and giving me the book said, "Under any other circumstances I should give it to Mrs. Bronson, but now I want to give it to you." [82]

So the small red book, later inscribed by Pen and placed in a decorative leather cover, was given to Fannie, who subsequently presented it to Wellesley College.

Later that day at five o'clock Browning whispered to Margherita Fiori, the homely Venetian nurse, that he felt much worse and knew now that he must die. At 6:30 a telegram from England arrived at the Rezzonico with news that the entire first edition of *Asolando* had been sold out on the day of publication. His son relayed the message. The dying man smiled and murmured, "How gratifying. I'm more than satisfied. My dear boy. My dear boy." [83] By eight o'clock he was unconscious and two hours later he was dead.

Robert and Pen Browning in Venice

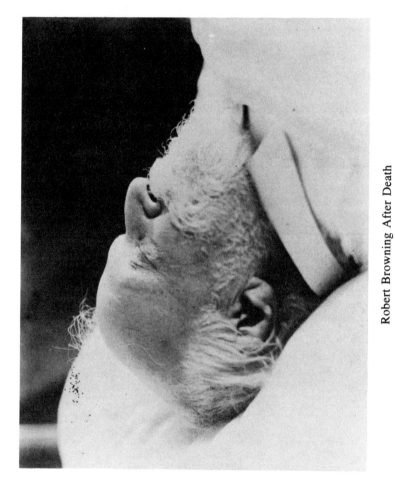

Robert Browning After Death

The circumstances of Browning's death raise several minor but relevant questions. What were the two different things Fannie claimed he wanted to see in the first copy of *Asolando*? Why didn't Browning send for Mrs. Bronson, who was after all only five minutes away from him by gondola, to give her the dedication copy? Indeed, why didn't Mrs. Bronson visit him during the twelve days of his final illness?

It seems logical from what we know about their relationship that the two things Browning wanted to see in *Asolando* were the dedication and the epilogue, where he tells Mrs. Bronson publicly his feelings for her. To summon her to his bedside to give her the book would have been little more than a sentimental gesture; after all, his feelings are printed there for all time. During his illness she received daily bulletins about his health and progress from a friend of Fannie's, Evelyn Barclay, who was staying at the Rezzonico and to whom she gave gifts of beef tea for the invalid. These bulletins were couched in optimistic terms and Mrs. Bronson may not have realized how seriously ill Browning really was. On the day before he died, for example, Pen wrote to Lady Layard when the illness was at its most serious:

> There is no change for the worse in my father's condition. The pulse is stronger, but he is very restless and when not waked talks incessantly in the strangest fashion often in Italian—rarely about common things.[84]

It may be, therefore, that Mrs. Bronson, who hated illness, did not want to see the sick man and did not realize how ill he really was. It is also possible that Fannie, neurotic and jealous Fannie, who was nominally in charge of the medical treatment and who so thoroughly enjoyed her role, kept her away—sensing an American rival.

Whatever the reason, Browning did not see Mrs. Bronson during the last fortnight of his life, although she was one of the mourners at the private funeral service at the Palazzo Rezzonico before his body was taken back to England for the official burial in Westminster Abbey.

She was overwhelmed by his death. On 14 December she wrote to young Zina Hulton:

> I thank you so much for your kind words of sympathy. I am indeed crushed by this to me sudden blow. The dear Poet was so brave and he always talked so confidently of the future—that the reserve—"if I live" always seemed to me a mere trick of speech, but with his far sight he no doubt felt the uncertainty of his tenure on life, not only because of his years, but of that oppression in breathing from which he has suffered– He has now been for so many years my guide, counsellor and friend that I feel a void more terrible than I can express. I can only thank God that I was permitted to study his comfort for those two months in Asolo. ... The epilogue in his new volume is very striking—you cannot yet have rec'd the book. It appeared only the day before yesterday—you heard him read some

of the poems from it, but it is never easy to understand true poetry
in that way unless you have read it before.[85]

The reference to the Epilogue to *Asolando* suggests that Mrs. Bronson
was beginning to understand the relevance of the poem to her, although
both she and Zina Hulton had heard Browning read it a few weeks before.
Gradually the realization of what Browning was intimating dawned on
her. She wrote to her friend Isabella Gardner in Boston:

> I have not seen him since the day he came last to see me—his last
> words to me were "Bless you, darling"—surely no woman ever had
> so pure and holy a love given to her as his for me. He loved me
> so—and I am left so lonely at heart without his everlasting affec-
> tion.[86]

For four days she saw no one, and then gradually she began to adapt
herself to the reality of his death. She sent mementoes of him to close
friends, either small personal trinkets or special silver-gilt hearts containing a fragment of his hair. She began to reply to the many letters of
condolence she received as Browning's friend—of which this, from
Henry James, is typical:

> *Your* loss was really the first reflection I made after I heard we shall
> never see Browning again. I thought immediately what it meant for
> you, before I thought what it meant for everyone else. And then,
> wrongfully, no doubt, even that sympathy was submerged in my
> sense of its being a supremely happy and enviable death.[87]

With Zina Hulton she began to make an elaborate scrapbook of his letters
to her, and she collected together her own personal mementoes: locks of
hair, a water-colour of one of Browning's blue eyes, dried eidelweiss
from Switzerland, the Love-in-the-mist from the Italian Tyrol, and presents given to her on her Saint's Day and on other festive occasions.
Some of these she displayed near her writing desk in the raised corner
of her study, which now became a "shrine" to Browning's memory, with
his portrait set between candlesticks above her desk. But, above all, she
kept alive his memory by maintaining a close friendship with Sarianna
and with Pen, which was to last until her own death.

FIN-DE-SIECLE

The last ten years of Katharine Bronson's life were a rather sad sequel
to the cosmopolitan life she had led before Browning's death. Recurrent
illness drove her frequently to fresh doctors and new health resorts, and
made her increasingly irritable with herself and occasionally with others.
Although she continued to entertain at Ca Alvisi until Edith's marriage
to Cosimo Rucellai in 1895, her lack of energy made her dinner-parties
smaller and the scope of her entertainment less lavish. It is difficult to
know just what afflicted her because it took a number of different forms—
coughs, rheumatism, general debility, headaches—but by 1896 she was

taking a heart cure in Germany, and it seems that, after such an energetic life, her body was slowly wearing out. She found her illnesses frustrating, particularly when they seemed general rather than localized:

> I feel "far from well" as the phrase is, and am in no way consoled by reading in a magazine article that the maladie du fin de siècle is that of feeling ill with no special name to attach to the malady. The fact that I am following the very last fashion is especially disagreeable, a form of banality one would gladly escape.[88]

Doctor Cini, who attended Browning, was her Venetian physician, but she also consulted the popular Dr. Baldwin of Florence, who became a close friend. He encouraged her to spend more time in the open air, and it was to him that she sent this account of her daily routine in 1893:

> You would praise me if you could see my daily life. I rise at 8½—sometimes earlier—go with my maid, Tou Fou and a basket of beef-tea and sandwiches to the Lido—sit by the lovely sea in a thatched cabin until 4 or 5—5 of late—to get home before the dews fall. I have my colour box and brushes, a few tiny paints, and paint small and not too hideous little daubs about the size of your 4 fingers; "a poor thing but mine own" I say of them. I will send you one of my cabin to amuse you one of these days. The great drawback is that I have too many visitors, idlers who think it a good way of passing the time to come and interrupt my happy communing with Mother Nature. ... I am forced to go back to the tittle-tattle of the town, and make tea for them all—and wish I was in a lighthouse tower away from everyone. You see I do not love *anyone* here. All my best friends have gone away—some to the other world—some to distant parts of this one—and so I live to be with them in memory at least.[89]

It is a sad picture, but slightly self-indulgent, because in 1893 Katharine Bronson still enjoyed life and people; her imagination was undimmed. Just occasionally, as in this instance, happy memories of the past cast shadows on the present. Browning remained in her mind:

> I hope he looks down upon us from some fair star—and knows how we revere and mourn him. He believed so firmly that we should meet again.[90]

In 1897 Sarianna's serious illness reminded her again of Browning's death:

> I get twice a day a bulletin from Pen—and a visit, exactly as when my beloved Poet lay ill and died at the Rezzonico. The same coloured paper—the same neat handwriting, the same concise sentences—the same expression of deep affection for *me*. I seem to live over again that terrible month in 1889.[91]

Asolo succeeded Venice as her chief love, and La Mura succeeded Ca Alvisi as a centre of entertainment in the Nineties. It was a tiny house and, although Mrs. Bronson enlarged it, very few guests could be accommodated and then not very comfortably; but her friends were happy to make the journey to Asolo and there were hundreds of happy parties and visits. The list of names in the La Mura visitors' book includes Eleanora Duse, Horatio Brown, the Layards, Isabella Gardner, the Storys, Henry James, Prince Gagarin, Ludwig Passini, J.McN. Whistler, Violet Paget, Luke Fildes, Sidney Colvin, Hamilton Aidé, H.B. Brabazon and a host of Italian, English and American friends. Mrs. Bronson delighted in the fancy, told her by many guests, that another Queen Katharine had come to Asolo, an American hostess with the charm of an Italian Renaissance aristocrat. Caterina Cornaro's castle was visible from her loggia, and Katharine Bronson often took her guests to the delightful eighteenth-century theatre built in its ruins.

Asolo accepted her gladly, as it welcomes most foreigners. For her part Katharine Bronson did all she could for the city, in particular helping to restore the ruined church of Santa Catherina near the house where Napoleon had spent a night during his Italian campaign:

> The nuns wrote to me the other day, 'we need a new pavement, a new roof and new church benches and we look to the Signora who bears the name of the saint'—I must say it *appeals* to me and so what I can will I do and "de tout coeur"—but it seems to me à première one what they call in the States "a large order," like the young couple who bought a grand piano before thinking of beds and bedding—I have already a fine picture for the church—"Sposalizio di S. Catherina" which will be more ornamental than useful. What really delights me is to do lots of good with a microscopic fortune and so I am quite happy in this what Edith calls "cookless solitude."[92]

When Asolo had a window-box competition, she offered a special prize for the best display of carnations, her favourite flower. Her social flair was as evident in the small hill-town as it had been in Venice, and she began to spend more and more time in Asolo.

Pen Browning was her neighbour across the valley. He had arranged the building of a large house, Pippa's Tower, on a site his father had chosen, which was ready for habitation in the spring of 1892. The previous April Sarianna, accompanied by seventy-six packing-cases of furniture, books and memories, had gone to live with Pen and Fannie at the Rezzonico. The cases remained unopened in storage, while Sarianna helped Pen organize the rooms and garden of the new Asolo hillside house. Seemingly frail after Robert's death, Sarianna had suffered an attack of Bell's palsy, which had paralysed half her face in 1890; but she had made a quick recovery and for twelve years was to provide strong support for Pen in Asolo and Venice.

Pen needed this support, for Fannie had become difficult to live with. There was a history of mental illness in her family and she was certainly nervous and high-strung, so much so that she had threatened suicide a number of times. A break came in 1893 when she accused Pen of infidelity with a maidservant in Asolo, a charge which he strongly denied, claiming her suspicions were merely the result of her jealous imagination. Sarianna totally believed him:

> From the first Fannie has been of a highly hysteric, excitable nature—in these fits of hysteria she does not know what she is saying or doing—at first they were more of a violent character—latterly more of a depressing turn—she would cry and sob for hours, five nights in the week. She tried several cures—Marienbad—Schwalbach—at last she tried the rest-cure—a very severe one, but she says it cured her outward illness, and have [sic] sent it to the brain– You were with us when Ginevra first came to us. I believe she told you the history herself– Fannie's normal nature is sweet and generous. She took a great love for the poor girl—at first taken on a visit,—afterwards kept as her right hand in looking after the housekeeping, which she managed admirably—she used to call Ginevra her greatest comfort, her younger sister, the *bimba* of the family, and expressed for her the strongest affection to the last moment of her stay at home. Before she left she made Ginevra promise to remain and take charge of the house till her return, however protracted the cure might be, without which promise she said she would not leave home– After her departure she wrote affectionately to her from Milan. Then came the two months of seclusion,—after which, she wrote that she saw things in a new light, and insisted that G. should be sent away. She seems to have taken an insane dislike and jealousy of her ... [Pen] has been very angry with Fannie's conduct, especially as tending to throw reproach on his own character. I believe he wrote very angrily to her—he says it was the first angry word he ever spoke to her, as he has had angelic patience, but she had taken offence, and instead of returning to us last month, is gone to England, refusing to return to her husband.[93]

Fannie sprinkled her accusations against Pen among many of their friends, who were therefore compelled to take sides. Mrs. Bronson strongly supported Pen, even though she was also fond of Fannie, and she considered the accusations most unjust.[94] She was living in Florence and too ill to give practical assistance when Fannie returned temporarily to the Rezzonico in 1899, before separating from Pen for ever.

Pen claimed sadly that he had always known that Fannie had been "in love with a name rather than with me";[95] and one suspects that Mrs. Bronson, too, liked Pen chiefly for his father's sake. She called him "PP"—Precious Pen—but there were times when the untidiness of his house or the casualness of his manners disappointed her. She knew his failings only too well:

> Still he is not happy! Who can be so if he has lost sense of proportion and fitness of things—or he be born without it, and yet unconscious of its absence.[96]

Also she wearied of Sarianna's repetitive talk. When the conversation turned to Browning, Mrs. Bronson found the situation intolerable:

> I drove to Bassano yesterday, taking Miss Browning with me. She spoke always on the same subject—it was very painful to me, as it took 5 hours. I was only kept up by the fund of *pity* I have in reserve for all who suffer, and in the thought that it must be a (rather grim) consolation to her to be *able* to talk. I did not succumb, but oh! . . .[97]

But for most of the time she was in Asolo and Venice, Katharine was on very friendly terms with the Brownings, and they exchanged letters and presents regularly. Indeed, Katharine Bronson's letters to Sarianna show her taking the initiative in retaining the friendship; she invited her over to spend the summer of 1890 in Asolo in order to recuperate, and made special provisions for Sarianna to revisit Asolo immediately on her return to Italy in 1891. Before Pen's house was built, the Brownings always stayed at La Mura, and Mrs. Bronson continued to visit the Rezzonico until Fannie's departure.

After Edith's marriage,[98] Katharine Bronson spent more time in Florence and gave up Ca Alvisi. She still retained La Mura and was there for the last time in the spring of 1899 when Henry James went to visit her. He had never liked the house, as it was too spartan for his precise tastes, but he was shocked by what he saw: "a great deal of rheumatism, an enormous appetite, not a scrap of possible action." Mrs. Bronson was being looked after by two nurses as well as a staff of servants, and was too ill to go out and explore the neighbouring countryside. Yet, in spite of all, James had to admit that she was still "alert for pleasant surprises and proved sincerities."[99] This was the view of most who saw her during those last two unhappy years; confined to bed or to a chair, she still retained an irrepressible zest for life, at the very moment that life was fast disappearing. Julien Gordon saw her shortly before her death: "Her cry of pleasure when I entered the dim twelfth-century drawing-room in Bellosguardo—her arms thrown up in tumultuous greeting—shook my heart. It was perhaps this naturalness, this impulsive simplicity, which so endeared Mrs. Bronson to those who knew her well. She did not understand cold friendship or half-hearted affection. She always said, however, 'Nothing must be forced. Above all, one must be oneself.'"[100]

It was in this state of mind in 1899 that she embraced the Roman Catholic faith. She had always been interested in Catholicism and had taken instruction from the monsignor in Asolo. Before leaving Venice for the last time she took her vows in the Armenian island church of S. Lazzaro. The nonconformist Sarianna Browning was disillusioned. "I wish she had turned Romanist from any serious motive, but it is only, I fear, to worship St. Anthony's little toe" was her tart comment.[101] This is most unfair. Mrs. Bronson's conversion was as seriously considered as much else in her outwardly carefree life; one suspects that Robert Browning, who understood the depths as well as the shallows, would not have been so ungenerous as his sister.

For the last eighteen months of her life Katharine Bronson lived in Florence. In June 1899 she rented the beautiful Villa Mercede in Bellosguardo, which had been designed by Michelozzo in the fourteenth century; there she exchanged her Venetian circle of expatriates for another, because Bellosguardo was still the social centre of Florence for the English and Americans, as it had once been in the time of Isa Blagden and the Brownings. Some of the inhabitants, like Walburga, Lady Paget, sensed a rival; but Katharine Bronson was too ill to contemplate serious entertaining, and spent much of her time with a few close friends, or sketched from her bedroom window. Eventually she needed a more central home, nearer the doctor and the necessities of life, and so moved into an apartment in the Via Solferino. Here, where she was attended by the faithful Natale Gavagnin and his wife Orsola from Ca Alvisi, her life ebbed away with the century. Even now she refused to submit passively to death. She organized an egg-hunt in her apartment for her little granddaughter Nannina on one of Edith's frequent visits, and she was photographed for the last time in an invalid chair, her face puffy and disfigured, but still smiling. She died in February 1901, aged sixty-six, and her body was taken to the small cemetery of Canneto where she was buried against the walls of the Rucellai chapel, her beautiful tomb engraved with a frieze of entwined carnations.

CONCLUSION

Katharine Bronson made a strong impression on all who knew her. "The secret of her beauty," wrote Julien Gordon, "was as elusive as is the serious smile in the eyes of the Mona Lisa. Mrs. Bronson's peculiar attraction remained always baffling. It seemed profanity to attempt to explain it."[102]

Her friends understood that she was a more complex personality than she appeared in her role as a society hostess. Henry James captured her public face well. "She sat for twenty years," he said, "at the mouth of the Grand Canal, holding out her hand, with endless good-nature, patience, charity to all decently accredited petitioners."[103] Yet he acknowledged that Katharine Bronson's social facility was "a defence, with serious thought and serious feeling quietly cherished behind it."[104] She hated gloom or pain as much as she disliked the banality and tawdriness of modern times,[105] and she therefore tried to make life happier, more meaningful, for those around her. To those she loved and admired Katharine Bronson gave more than mere kindness or friendship. Lilian Whiting felt she possessed the gift of liberating individuality and allowing a person to reinterpret himself.[106] Other friends mentioned the influence on them of Katharine Bronson's mind with "its flashes of unexpected fun, its touches of unlooked-for pathos."[107]

She was probably at her happiest and most influential during the 1880's, the period of her friendship with Robert Browning. After years of pleasurable but aimless travel, she found in Venice a security and a position she had not known before. There she was free to indulge her generosity and kindness a hundred different ways. The "inner essence of her charity" was her love and tenderness for Venice:

> The old bright tradition, the wonderful Venetian legend, had appealed to her from the first, closing round her house and her well-plashed water-steps, where the waiting gondolas were thick; quite as if ... the ghost of the defunct Carnival ... still played some haunting part.[108]

She responded intuitively to others who felt as she did, and this is why from the very beginning she and Robert Browning had such a close affinity.

Their mutual love of Venice and her instinctive understanding of him drew Browning and Mrs. Bronson together. He quickly recognized the seriousness which lay behind her easy charm, which made her so different from the society hostesses he knew in London. His open, frank acceptance of her, his keen interest in all she said or did, gave Katharine Bronson an added confidence, not only with Browning but with others, during their ten-year friendship. Each supported the other and brought the best out of each other.

Mrs. Bronson entered Browning's life at an opportune moment. As he approached late middle-age he had become very set in his ways, and there had been a noticeable falling-off in the quality of his poetry written in the 1870's. The deaths of Isa Blagden, Annie Egerton-Smith and Mrs. Benzon had deprived him of the friendships of three women who had in their different ways meant much to him. As his life settled into a routine, he was becoming increasingly disenchanted and more querulous. It was not surprising that Asolo had lost its charm for him in 1878.

His rediscovery of Venice was entirely Mrs. Bronson's doing. The city took on a different aspect for him in her presence.[109] Attracted first by her personality, Browning found his former feelings for Venice awakened by the kindness and hospitality she offered him at Ca Alvisi. His holidays were restorative. He found a peace and happiness with her, and memories of Venice helped him to survive bleak winter days in London on his return.

More important was the effect of their friendship on Browning's poetry. Although he wrote a few personal poems to or about her, Katharine Bronson's influence was wider-ranging and prompted the direction and structure of his last three books. The reawakening of his youthful feelings for Venice, and later for Asolo, suggested to Browning a reordering and reshaping of his experience, which led him to summarize his life's work in *Ferishtah's Fancies*, *Parleyings* and *Asolando*. It is therefore understandable that he wished to associate her name with his in the final book he wrote.

Although their friendship was such a productive and happy one, neither Katharine Bronson nor Browning was quite able to come to terms with its full implications. Mrs. Bronson found Browning's interest and gratitude immensely pleasing, but she allowed her romantic nature to idealize him; and so, the more she knew him, the more she thought of him as a poet rather than as a man. Browning, for his part, valued all that Katharine did for him, and struggled to express feelings which twice, in 1884 and 1889, threatened to get the better of him. Luckily they did not. He was able to commit any frustration he felt to his poetry and, therefore, to preserve a friendship whose tenderness, warmth and good humour is so clearly shown in the letters which follow.

1. Letter 29, 16 September 1884.

2. Leon Edel (ed.), *The Complete Tales of Henry James*, Vol. 6, London, 1963, p. 276.

3. For details of Henry James's projected novel about Katharine Bronson, see F.O. Matthiessen and Kenneth B.Murdock, *The Notebooks of Henry James*, New York, 1961, p. 333 and pp. 343–360. Starting with "the 'humiliations' of Mrs. B without her *amanti*— in the midst of the *amanti* of others," Henry James developed what he called "The K.B. Case": "My question is that of a still youngish and still 'living' American woman who is suddenly thrown upon the world, and upon her first real freedom, by the death of a husband with whom she has had a bad time and as to whom she has yet been, by her nature and her conscience, devoted and irreproachable." The final situation does not tally in all respects with Mrs. Bronson's. James's emphasis on her unhappy relations with her husband is interesting, as Mrs. Bronson was discreet and uncommunicative about her married life.

4. Letter to Alice James, quoted in Edel, Vol. 1, p. 537.

5. Leon Edel (ed.), *The Complete Tales of Henry James*, Vol. 8, London, 1963, p. 225.

6. Browning and James were in Venice at the same time for about three weeks in September and early October 1881, Browning staying at the Universo and James at 4161 Riva degli Schiavoni. Harry T. Moore in *Henry James and his World*, London, 1974, p. 61 claims that James "often sat with Mrs. Bronson and Robert Browning" on the front balcony of Ca Alvisi that autumn, but I can find no evidence to support this statement.

7. Typescript of letter from Henry James to Katharine Bronson, 12 January 1890 (Rucellai).

8. Unpublished manuscript by Katharine Bronson, "Recollections of my childhood in its first decade," written at Gleichenberg, 12–24 July 1890 (Fossi). In reconstructing Katharine Bronson's early life I have made extensive use of this manuscript and of Nannina Fossi's privately circulated typescript, "Cousin Edith," the translation of her memoir of her mother, originally written in Italian as "Zibaldino."

9. P. de Kay Wheelock, "Commodore George de Kay and the Voyage of the *Macedonian* to Ireland," *The American Neptune*, Vol. XIII, No. 4 (October 1953), p. 265.

10. This and the following four quotations are taken from an unpublished manuscript journal kept by Katharine Bronson from 5 August 1856 to 10 July 1857 (Fossi). It clearly has been edited by Mrs. Bronson at a later date, as there are alterations and erasures. I have avoided such passages in my quotations, which therefore reflect her thoughts at the time of writing.

11. Typescript, Rucellai. Manuscript sold at Christie's, London, 6 April 1977, lot 50.

12. Henry James, *Italian Hours*, New York, 1979, pp. 78–79.

13. Even today some of her phrases are remembered with affection in the Rucellai family. For example, she used to order Giuseppe to carry Mrs. Bronson's dogs down to the courtyard to take exercise in the following abrupt words with their deliberate English vowels: "Portate Contenta anche Trolley in corte."

14. Letter to Zina Hulton, 8 February 1889 (Balliol).

15. Ms. Fossi.

16. Letter to Katharine Bronson, 11 February 1880 (Morgan).

17. Catharine Cornaro, "The Revival of Burano Lace," *The Century Magazine*, 23 (January 1882), pp. 333–343, illustrated by the Misses Montalba and the Princess Louise, Marchioness of Lorne. It is interesting that Mrs. Bronson uses Catharine Cornaro, Queen of Cypress and patroness of Asolo, as her nom-de-plume. She would have learned from Browning (or from his *Pippa Passes*) that Asolo had once been famous for its lace, but this is the first time she refers even indirectly to the city which was later to mean so much to her.

18. All the notes and drafts she made are extant, as is a fair copy of the finished work, which bears the date 1885 and this dedication:

To the
great and good
Robert Browning
who in his verse has immortalised
Venice
I dedicate with reverence
and affection
This volume.

19. The Hon. Emily Lawless, *Ireland*, with some additions by Mrs. Arthur Bronson, Putnams, New York, 1898. The book was simultaneously published in London by T. Fisher Unwin.

20. Hulton, p. 47.

21. Mrs. Sutherland Orr is the first of many biographers who mention the Story introduction. She believes that Emelyn Story was responsible (Orr, p. 313). Nannina Fossi in "Cousin Edith," p. 13, states that Trollope's letter led to the meeting and "his letter of introduction is kept among the treasures belonging to that period." I have not seen the letter, as it was not among the Bronson papers at Asolo.

22. Betty Miller quotes Florence Nightingale as the source of the story that the tune the Venetian children whistled was by Galuppi. (Miller, pp. 66–67.)

23. Frederic G. Kenyon (ed.), *Letters of Elizabeth Barrett Browning*, London, 1897, Vol. 2, p. 8.

24. Browning's sickness in Venice was unusual, and has similarities with the psychosomatic headaches and illnesses he experienced as a young man. Elizabeth first mentions it in a letter to Miss Mitford on 4 June: "Robert, after sharing the ecstasy, grows uncomfortable, and nervous, and unable to sleep or eat." Later she told John Kenyon that "Robert could not sleep at nights." To Mrs. Ogilvy she was even more explicit: "He lay awake night after night, suffering nervous pains in the face and head." His illness seems very different from the biliousness the maid Elizabeth Wilson was suffering at the same time. No sooner did he leave Venice, than he was cured.

25. Letter to G.W. Curtis, 9 August 1847 (*Harper's Monthly*, March 1890, p. 638).

26. All quotations from Browning's poetry are from the 1888–89 edition, unless otherwise stated. The first edition of *Asolando* is used.

27. In the first edition of 1842 these lines read:

Heart to heart,
And lips to lips! Once, ere we part,
Make me thine as mine thou art!

This has a greater immediacy than the final version, a stronger emphasis on the simultaneous moment of love and death. All the original readings are less sophisticated and more immediate, reinforcing the sensual power of the poem. See Appendix D.

28. The problem exists even in "A Toccata of Galuppi's." Browning uses a rational Victorian scientist as narrator, who hears criticism of the eighteenth-century Venetians in Galuppi's music, but who is tolerant and refuses to condemn them. His air of slight condescension and superiority directs the reader's sympathies even more towards the "immoral" lovers. The poem is best seen as a comment on the transitory nature of life rather than a moral judgment.

29. Letter 2, 16 November 1881.

30. Mrs. Bronson sent this poem and another by Longfellow to her brother-in-law, R.W. Gilder, editor of *The Century Magazine*, who published them in the November 1882 issue. For an account of this and of Browning's annoyance, see *BT*, pp. 61–62. There is no reference to his displeasure in any surviving letter to Mrs. Bronson.

31. Ms. rough draft, Meredith.

32. Letter 2, 16 November 1881.

33. Letter 5, 1 January 1882.

34. Letter 4, 23 December 1881.

35. Letter 8, 19 April 1882.

36. *LL*, p. 169.

37. *Ibid.*, p. 173.

38. Letter 17, 1 January 1884.

39. Letter 16, 27 December 1883.

40. Letter 15, [12 December 1883].

41. Ms. ABL, dated 4 November 1883.

42. Letter 18, 6 January 1884.

43. Browning tended to remember Elizabeth in moments of emotional crisis. His rejection of Lady Ashburton's proposal of marriage was one such occasion, and feelings of strain at this time led to references to Elizabeth in the prologue and epilogue to *Fifine at the Fair*. It is not surprising, therefore, when Mrs. Bronson is engaging his emotions, that he should again introduce memories of Elizabeth into his poetry.

44. Betty Miller, in particular, exaggerates the closeness of the relationship between Browning and Mrs. Bloomfield-Moore. Basing most of her information on Mrs. Moore's inaccurate and distorted article published in 1890, she accepts the fantasies of this neurotic, self-dramatizing woman as facts. Mrs. Moore meant no more to Browning than any other close female friend. He was kind to her and valued her support of Pen's art, but her enthusiasms (particularly her obsession with Keely's air-pump) embarrassed him. He was happy to stay with her at St. Moritz and to dine with her in London; sadly she allowed her overwrought feelings to get the better of her. Browning's surviving letters to her are friendly, but lack any note of intimacy or any of the playfulness which characterizes his letters to Mrs. Bronson. He was aware of her mental instability. "There is little doubt that she has been suffering from some strange fancy, or hallucination—from which she is recovered," he wrote to Fannie Browning on 10 October 1887 (Balliol). A letter written two months later to Pen and Fannie (Balliol) clearly shows Browning's position: "Mrs. Moore has called, and written, as usual—and I dine with her quietly tomorrow—by her desire, . . I enclose her note: what does it allude to? But I will ask her. She is so rash in her confidences and communications that she exposes herself and her friends to plenty of annoyance,—and nothing is likely to change her habits." Mrs. Moore's claim that "Not with my Soul, Love!" was written for and to her should be treated with considerable scepticism. A study of the manuscript and proof of *Ferishtah's Fancies* does not substantiate her claim. Browning did not give her one of his twenty-four presentation copies of the book. Instead, he gave her a second edition as a Christmas present, inscribed "with RB's grateful and affectionate regards," sentiments identical to those he wrote for Mrs. FitzGerald and Lady Martin.

45. Letter 28, 6 September 1884.

46. Letter 33, 7 October 1884.

47. Letter 18, 6 January 1884.

48. Letter 23, 21 February 1884.

49. Letter 39, 4 September 1885.

50. Letter to J. Dykes Campbell (*LRB*, p. 240). Browning conveys some of the depression of his stay in Venice in a letter to Miss Leigh Smith, 27 November 1885 (ABL): "We left Venice on the 23rd, arriving here on the 25th. Mrs. Bronson was much oppressed by a bad cold and cough. Edith was happily convalescent,—and Venice,—I

grieve to say, was more cold and rainy than at any time I remember."

51. It would be wrong to suggest that there was a break between the Brownings and the Bronsons during this period; it may be that they corresponded and the letters are lost. References to Katharine Bronson occur in Browning's letters to Pen and Fannie (Balliol): 10 October 1887: "Do remember me kindly to all friends—to Mrs. B. and Edith"; 17 October 1887: "My kindest love is with the Bronsons, and needs no 'sending'"; 12 November 1887: "Miss Ker ... gives rather a bad account of Edith Bronson, and says the mother seems slow to perceive the danger"; 14 May 1888: "Mrs Bronson wrote to us last week—we answered at once. She told us about Edith's intended departure"; 21 May 1888: "Give my love to Mrs Bronson and Edith."; 17 June 1888: "Always give my best love to Mrs Bronson: I quite agree with you about the waste of money on the house—but if she sticks to old friends as she does old rooms, well and good."

52. Letter 47, 8 August 1888.

53. Browning's lassitude and indecision can be seen in this letter of 1 August 1888 from Sarianna to Fannie Browning (Balliol): "Father is better, but will not be quite well till he leaves London: between ourselves, it serves him right for the way in which he keeps hesitating and refusing to make up his mind. *You* know, it will not be my fault if we do not come to you."

54. Letter 48, 21 August 1888.

55. *Idem.*

56. Letter to George Smith, 28 October 1888 (Murray).

57. Letter to Felix Moscheles, 29 October 1888, quoted in Felix Moscheles, *Fragments of an Autobiography*, London, 1899, pp. 244–245.

58. Letter 52, 15 December 1888.

59. Ms. Fossi.

60. Letter 53, 4 January 1889.

61. Appendix A, p. 128.

62. Letter 56, 10 June 1889.

63. *Idem.*

64. Letter 57, 17 July 1889.

65. Letter to Pen Browning, 15 September 1889 (Balliol).

66. Letter to Pen Browning, 8 September 1889 (Balliol).

67. Appendix A, p. 138.

68. *Ibid.*, p. 130.

69. *Asolando* is more carefully structured than at first appears. After Browning's introduction of his theme of fact and fancy in the autobiographical Prologue, when he comes to terms with the loss of the romantic power Asolo once had for him, the book plays constant variations on the theme in different keys and moods. The autobiographical poem which concludes each section does more than relate the topic to Browning's own experiences. "Development," for example, not merely explains how the young Browning learned Greek in different stages, but shows how one can gain philosophic truth from myth and story more easily and fruitfully than from ethical treatises. In this way the reader is shown how to read and come to terms with the fancies of the previous eleven poems; even the most trivial poem should not be ignored. It is this interplay between the poems which makes *Asolando* such a successful book.

70. See De Vane, pp. 490–524.

71. It was first made by Betty Miller (Miller pp. 277–278). Her suggestion that Mrs. Bronson deliberately ignored Browning's passionate feelings in order to preserve "the equanimity of the relationship" is ingenious, but is unsupported by biographical evidence.

72. Browning knew Violet Paget but found her difficult to talk to. She greatly admired him and his poetry, and told Mrs. Bronson on 7 January 1890: "I have always kept preciously some flowers which he once gave me out of his button-hole three or four years ago" (Meredith). In the same letter she says, "I was so surprised and delighted to find my name in *Asolando*."

73. The meaning of the first two verses is often ignored or a wrong identification is made, usually with Elizabeth Barrett (e.g. De Vane, p. 552: "He admits his mistakes of judgment in his relationship with his wife, but never a lessening of his love.") As the woman in the poem is clearly alive, such speculation is fruitless. Other interpretations, which make Browning's love a more general love towards humanity, run into further difficulties. James Reeves in his Heinemann edition of the *Selected Poems*, London, 1955, gives a prose paraphrase (p. 152) which ties itself up in knots. When one realizes that the poet is addressing Mrs. Bronson, all is made clear. I have recently discovered that R.B. Pearsall, *Robert Browning*, Boston, 1974, shares my view, but he does not elaborate the point, says the woman is "probably Mrs. Bronson," but gives no reasons.

74. Appendix A, p. 144.

75. Ms. Fossi. The manuscript of Mrs. Bronson's two articles on Browning originated in a long letter she started to write to Fannie Browning in November 1890, which starts: "Your desire my dear Fannie that I should write to you all I remember of your father-in-law, is a natural one on your part, but you little know how difficult it is for me to accede to your request. My memory, my mental vision, seems clouded when I think of the friend I have lost, of his wondrous personality, of his surpassing genius."

76. Ms. Fossi.

77. Appendix B, p. 149.

78. *Personalia*, pp. 77–78.

79. William H. Grove, *My Memories of Robert Browning*, two-page typescript (Scripps).

80. William Sharp, *Robert Browning*, 1890, pp. 195–196.

81. Letter to Margaret Keep, quoted in Orr, p. 398.

82. *Memories*, pp. 29–30.

83. As reported by Evelyn Barclay in her diary.

84. Letter to Lady Layard, 11 [December 1889] (ABL).

85. Letter to Zina Hulton, 14 December 1889 (Balliol).

86. Letter to Isabella Gardner, 14 December 1889 (IGM).

87. Typescript of letter to Katharine Bronson, 12 January 1890 (Rucellai).

88. Letter to Isabella Gardner, Sunday, September 1892 (IGM).

89. Letter to Dr. Baldwin, 12 October [1893] (Morgan).

90. Letter to Isabella Gardner, 8 February 1890 (IGM).

91. Letter to Isabella Gardner, 26 September 1897 (IGM).

92. Letter to Isabella Gardner, undated 1892 (IGM). Mrs. Bronson's oil-painting still adorns the wall behind the altar in the crumbling church of S. Catherina in Asolo. A late photograph of her in an ugly frame hangs in the mayor's office. Her memory survives almost a hundred years after her death.

93. Letter from Sarianna Browning to Mrs. Miller Morrison, 17 December 1893 (Harry Ransom Humanities Research Center, University of Texas).

94. See her letter to W. Hall Griffin, 7 January 1894: "She has accused I think unjustly her husband of having been faithless to her during her absence" (BL).

95. Letter to Miss Leigh Smith, 14 May 1907 (ABL).

96. Letter to Isabella Gardner, 29 August 1892 (IGM).

97. Letter to Isabella Gardner, undated 1892 (IGM).

98. To begin with, Mrs. Bronson opposed Edith's engagement to Count Cosimo Rucellai, and there is no doubt that the loss of her daughter made her feel more insecure and vulnerable than ever before. Edith appealed to Isabel Gardner, Henry James and other friends of her mother's to persuade Katharine to relent: "She doesn't dislike him, but she feels the strangeness that I so much feared she would feel." The great happiness of Edith's marriage entirely justified her initial feelings for Cosimo Rucellai.

99. Edel, Vol. 2, p. 315.

100. Julien Gordon, "Recollections of the late Katharine de Kay Bronson," 1901, from unidentified newspaper cutting among the Fossi papers.

101. Letter to Mrs. Miller Morrison, 6 August 1899 (Harry Ransom Humanities Research Center, University of Texas).

102. Julien Gordon, *op. cit.*

103. Henry James, *Italian Hours*, p. 77.

104. *Ibid.*, p. 79.

105. This is clearly shown in a letter Katharine Bronson wrote to Dr. Baldwin, 12 October [1893] (Morgan): "It is not a base feeling that makes one like things that are unique, not because we like to triumph over others, but because we like to be able to triumph, for ourselves, over the banality which is the curse of our epoch. The old time was *not* banal, everyone worked out his own ideas—and others delighted in them, when they could afford it—now everyone aimlessly and ignorantly seeks to possess the beautiful—and the result is overstocked markets and drawing-rooms with the altogether hideous."

106. Lilian Whiting, "A Friend of Browning's," *The Springfield Sunday Republican*, 6 October 1918.

107. Julien Gordon, *Idem.*

108. Henry James, *Italian Hours*, p. 79.

109. See Letter 62: "Venice is not herself without you, in my eyes– I daresay this is a customary phrase—but you well know what reason I have to use it with a freshness as if it were inspired for the first time."

More Than Friend

Letter 1

ROBERT BROWNING TO KATHARINE BRONSON

Universo, Oct. 10, '81

Dear Mrs Bronson,

We were greatly concerned yesterday to find you were unwell: *that* is a far greater drawback to our enjoyment of Venice than either the cold or rain.[1] May I beg of your kindness a verbal answer to the enquiry I shall presently make as to your condition this morning? If the news should be happily so good as to allow of our looking in, and personally satisfying ourselves, at about 8 o'clock, we trust to be allowed to do so. Pray accept for yourself and Miss Bronson our best of regards and all good wishes from my Sister as well as from

Yours affectionately
Robert Browning.

Publication: None traced.
Manuscript: Armstrong Browning Library.

1. The autumn of 1881 was uncharacteristically cold and stormy in Venice. On the day after writing to Mrs. Bronson, Browning told Furnivall: "Our weather is mending somewhat, but continues a month behind hand, and very little characteristic of Venice. I walk, even in wind and rain, for a couple of hours on Lido, and enjoy the break of sea on the strip of sand as much as Shelley did in those days" (*BT*, p. 35).

Letter 2

ROBERT BROWNING TO KATHARINE BRONSON

19, Warwick Crescent. W.
Nov. 16, '81

I would not write at first arriving, Dear Friend, because I fancied that I might say too much all at once, and afterwards be afraid of beginning again till some interval: this fortnight since I saw you must pass however for a long interval indeed. I will try and tell you as quietly as possible that I never shall feel your kindness,—such kindness!—one whit less than I do now: perhaps I feel it "now" even more deeply than I could—at all events, *realize* that I was feeling. You have given Venice an association which will live in my mind with every delight of that dearest place in the

[1]

world. But all the same you remain for me a dearest of friends whether I see you *framed* by your Venice, or brightening up our black London, should you come there. In Venice, however, should I live and you be there next Autumn, it will go hard with me if I do not meet you again. What a book of memories—and instigations to get still more memories,—does your most beautiful and precious of books prove to me![1] I never supposed that photographers would have the good sense to use their art on so many out-of-the[-]way scenes and sights—just those I love most. They were painfully (almost so!) true as I looked at them a few minutes ago. Well, I must speak a little about myself—as an "instigation" to you of whom I want to hear as much as a letter will hold. I said "black London" just now rather ungratefully: it has been sunny and warm as October ever since our return. My sister managed to catch a bad cold either on the journey or soon after it,—she is better however: and we sit alone on the evenings,—each at a table, book in hand. How long this blessed "retreat",—as the religious would call it,—will last depends on my resolution to enjoy myself and my memories: at all events, I go out next Saturday for the first time—and under protest.

You—you have lost Lowell, and Field,[2] and the rest of the good fellowship: but you will be sure of a succession of the sort. Now,—do not sit up too late more than you can help! As *I* never trespassed that way, you will not call me jealous, surely: and avoid the headaches, if a little walking may be helpful in the case. I get as nearly angry as it is in me to become with people I love, when they trifle with their health—that is, with their life,—like children playing with jewels over a bridge-side—jewels which, once in the water, how can *we*, the poor lookers-on, hope to recover? You don't know how absolutely *well* I am after my walking,—not on the mountains merely but on the beloved Lido. Go there, if only to stand and be blown about by the sea-wind. I see it all,—and Miss Kerr's[3] dog rushing down the sand bank by the fortress to jump on you! And your own little creatures will be the better for the air and exercise: then go back and write verses,—would I could imitate you!

I have paid your subscription to the notable "B" Society,[4] and am assured that the "Bibliography" has been posted to you. My sister wrote, and sent some of the latest photographs of "B." himself. "B" has already given a three-hours' sitting to one R.A.,[5] and is obliged to give another artist[6] (whom he has never seen) another set of sittings next week. Oh, for the recesses of the Gondola! I have not seen any of the Russells yet,—and rather think the Duke[7] is yachting. As soon as I am sure of his whereabout, he shall have your book. Did you know of the sudden departure of the Curtises[8] for Paris when you wrote? We were glad to hear from them, a few days ago, that the son was much better. What a surprise it was to meet them on the platform at Macon! And here is the paper's end, and what have I put down of the so much that I wanted to say? Understand, supply the defects of, and remember as he will ever remember you—

Yours affectionately

R Browning.

Is this corner room enough[9] to beg that Miss Bronson will remember me also in some degree? I wish her all good in the world—and continue to see her, in my mind, in the perfect little house by the Riva.[10] When shall I again drink tea and eat *the* bread and butter there? Well, such good things *have been*, at least!

I enclose the note of Ruskin's I promised to Mad^e de Pilat.[11] It is an old one, but the first I lay hands on. What have I said for your cypress, and olive? But what have I said for anything! Ah,—*wait for the reply to your next letter!*

Publication: Whiting, p. 243 (in part, as 18 November 1881).
Manuscript: Armstrong Browning Library.

1. An album of 39 photographs, the cover of which reads *Views of Venice*, given to Browning by Mrs. Bronson before he left Venice. It is now in the English Poetry Collection, Wellesley College Library.
2. James Russell Lowell (1819–1891) and John W. Field (1815–1887) were regular visitors to Ca Alvisi during September and October 1881. Lowell, distinguished New England poet and former Harvard professor, was United States Minister in London. Field, who had once been part of Newport society, spent much of his life travelling in Europe, and had been one of the first Americans to explore the wilder parts of Sicily. In the early 1880's he spent the summers in Venice, and commissioned paintings of Browning from Harper Pennington and Julian Story. In November 1881, when Browning left for England, Lowell and Field joined their friend William Wetmore Story and his family in Rome for a short holiday, before Lowell resumed his diplomatic career in London. A table-plan from 1881 in the editor's possession shows Mrs. Bronson and Edith entertaining the Brownings, Lowell, Field and the Curtises to dinner at Ca Alvisi.
3. Olga ("Nini") Kerr was a friend of Edith's. Her brother, Gervase Kerr, was an Englishman, "sensitive and subdued," who lived in Venice, spoke the Venetian dialect and dressed as a gondolier. A fine craftsman in wood, he made inlaid boxes and gave some to the Bronsons. A particular favourite of Edith's, he kept in touch with her for over fifty years until his death in a Fascist concentration camp in 1940.
4. The Browning Society had been founded in London by Emily Hickey and F. J. Furnivall earlier in the year and had held its inaugural meeting on 28 October. A few days before this meeting, Furnivall had circulated to all members copies of his *Bibliography of Robert Browning from 1833 to 1881*, which listed all Browning's works, his printed letters and some selected criticism. Browning's enrolling of Mrs. Bronson was almost certainly at her request and as an appreciation of her kindnesses to him in Venice. In usual circumstances Browning was slightly embarrassed by the adulation of the Society and reluctant to recommend his friends to join.
5. William Powell Frith (1819–1909), famous for his vast canvasses of Victorian life, such as "Derby Day" and "Ramsgate Sands." In 1881 he began his painting of "The Private View of the Royal Academy Exhibition" and wrote to Browning on 30 October to ask if he would agree to be included among the eminent people seen at the Academy: "If I should be so happy as to get your consent, will you in your reply tell

me your *exact height*? This information is necessary so that I preserve the relative proportions of the figures. Trollope has already sat for me and the Archbishop of York sits on Thursday" (Charnwood, p. 257). Browning agreed to a sitting at 10:30 a.m. on Monday, 14 November. In the finished painting he is standing in the middle-distance, talking to a young woman, with the noticeably taller Matthew Arnold on his left.

6. The unknown artist was Frederick Sandys (1832–1904) who had been commissioned by the publisher George Lillie Craik and his wife Dinah Mulock Craik to make a pencil sketch of Browning. The completed drawing was in their hands by 15 December. It is reproduced in Wilson, p. 124. Sandys persuaded Browning to join the Society for the Promotion of Hellenic Studies in January 1882.

7. Francis Charles Hastings Russell, 9th Duke of Bedford (1819–1891). Mrs. Bronson had discovered a book which had formerly belonged to his family, which Browning had agreed to return to the library at Woburn. Browning had known the Duke's mother, Lady William Russell, in London in the 1860's and had corresponded with her until her death in 1874.

8. Daniel Sargent Curtis (1825–1908) and his wife Ariana (1833–1922) were former Bostonians who settled in Venice and became part of the resident American colony. They were introduced to Browning by William Wetmore Story in 1879 or 1880, became good friends, and were regularly entertained at Warwick Crescent on their visits to London. Interested in literature and the arts, they wrote plays; their son, Ralph Curtis, became a friend of Edith Bronson. At this time they lived at Barbier's, opposite the Brownings' hotel, but later they rented (and eventually bought) an apartment in the Palazzo Barbaro on the Grand Canal. Daniel Curtis's reminiscences of Browning are printed in Appendix C.

9. The postscript is written at top of first and second pages.

10. Ca Alvisi.

11. Madame de Pilat is presumably the Fanny Pilat who signed Mrs. Bronson's birthday book. Everything suggests that she was a Frenchwoman of slender means who gave language lessons in her spare time. She is known to have lived in Venice between 1878 and 1892 and she became part of the American circle, in spite of her lowly circumstances.

Letter 3

ROBERT BROWNING TO KATHARINE BRONSON

19, Warwick Crescent, W.
Dec.4. '81.

Now let us shut the Gondola glasses,—I forget the technical word,—and talk, dear Friend! Here are your dear labours of love, the letters and enclosures, and here is my very first day of leisure this long fortnight: for, would you believe it?—I have been silly enough to sit every morning for three hours to one painter—who took an additional two hours and a half yesterday in order to get done: before which exercise of patience I had sat to another gentleman—who will summon me again in due time: all this since my return from Venice and the youthful *five!*[1] However, when two days ago there came yet another application to sit—the bear within the "lion" came out and I declined—as little gruffly as I was able. And so the end is, I can talk and enjoy myself—even at a distance—with a friend as suddenly dear as all hands from the clouds must needs be. I will not try and thank you for what you know I so gratefully have accepted and shall keep forever, I trust. Well,—here is the Duke's letter:[2] he is a man of few words and less protestation, but feels as he should your kindness, and will gladly acknowledge it should you come to England. And it seems that you *may!* But what will Venice be to us without you next year, if we return there as we hoped to do? How bright the City has become, despite the rain and the cold, since we left it—and have only you to remember!

Don't you remember we heard and conversed about Mrs Bloomfield Moore?[3] She passed through London some three weeks ago, and at once wrote to me about what pictures of Robert might be visible. She at once bought the huge "Delivery to the Secular Arm"[4] for the Philadelphia Academy of Fine Arts, and the "Dinant Market-Woman" for herself: and this so spontaneously and pleasantly that I could not help remembering the stories about capriciousness, and half expected to hear of some change of mind: whereas what I did hear in a day or two was that she was convinced I had not asked half enough for the pictures! She had enquired at the Gallery where the larger one was exhibited, and they estimated its value at so much. I told her their estimate was not mine, and that Robert was thoroughly remunerated—to say nothing of what he would think of all this graciousness. And, since her departure, I have had an extremely gratifying letter full of satisfaction at her purchases.[5] I put down this in mere justice to a lady concerning whom the reports hardly led me to expect such behaviour—did they?

Now for the dramatic stories—how good, good and good again you are! I shall examine them carefully and tell you if I can manage to turn them to account,[6]—in any case, thank you heartily! and all the while you were suffering from cold, and saddened by that calamitous fire and the loss of so many precious things—loss never to be repaired! In the midst of this, you employ yourself in helping me: what am I to say? How I feel, I know. Pray let me hear from you soon,—news never so minute of how you are—if you just write "I went to the Lido" I shall see the beloved back of the gondolier considerably in the way of my look-out—so that I shall look in—where the cushion is softest and somebody is sitting. Do you know that our London November has been warm and May-like beyond example, and in no way deserving the ill words I gave it, by anticipation, all the journey homeward. Golden as it is, may yours be refined and gilded true Venetian for your sake! But enough aloud: Good bye, dear friend! Give my truest regards to your Edith whom I continue to see in the cap, and the short sleeves and—well, and all the pretty rest. My sister loves you really, and bids me say so. And, saying or keeping silence, I am ever yours affectionately

Robert Browning.

I perhaps misunderstand a passage in your letter which mentions your sending some hand-made Venetian paper—none has arrived, unless it is the paper made valuable by the hand of the writer. By the bye, if you see Clerlé, pray tell him that his wares have come to hand in perfect condition—thanks to his care: also Rietti's[7] wood is safely here, and, it is thought, will answer its intended purpose well enough.

Publication: Whiting, pp. 265–266 (in part, as 4 December 1887).
Manuscript: Armstrong Browning Library.

1. One day in October 1881 Browning sat to four young artists in Ca Alvisi at Mrs. Bronson's request. These were Harper Pennington, Julian Story, Ralph Curtis and Charles Forbes, all friends of Edith Bronson. The identity of the fifth is less easy to ascertain. It is possible that Edith joined her friends in what clearly began as an artistic game or competition. As her gift was for flower painting and her portraits aren't very accomplished, it is probable that she destroyed any likeness she made. Alternatively, the fifth painter may have been Richard Peters, about whom little is known, but whose oil painting of Browning at the Armstrong Browning Library, wrongly attributed to 1884, has marked similarities to the other four canvasses. The results of this artistic mass production were better than anyone anticipated. Mrs. Bronson was particularly fond of the Harper Pennington likeness and hung it above her desk. Artists' copies of the Pennington and Story portraits, now at Williams College, were commissioned by John Field.

2. Still preserved with Browning's letter, it reads as follows: "Woburn Abbey. / Novr 29 1881 / Dear Mr Browning / If ever an opportunity should occur, on which I might, personally—express my gratitude to Mrs Bronson for so kind a thought and gift—may I trust to you, not to let it pass, without enabling me to take advantage of it? In the mean while will you be the kind channel of communication and convey my thanks? Wriothesley Duke of Bedford* collected books—and many, in Woburn Abbey library, bear his bookplate of 1703. By incorporating your letter of 27 November 1881, (containing its singular adventures) with this work of 1687—I shall give the volume a value it never would have acquired sleeping for centuries upon the Abbey shelves– Pray thank Mrs Bronson most gratefully for having so graciously added an interest to the old Abbey library and / Believe me / Yours very truly / Bedford." *At this point and below the line Browning has written "(*volti*)."

3. Clara Bloomfield-Moore (1824–1899), daughter and wife of American paper manufacturers, was a millionaire from Philadelphia who came to England in 1879 after the death of her husband. She endeared herself to Browning by buying some of Pen's pictures, and later entertained Browning and Sarianna at St. Moritz in 1884 and 1887. In an article in *Lippincott's Magazine* (vol. XLV, no. 46, May 1890) she claimed a particularly close relationship with Browning, stating that he asked her to make her home in London "in order that we might live near to each other to the end of our lives upon earth." She also maintained that *Ferishtah's Fancies* was her tribute from Browning, and implied that the lyric "Not with my Soul, Love!" was written to her. As her article is marred with factual inaccuracy, and as her son Clarence later claimed in a court case that his mother was certifiable, we may assume that she greatly exaggerated Browning's affection for her and indulged in wishful thinking. She was present in 1882 when Browning received his D.C.L., but she seems to have been a source of embarrassment to Browning in later years when she wrote poems to him, such as the melodramatic "On the Heights." After Browning's death Pen told her that "My father was a very true friend of yours, and you were in his mind during his last hours." But he also wrote similar

sentiments to the Layards and other friends and acquaintances, so no particular conclusions need be drawn.

4. "The Delivery to the Secular Arm," which shows a girl being handed over to the civil authorities by the Inquisition, was painted in Antwerp in 1880. It was exhibited at the Hanover Gallery in the same year, but failed to find a purchaser because of its size (10'6" x 7'6") and because of a poor review in *The Times* which said that the figures were the merest puppets and "we discover no merit of any kind in the picture except a somewhat careful and level execution of the technical portion of the painting." Edward C. McAleer (*LL*, p. 106) states that the picture has been rolled up in a case in the Pennsylvania Academy of Fine Arts since 1944. "Dinant Market-Woman" is unrecorded in the Catalogue Raisonné of Pen's works (*Reconstruction*, pp. 536–548) and so presumably is lost.

5. Mrs. Bloomfield-Moore's version of the purchase differs from Browning's. She says that Browning offered to give her the larger painting as a present and that, when she refused, he named a moderate sum which she then paid.

6. Mrs. Bronson had sent Browning fictional and historical anecdotes as possible subjects for poems, knowing that he had a love of the unusual, and that many of his poems originated from his reading.

7. Clerlé and Rietti were Venetian tradesmen from whom Browning had made purchases.

Letter 4

ROBERT BROWNING TO KATHARINE BRONSON

19. Warwick Crescent, W.
Dec. 23. '81.

Dear, kindest of friends—this is not the letter I was meaning to write concerning the records and the stories, and the goodness attending the gift: I will try *that* with a quieter pulse than your gift, of this morning, sets in motion. I would say "How *could* you"—"why did you"—or some such attempt at sober remonstrance: but you break down all my guards and I shall simply thank you—not promising to love you the more, which would be hardly possible—but engaging to render forgetfulness of your gift *mechanically* out of the question—since I will wear your beautiful ornaments every evening of my gayer life, as the earlier and equally valued ones remind me of you all the daytime.[1] This is no letter,—once again,—only an outcry: you will understand it, however—and that I wish you and yours all happiness from the bottom of my heart.

Ever affectionately yours
Robert Browning.

Publication: None traced.
Manuscript: Armstrong Browning Library.

1. Presumably evening studs and cuff-links sent as a Christmas present.

Letter 5

ROBERT BROWNING TO KATHARINE BRONSON

London, 19. Warwick Crescent, W.
New Year's Day, '82.

Dear Friend, I will not be overwhelmed and stifled by your kindness upon kindness, but ever and anon send up a feeble word of thanks from under the heap. The best thing the Old Year gave me was the confirmation of your friendship for me, which I dared hardly be sure of when we first met nine or ten months before: now I fully believe nothing will change it, be the years to come many or few. You will not suppose this comes of your giving me these good things—valued to the height as they are—but there is an effluence (I can't help the hard word) which pervades and makes quite alike precious paper and—pearls:[1] and as I seize and appreciate *that*—I shall not doubt but you also think what I would speak, and understand much of what I feel: there! I will not be discouraged because I can only wish you all happiness and have no diamonds to weight wishes on their journey to that dear Venice which your wonder of an Album helps me to enjoy when I please—which is nearly every day.

The extracts are all very characteristic and valuable: if I do not immediately turn them to use, it is because of an old peculiarity in my mental digestion—a long and obscure process. There comes up unexpectedly some subject for poetry which has been dormant and apparently dead for perhaps dozens of years: I wrote,—about a story I heard more than forty years ago and never dreamed of trying to repeat,—a poem of some two hundred lines a month ago[2]—wondering how it had so long escaped me,—and so it has been with my best things. These "petits faits vrais" are precious.

I have been meeting, these two last days, at the Private Views of the Grosvenor[3] and R. Academy Exhibitions, many of your intimates— Whistler,[4] Lowell, the Burys,[5] in whatever degree of intimacy they may be—and Mr Field has sent kind letters and pretty cards. I hear nothing from the Storys—I told you, I think, of Waldo's enthusiastic letter,—but who the lady is, English or American, is as yet undiscoverable.[6]

One sad piece of news reached me, however—that the poor "Universo" has gone to ruin absolutely—the furniture sold, the quality of Albergo departed forever.[7] Is it so? I suppose we shall have no difficulty in finding an apartment: but no "Europa"[8]—for our quiet ways, be sure! Another thing did I tell you—that a railway is about to run through my house,[9] just as I had made up my mind that twenty years' occupation of it was proof that I *could* live out my life there! "The world is all before us where to choose."[10] You remember the Grahams? I was present last Thursday at the wedding of the younger daughter, to a brother of your Mrs Eden[11]—who seems by all accounts worthy of his sister—which is something to say. Dear Friend, I shake the warmest of hands (*mine* is, anyhow) with you, over the land and sea. You know you have my sister's love: my son is with me—as Edith with you. Let us all be thankful, and may you and yours be happy—to the joy of yours affectionately ever

Robert Browning.

Publication: "Browning in Venice," p. 574–575 (in part).
Manuscript: Armstrong Browning Library.

1. Mrs. Bronson particularly loved pearls and always wore them. It is possible that the evening "ornaments" she gave Browning (Letter 4) were mounted seed-pearls.

2. "Donald," which was later published in *Jocoseria* (1883). Browning probably remembered reading the story in prose by Sir Walter Scott in *The Keepsake* for 1832, an annual to which he later contributed. However, he claimed to Daniel Curtis that he heard it from a man who had known Donald: "The man told me his story forty years ago" (Appendix C, p. 170).

3. The Grosvenor had opened in Bond Street in May 1877 as a gallery to support the younger school of painters. It was owned and managed by Sir Coutts Lindsay (1824–1913), and its building had been financed and designed by his wife Blanche (1844–1912), the daughter of Hannah Rothschild. During the last twenty years of the century it rivalled the Royal Academy and was even preferred by a number of painters, because the works of each artist were grouped together and divided from the rest by blank spaces, instead of being randomly hung as was customary at Burlington House. The Grosvenor Gallery was superbly appointed: "Green marble was brought from Genoa to make the columns in the entrance hall. The ceiling was painted blue with gold stars. The wall panels were divided by Ionic pilasters, fluted with gilt, from the old Italian opera house in Paris. The walls themselves were entirely covered with deep crimson silk damask" (Henrey, p. 84). Browning attended the private view of the opening exhibition, and a number of Pen's works were exhibited at the Grosvenor in the 1880's. Browning's friendship with the Lindsays lost much of its spontaneity after 1884, when Lady Lindsay left her husband. His sympathies lay with Blanche Lindsay, but he still needed Sir Coutts' encouragement and support to further Pen's career.

4. James Abbott McNeill Whistler (1834–1903), American painter and etcher, had been entertained by Mrs. Bronson at Ca Alvisi and remained a friend. They later met in London; he told her in an undated letter: "How very glad I shall be to see you again—you who have always been so *bienvieillante* for me—and whose kindness and hospitality to me in Venice I shall never forget" (Rucellai). His pleasure is not surprising, because he was unpopular and bankrupt in 1879 when he was sent to Venice by the Fine Arts Society of London to do a series of etchings. Shabbily dressed and desperately poor, he worked directly on small copper plates he carried around in his pockets. Mrs. Bronson's welcome to him at Ca Alvisi shows how unconcerned she was with the wealth or social prestige of her guests. She also helped Whistler financially by buying some of his pastels, and consulted Sargent as to which he thought the best.

5. The Burys were also Americans. Their son, Basil, was to marry Phyllis de Kay, Mrs. Bronson's niece.

6. Waldo Story (1854–1915), second son of William Wetmore Story, announced his engagement to Ada Maud Broadwood in December 1881. Browning's uncertainty as to Ada's nationality is understandable, as her father was English and her mother American. The Storys were married in Rome in 1883.

7. Browning's favourite albergo in Venice was always slightly seedy, and its collapse in 1881 had been anticipated. It was owned by an impoverished aristocratic couple from Dalmatia. According to Daniel Curtis, the husband was constantly away, sailing his boats on the Lagoon, leaving his wife to cook and do the housekeeping. The food was bad, guests few, and the spacious halls and rooms barely furnished and intensely cold. Apparently Browning didn't mind the Spartan surroundings.

8. A smart hotel on the opposite side of the Grand Canal from the "Universo."

9. This is the first intimation that, owing to the passing of the Regents Park Bill, Warwick Crescent was scheduled for demolition. Browning spent much of 1882 thinking about a new home and regretting in particular the destruction of his small garden, recently planted with shrubs from Shalstone, given to him by Mrs. FitzGerald. Eventually he moved in 1887, but 19 Warwick Crescent wasn't demolished until 1960. The building of the proposed railway was postponed, then revived in 1887, and finally abandoned.

10. An adaptation of Milton's lines at the end of Book 12 of *Paradise Lost*, when Adam and Eve are driven out of Eden:

> The world was all before them, where to choose
> Their place of rest, and Providence their guide.

11. Agnes, the youngest daughter of William Graham, married Captain Herbert Jekyll on 29 December at St. Peter's, Eaton Square. (*The Times*, 31 December 1881, p.1). William Graham (1825–1907), a naval officer whose first wife died in 1880, had met Browning and Mrs. Bronson in Venice. He was just at the beginning of a distinguished career, which included the posts of Controller of the Navy, Lord of the Admiralty and President of the Royal Naval College. He retired with a knighthood and the rank of Admiral. For Mrs. Eden, see Letter 17, n. 2.

Letter 6

ROBERT BROWNING TO KATHARINE BRONSON

19. Warwick Crescent, W.
Jan. 30. '82.

The day before your letter to my Sister arrived, she observed to me "How long since we have heard from Venice!"—and on my telling her that your last letter to myself remained unanswered, two such great eyes were at once observable in her that I made haste to explain: Mrs Bronson's dear goodness was not exactly a Fortunatus'[1] purse into which one might with impunity dip and dip again; and her letters and the news in them were such a delight that it behoved one to be moderate in trying for them: but (said I) I may perhaps venture to write tomorrow,—and then followed the letter. Another coincidence,—which I notice because of a paragraph referring to your Edith,—that same evening we had a visit from a young lady of various and considerable pretentions: and, after it, my Sister and I, meeting on the staircase, broke out simultaneously—"What comparison between her and Miss Bronson!"—and we exchanged impressions about the latter—if the comparing impressions and finding them to be quite

Ca Alvisi

Mrs. Bronson's Study

alike can be called "an exchange." Dear Friend, there is no place and time, in these latter years,—which I so thoroughly enjoy remembering with every minute circumstance therewith connected, as Cà Alvisi and the beloved couple there: all the charms of Venice, like so many currents,—drop into the memory of Venice where I may,—these one and all converge there, and, beginning, say, at Murano,[2] in a trice I am on the low soft chair in the room over the canal with the delicate cigarette-smoke with which I began to be seduced. Well, are these things really impossible for next Autumn? If so, Venice itself must go unvisited, I believe. Yet it will be something to see you in May[3]—though that hurried uncomfortable sort of bird-on-the[-]branch tarrying in this great distracting London will rather tantalize than satisfy my eyes and ears. But as somebody replied—to someone who proposed "Wine or Punch?'[']—"Wine—while the Punch is making",—so I would fain arrange for May here—and the chair, the room, and the cigarette-smoke when the gondola conducts to them. See, Mrs Bronson, what comes of pampering people—whether poets or *pigs*—for these latter, I am told, if indulged to the full, will munch the rosy side of an apple and disdain the rest—just as I reject the green Venice—missing the ripe Cà Alvisi. I say very little—would much be necessary?—of my concern about that illness through the water in the Gondola: I am simply happy that it is over.

Yes, our Winter, for once, has been no Winter at all: but there are vile fogs. My sister was—and indeed still is—suffering from neuralgia and a cold, but, as her way is, bears up womanfully. Our "season" is going to begin and quiet to end. Robert is at Paris, studying how to *model* under a clever artist:[4] he arrived one night, arranged with the sculptor next day, set to work on the following morning, and two days after (last Saturday) was "engaged on a figure half-life size from the model in motion": such is the earnestness of the fellow! His pictures[5]—two for the Academy and one for the Grosvenor Gallery—were ready by Christmas,—and this way he takes a holiday. Now, dear Friend, have you enough of me and mine? Give me all you can of yourself and your Edith—whose value was very apparent to me, little as our intercourse may have been. Well, I feel very affectionately to you both—*that* I know,—my sister will probably tell you something more like "news" than *that*—or that I am ever yours

Robert Browning.

Publication: None traced.
Manuscript: Armstrong Browning Library.

1. The hero of a popular European chapbook. He was a native of Famagusta in Cyprus who, meeting the Goddess of Fortune, received a purse which was replenished as often as he drew from it. Fortunatus was the subject of a number of plays and poems, including

an unfinished narrative "Fortunatus and his Sons" by the nineteenth-century German poet Johann Uhland. As Uhland was one of Mrs. Bronson's favourite poets, it is probable that she knew the poem, and that Browning therefore deliberately chose this metaphor in writing to her.

2. The largest island of the Lagoon, noted for its glass.

3. Mrs. Bronson was in London with her brother Charles de Kay in May and June 1882, and passed through again in August when Browning was in France.

4. Auguste Rodin (1840–1917). Pen was working in a friend's studio in Paris under Rodin. He told Waldo Story: "I am going in for a dose of modelling which, I take it, is a surer road to knowledge of the figure than drawing in black and white" (*BAF*, p. 180).

5. One of these was "Vespers," which depicts an elderly monk pulling a bell-rope for evening service in a church. The other two could be "The Reaper" and a portrait of his father.

Letter 7

ROBERT BROWNING TO KATHARINE BRONSON

19. Warwick Crescent, W.
April 2. '82

Dear Mrs Bronson,—it is so long ago since we heard from you! I wrote, and got no answer: my sister,—who had heard later,—wrote, and not a word comes to say how you are—though the last fears about the result of your accident in the gondola could not but continue—or increase, as they do. You must be your kind self again and write if possible,—or let Miss Bronson write, if only a line—till the arrival of which any gossip of mine is altogether impossible, understand!

Ever yours affectionately
RB.

Publication: None traced.
Manuscript: Armstrong Browning Library.

Letter 8

ROBERT BROWNING TO KATHARINE BRONSON

19. Warwick Crescent, W.
Apr. 19. '82.

Your letter did really set me at ease:[1] perhaps I am so little used to illness of any sort in this house that the intelligence of your accident and its effects remained unreasonably on my mind: besides, you were occasionally *indisposed* (at least) while I remained at Venice. I shall hardly go on to say whether I am glad or no that I had my bit of apprehensiveness for nothing—or rather for something—to wit, the letter with its news that I am to see you a month hence. But *not* at Venice! If you succeeded in getting the stray letter of mine (which I suppose, since it has not been returned to me) you will have heard the plain truth that, in all probability, I shall forego Venice this year, since—well, find out some better reason than what I gave you! As for occupying Cà Alvisi with all Cà Alvisi-ishness out of it,—any other place in the Universe—even the *Universo!*

Thinking of which too likely absence,—what if I give a proof of its unlikelihood by saying just something which I shall not call asking you a favor—so little shall I care if you forget it. You *may* see the redoubtable Clerlé: he promised me, on bidding me good bye, that he would retain for me, till my next visit, two old brass   —what shall I call them?—salvers, engraved on the inside   —not big at all, whereof the price was stipulated for at   (I *think*) *50 lire* the pair. They suit with things I have, and,   failing my appearance, he may dispose of them. So, if they were (look me in the eyes, Friend, and be frank!) not too burthensome for carriage I should be glad to have them—I won't even say, through your goodness,—not choosing to borrow your gondola to bring me potatoes! You will understand—as *I* understand what a business must your departure be.

This paper I write on—now, have I acted ungratefully in making certain painters grateful to me by a gift of a portion of what they pronounced worthy of all gratitude?[2] Thus it fell out: "silver-point" drawing is rarely practised, it seems, because the paper for it is hard to get: and conversation turning on the pity of *that*, at a dinner where Burne Jones[3] was (and your Princess Louise)[4] I said I fancied I had some of exactly the sort, through the artistic proclivities of a lady who &c. &c whereon arose a yearning,—whence followed this acceding to it, that I sent one parcel to the said Burne Jones, another to our host George Howard,[5] and another to Leighton[6]—whose beautiful drawing had caused the talk. All three abound in thankful praise—which I honestly return where it is due. If more thanks are wanted—so many shall be heaped on you for the word which is to tell me when you leave Venice, when you will arrive here, and when I may, after as few minutes' delay as possible, see you with the eyes of

Yours affectionately
Robert Browning.

All love to the Daughter—how else?

Publication: None traced.
Manuscript: Armstrong Browning Library.

1. This letter is missing.
2. Mrs. Bronson had sent Browning a large quantity of hand-made Venetian paper (see postscript to Letter 3), some of which he had given away to three artist friends.
3. Edward Burne-Jones (1833–1898), the distinguished Pre-Raphaelite painter, was first introduced to Browning by D. G. Rossetti in London in 1856. A few weeks later, Browning and Elizabeth entertained Burne-Jones and William Morris, both of whom were admirers of *Men and Women*, at 39 Devonshire Place. Burne-Jones illustrated two of Browning's poems, "Childe Roland" (1861) and "Love among the Ruins" (1870–73). He was given a baronetcy in 1894.
4. Princess Louise Battenberg, who illustrated Mrs. Bronson's article on Burano lacework in *The Century Magazine* with pen-and-ink drawings.
5. George James Howard, 9th Earl of Carlisle (1843–1911). He was a Liberal M.P. between 1879 and 1885, and was a good amateur artist, well known for his landscape watercolours. He admired Italy and all things Italian and was a friend of Burne-Jones, Leighton and G. F. Watts. Browning stayed at his home, Naworth Castle, for a month in 1869, during which Howard drew a pencil sketch of him illustrated in *Reconstruction*, plate 15.
6. Sir Frederick Leighton (1830–1896), President of the Royal Academy, later Lord Leighton, was a close friend of Browning from Florence and Rome days in the 1850's, when he made a much admired pencil sketch of Browning (Wilson, p. 59). Leighton designed the monument placed on Elizabeth's grave in the Protestant Cemetery in Florence at Browning's request. Browning paid tribute to Leighton's art in *Balaustion's Adventure*, and the two remained friends until Browning's death. Leighton was one of his pall-bearers in Westminster Abbey.

Letter 9

SARIANNA & ROBERT BROWNING TO KATHARINE BRONSON

[In Sarianna's hand.]   19. Warwick Crescent. W.
                                           Oct 9th [1882]

Dearest Mrs Bronson,

Oh, the bitter, bitter disappointment! I can hardly bear to speak of it. Venice has been in our hearts and plans all the year long— We never dreamt that we should wait twelve days in vain, first at Turin then at Bologna, for the possibility of entrance, finding all the roads broken up.[1] But I hope you are now safely housed in dear Casa Alvisi, and you will have learnt the history of our baulked plans. Our sojourn among the mountains in Dauphigny was delightful.[2] We purposed after leaving them, to pay a visit to a friend who had a villa at Ischia, but a fatal accident to one of his guests made us give it up.[3] Mrs Curtis most kindly procured rooms for us at Barbier's, and I comforted myself for losing Ischia by thinking we should see more of dear Venice. It is a pang in my heart.

"Another year" is no consolation—life is too short and uncertain to look forward to another year. We began to be very anxious at not hearing from you. Do tell me all about yourselves—your health and your journey. Have you and dear Edith lost your colds, and do you not feel it a delight to be in Venice again? Did you see Miss Montalba's bust[4] as you passed through London?

With very best love to dear Edith, and more than I can express, ever

Your affectionate

Sarianna Browning.

[Continued by RB.]

Dear Mrs Bronson,

I just add my true regrets, and earnest hopes of repairing in some degree all this misfortune next year. Italy should leave off building her big ships, and try again at *Murazzi*[5] which might do some good. I see a little notice of your Brother's Poems,[6] and send you the paper (—one which Carlyle used to get all his information about modern literature from!) All love to you & Miss Bronson from yours

affectionately ever

RB.

Publication: None traced.
Manuscript: Armstrong Browning Library.

1. There were heavy floods in Italy. The Verona road was impassable, temporarily cutting off Venice and the surrounding region.

2. At St. Pierre de Chartreuse, Isère, where Browning had also stayed in 1881. He wrote to Mrs. FitzGerald on 3 September (*LL*, p. 152): "It is the loveliest country I ever had experience of."

3. Reginald Cholmondeley (1826–1896), whose guest Miss Wade, daughter of the Revd. Nugent Wade (1845–1891), fell to her death while sketching the sunset behind his villa on 12 August. After the funeral Cholmondeley decided to leave Ischia, but offered the Villa Sauvé to Browning and Sarianna for the autumn and winter. Browning refused with a certain relief, because, to reach Naples and Ischia, he and Sarianna would have had to pass by Florence and Rome, which would have awakened old memories. Browning did not visit either city again after Elizabeth's death, but he felt guilty that he deprived Sarianna of the pleasure of seeing them.

4. Henrietta Montalba (1856–1893) was the youngest of four artist sisters who lived in Venice and London. The bust was made in London at the request of Mrs. Bronson and was finished by July 1882. On 26 July her sister Clara Montalba described the bust to Mrs. Bronson: "I think you will be pleased with Mr. Browning's bust; it is dignified and amiable and very like indeed. Everyone sees everyone with their own eyes; it is to be hoped that what you particularly care for in his face is there" (Meredith). A cast of the bust in bronze is now in the Examination Schools, Oxford University.

5. *Murazzi* are the embankments of Venetian lagoons. This may, therefore, refer to the flooding which had affected Venice as well as the Veneto.

6. Mrs. Bronson's youngest brother Charles de Kay (1848–1935). The poems are presumably *The Vision of Esther* which Charles de Kay published in New York in 1882. This was a continuation of his *The Vision of Nimrod* and the second part of a vast epic poem set in Ancient Babylon, which was intended to have a bearing on problems of

modern America, such as the corrupt judiciary and the status of women. The book received kind but puzzled reviews in America and England, but it is not clear which of the reviews Browning read. Charles de Kay is better known as a writer of occasional verse.

Letter 10

ROBERT BROWNING TO KATHARINE BRONSON

19, Warwick Crescent, W.
Nov. 10. '82.

Dear Friend, how good and kind you are to think of me—but how mistaken if you fancy I need any incitement to think of you—such a help, for instance, as this beautiful little dish which is full in my eyes while I write: it will never hold "olives," I assure you, but front me as a most happy and natural completion of a certain family cup which I value greatly. Thank you—always with the reservation of any atom of thanks that would go to the fear I should forget you if my memory were not stirred this way. As for the failure to get to Venice, we,—my sister & I,—have only regretted it once—that is, uninterruptedly ever since. You must know, that beside the adverse floods and bridge-breakings I was for the first time in my life literally lamed by what I took for an attack of rheumatism which I caught just before leaving S! Pierre de Chartreuse through my own stupid inadvertence in sitting with a window open at my back,—reading the Iliad,[1] all my excuse!,—while clad in a thin summer suit,—and snow on the hills and bitterness everywhere. My doctor here will have it that "the liver was attacked"—and I am not out of his drugging even now,—though all to complain of is a moderate aching—rather when I move than when I keep quiet:⟨—no, the reverse,—"when I keep quiet" goes first!⟩[2] but this was no such slight matter at Bologna, and I fancied I might be absolutely crippled at Venice, if I even managed to overcome all obstacles and get there. Of course, now that what is done is done,[3] I am tantalized with fancies of what might have been done otherwise. But, if I live and do well, be sure, Dear Friend, that I will go as early to Venice next year, and stay as late, as circumstances will allow. And you,—the first news was that you were ill, and inconvenienced in various ways. In this little note, you say nothing of yourself. Now, do believe the simple truth that a word from you, if possible, a word to the effect that you are well again and happy,—will light up November as if it were May: and, that good intelligence duly set down, you must go on and tell me every particle of Venetian occurrences to the minutest: for if you only chronicle the capture of a crab (mark the alliteration) it will interest me nearly as much as Gladstone's capture of a vote in to-night's division[4]— though I am properly interested in *that*, I hope. How is Miss Bronson—but I won't begin with a whale instead of a crab,—*all* you can tell will give me a pleasant thrill. I was sorry to be away when Mr Woods[5] called with your parcel,—I could have pumped him dry—even now, something may be got out of him when I see him, if I am so lucky: and Robert writes from Paris that Mr Sargent[6] is arrived there,—and he too has Venice hanging about him. Well, I too catch it a little in writing thus. My Sister will write for herself. All love to you from yours ever affectionately

Robert Browning.

Publication: None traced.
Manuscript: Armstrong Browning Library.

1. The *Iliad* was one of Browning's favourite Greek texts. He used to travel with a small copy bound in limp morocco, which he purchased in June 1873 before going to France. He had this with him at St. Pierre in 1881 and 1882.
2. Interpolated phrase is shown in angle brackets.
3. Shakespeare: *Macbeth*, III, ii, 12.
4. Gladstone's government was under strong attack from the Tories at this time, and the Prime Minister was himself unpopular among leading Liberals for his Irish and Egyptian policies and for the introduction of new taxes. Yet he had strong popular support, as had been shown at the Lord Mayor's Banquet at the London Guildhall the previous evening, where his speech had been warmly applauded.
5. Henry Woods (1846–1921), artist, was originally a book illustrator on the staff of *The Graphic*. A journey to Italy made him realize the charm of Venice, and he lived there almost continuously from 1876, each year sending his atmospheric paintings of Venetian buildings, scenes and people to the Royal Academy. He was elected A.R.A. in 1882 and R.A. in 1893. It was only natural that he should have joined Mrs. Bronson's circle; he was among the many friends who signed her birthday book in Asolo. See H. Ward, *History of the Athenaeum 1824–1925*, London, 1926, pp. 319–320.
6. John Singer Sargent (1856–1925), distinguished portrait painter, was born in Florence of American parents. He studied in Florence and Paris, and saw much of Europe before going to London (1885) and settling permanently in J. M. Whistler's former studio in Tite Street. Sargent had been staying in Venice in 1882, living in rooms at the top of the Palazzo Rezzonico. When Pen Browning bought the Rezzonico six years later, he preserved Sargent's scratched signature in the attic room. Writing to Mrs. Bronson from Paris about this time, Sargent recalled his Venetian holiday: "Ralph Curtis tells me that you are surrounded with your guests as ever. It is difficult for me even to fancy your parlour without a glowing fire, yourself sitting near it in a particular chair; asking the Montalbas and me to write witty and beautiful verses, while . . . Miss Chapman brews pick-me-up at the Arabian bar" (Rucellai).

Letter 11

ROBERT BROWNING TO KATHARINE BRONSON

19, Warwick Crescent, W.
Dec. 17. '82

Dear Friend of mine, when I read your letter once more, as I have just done, it seems the most surprisingly unaccountable of follies that I have let full three weeks go by without making any effort to procure myself such another delight as I had in receiving it. Put the kindness in it aside,—and the mere talk about Venice, and my friends, and your friends old and new,—this alone would be a cordial to me in the dispiriting fog and cold of our London just now,—while, put all this aside, and the kindness by itself would act as a true *elixir vitæ*: I mean what I say—and can only suppose that I have feared to look greedy in crying out at once for more—more—as the "daughters of the horse-leech"[1] are said to do. There was an enquiry about my health in a letter which my Sister showed me: I am quite well again,—there was a punishment (did I not tell you?) of an egregious stupidity I committed in reading at St. Pierre for some hours on a bitterly cold day with an open window at my back—which back was clothed in its summer costume, though snow had fallen a week before: and the result, a full fortnight after, was actual & painful lameness of one hip and thigh: *that*—and no amount of mere rain—*might* have kept me miserably a prisoner at Venice; I remembered when I decided on going home ingloriously: at home, the pain became worse, and I consulted "my" doctor—who rarely has other than a sinecure of doctoring as regards me—and he at once pronounced "not rheumatism,—a cold on the liver,—which is to be treated, and no leg at all": and so he treated it—and so the event corresponded,—for, after a short course of "acids"— the whole annoyance ceased as by magic—leaving me a gladder and wiser man[2] when open windows at my back are concerned. I went to thank him for his penetration—and he said "Didn't I tell you I should cure you?"– All the same, I feel increasingly the "filthy air"[3] of this London—and, in proportion, long—and indeed begin to plan for an escape next Winter. There, you are paid for your care of my poor unworthiness! Anything ought to be more to the purpose than *that*: yet I can't begin to think, even, of our London news without sadness enough: for poor Trollope[4] was your friend, as indeed he was mine: two days only before his seizure I dined with him at his Club—we had a gay party, and I thought him in his usual florid health: but he had over-tasked his wonderful capacity for work—applying it, of late, to uncongenial matters with which he had properly no concern—managing the disordered financial accounts of a bookseller's firm. Then, the Archbishop[5] was used to show me the mellow light of his countenance. My old friend Houghton[6] seems saved (for the time being) "so as by fire"—for his imprudence is past remedy. Well,—through the unwonted Autumnal Session of Parliament we have had an Autumnal season, you know: the great event of which has been the Opening of the Law Courts:[7] I avoid shows generally: but as the people sent me two of the best tickets,—which were fought for tooth and nail,—I thought it ungracious to refuse them—so, my sister & I saw—and perhaps enjoyed—what was generally allowed to be imposing enough. Two days after, I would have you know, I was Vice-Chancellor—for an evening: the real Dignitary[8] being summoned to Windsor just when he had a dinner-party—I was besought to "be Chancellor for the occasion"—with a very unnecessary regret that they could not give the Great Seal. Last Monday, we gave our genial little hero, Wolseley,[9] a dinner—we of the Cosmopolitan Club[10]—and it went off well: he quite sparkles with vivacity and goodnature, and our fat Prince[11] is pleasant-mannered if little else. This enormous Belt trial[12] is exercising us,—it will clear the air of much nonsense, showing as it does the ineptitude of our art-patrons and dishonesty of our art-practitioners—though one might have attained that knowledge without exactly paying some twenty five thousand pounds for it,—the expense of the proceedings amounting to nearly that already. By the bye, an important piece of news to my *grand* fatherly heart, came in the shape of a telegram last night to announce the purchase—by some stranger—of his picture at the Manchester Exhibition. Himself returns early next week—that is, *this* week—for a few days' visit: he has painted & modelled very diligently; and seems to have taken a new departure altogether, in his passion for "the figure." I have no notion when this house will be required of me—so, am still, as a bird on the branch, unsettled and uncertain. Does one get tired of Cà Dario[13] in a couple of years? Dear friend, *I* should not wish myself away from such a delicious haven of rest as Edith's house in a couple of centuries, I verily believe. Now, all this talk about myself (of my sister, I shall say no word: she ought to write and thereby get me a double allowance of letters from you)—this talk, I say, is to informally claim a like collection of all minutenesses about yourself—and that dear Edith too. Make the Christmas here effectively "merry," and happy, by a letter,— and my heart shall leap over the long way between us,—indeed it shall!

Spite of what I have just said,—here is my Sister who *does* send her best & warmest love to you both—and with it goes that of

yours ever aff.ʸ

R Browning.

Publication: None traced.
Manuscript: Armstrong Browning Library.

1. Browning refers to Proverbs 30:15—"The Horse-leach hath two daughters, crying 'Give, Give!'"

2. A pastiche of the final lines of Coleridge's "The Ancient Mariner" in which the wedding guest is described:

> A sadder and a wiser man,
> He rose the morrow morn.

3. Shakespeare: *Macbeth*, I, i, 12.

4. Anthony Trollope (1815–1882) had died on 6 December; and Browning had dined with him at the Garrick Club on 1 November, the day before Trollope suffered the stroke which paralysed him. Trollope had crossed to England with the Bronsons on the Cunard steamer *Bothnia* in 1875, and had corresponded with Mrs. Bronson as recently as 16 June 1882.

5. The Most Revd. Archibald Campbell Tait (1811–1882), formerly Headmaster of Rugby School and Bishop of London, had been Archbishop of Canterbury since 1868. He died on 3 December, having been ill for some time. On 3 September Browning wrote to Mrs. FitzGerald: "I am very anxious about the Archbishop, who has always been strangely kind to me" (*LL*, p. 53).

6. Richard Monckton Milnes (1809–1885), 1st Lord Houghton, whose friendship with Browning went back to the 1830's. Milnes had organized Browning's election to the Athenaeum in 1862 and the two men were regular correspondents. Early in 1882 Milnes had suffered a severe attack of angina pectoris in Athens. He returned to England and, instead of taking life easily at home, he made a strenuous trip to Scotland to stay with Lady Ashburton, visiting other friends on the way—which explains Browning's comment on his "imprudence." Early in 1883 he travelled extensively in Italy, and he even made plans for a visit to India, which he reluctantly abandoned on medical advice.

7. The new Law Courts in the Strand, designed by G. E. Street, R.A., were opened on Monday 4 December by the Queen. The occasion was described by a writer in *The Illustrated London News* as "an informal and spontaneous meeting of Her Majesty and myriads of her subjects from town and country." Browning was invited as a representative of persons eminent in literature, art and science, and was seated during the ceremony in the quadrangle inside the new buildings.

8. The Earl of Selborne (1812–1895), the Lord Chancellor, was invited to join Queen Victoria at Windsor Castle for dinner on 7 December with the Italian Minister and Sir William and Lady Harcourt. He could hardly refuse the royal command, although he had already arranged a dinner party himself for that evening, at which Browning deputized.

9. Garnet Joseph Wolseley (1833–1913), distinguished soldier, was appointed to the command in Egypt in 1882, on the outbreak of the rebellion of Arabi Pasha, whom he decisively defeated at Tel-el-Kebir—thus prompting the celebrations mentioned by Browning. He later was in charge of the Nile Expedition (1884–85) for the relief of General Gordon and became a Viscount, Field-Marshal and finally Commander-in-Chief of the Army. Browning held him in great esteem and willingly agreed to send him some autographs in November 1880.

10. The Cosmopolitan Club was a London club, founded in 1852 in Charles Street, Berkeley Square, as an after-dinner retreat for a group of young artists and politicians, including Milnes, Thackeray, Holman Hunt and Watts. Members met in a stuffy window-less room, formerly Watts's studio, for an informal smoke late in the evening. Browning became a member in 1863 but resigned in 1883 "from sheer shame at having belonged to it for years together without paying it a visit" (letter to Mrs. Wynne Finch, 30 May 1885, ABL). The club was dissolved at the end of the century.

11. The Prince of Wales, later King Edward VII.

12. Richard Claude Belt, sculptor of the Byron statue in Hyde Park, claimed damages from the proprietor of *Vanity Fair* for libel by Charles Lawes, who stated in an article that Belt passed off the works of other artists as his own. The trial occupied the court for forty-three sittings, and on 28 December the jury decided in Belt's favour and

awarded him £5,000 damages. The case was the last heard at the old Law Courts at Westminster.

13. Ca Dario, on the opposite side of the Grand Canal from Ca Alvisi was the lifelong home of Rawdon Brown (see Letter 20, n. 1 and Letter 23, n. 5). It was briefly the home of Pen and Fannie Browning in 1888 when they were waiting to move into the Palazzo Rezzonico.

Letter 12

ROBERT BROWNING TO KATHARINE BRONSON

London, 19. Warwick Crescent, W.
Feb. 20. '83.

Dear Mrs Bronson, am I never to hear from you again? This is the judicious way of slurring over the circumstance that it is, very likely, my own stupid fault that I have not heard long ago: for I know your kindness too thoroughly to doubt that, if I had begged for a word from you, I should have got one. I have been hearing *of* you—from the Layards'[1]—and gather, from the account of your hospitalities and entertainments, that you are well again: I do hope so, with all my heart. My own tardiness in writing comes of the quantity of merely necessary scribbling I have to effect—before setting to work at which, I say "This kind of thing *first*"— and when the five or six letters lie done and done with before me—I say "*Not* this other quite different thing when my mind aches even more than my fingers—wait till they are both fresh!"—So, the mornings come and go,—and, this particular morning, I determined that when the five troublesome businesses were dispatched, the compensatory word or two should follow at all risks: and why compensatory unless because it appeals to your goodness for a return (in Homeric language) of gold for brass? As if *you* have not infinitely more pressing troubles with your schools and poor folks[2] and guests and—what know I? But then *you*—you are goodness and I am anything but that, when I do my duty with grudging and groaning. We have had vile weather, worse public news, and,—in my case,—worst of all misfortunes in the sudden death of friends,—the most prominent being that of Professor Smith[3]—one of the rarest of scholars and best of men. Now, your Wagner[4]—of whom I saw a little but enough in London once on a time, was a great genius but greater curmudgeon— and such a monster of peacock-like vanity that one finds it hard to fancy the substance that was hidden by the blue and yellow feathers.

Pray did I say anything—or anything like enough—about your offer of the House? At all events I breathed out a "*Magari*"[5] that no words could properly represent. We are still in the same uncertainty as to when they will turn us out here: they can when they please—but that pleasure exercises itself tyrannously enough in this land where so much fuss is made about the "rights of property": and my laziness increases every day. Do you know anything of the Storys? They talked of returning in the late Autumn: what are they doing? Even the young men are out of sight and knowledge,—except that I see Waldo has been an exhibitor at Rome. Here is the sheet all but full—and nothing said—but much thought—concerning your Daughter—oh, and concerning everything! There is a tradesman in our neighbourhood who styles himself "Universal Provider": do particularly provide for one who will gluttonously devour every scrap you throw to yours affectionately ever

Robert Browning.

My Sister desires her kindest love to you and to Edith.

Publication: None traced.
Manuscript: Armstrong Browning Library.

    1. Sir Austen Henry Layard (1817–1894), excavator of Nineveh and Ambassador to Madrid and Constantinople. He and his wife Enid lived in their retirement in the Palazzo Capello on the Grand Canal. Browning renewed his acquaintanceship with them in Venice, and they were also close friends of Mrs. Bronson. The Layards possessed a fine collection of Italian paintings, and Lady Layard helped to found a hospice for seamen on the Guidecca.

    2. Mrs. Bronson looked after the Venetian poor, particularly the families of the gondoliers, sometimes giving them food and lodging in the winter months at Ca Alvisi. She also organized basic schooling for their children, supervised by a local teacher. Photographs exist in the Fossi collection of classes of small children, dressed all alike in a special school uniform provided by Mrs. Bronson.

    3. Henry John Stephen Smith (1826–1883), Fellow of Balliol College, Oxford, Tutor in Mathematics and Savilian Professor of Geometry. An inspiring teacher, Smith was one of the leading reformers in nineteenth century Oxford and sat on the Royal Commission which shaped science education in the latter part of the century. Among the many posts he held were Chairman of the Meteorological Office and Curator of the University Museum. In 1878 he tried unsuccessfully to enter parliament as Liberal M.P. for the university; Browning endorsed his candidature and voted for him. Jowett described Smith to Browning as "one of the kindest men I have known" and claimed that his death on 9 February was "more deeply felt in Oxford than any stranger to the place can easily imagine" (ABL). See Keith Hannabus, "The Harmonious Mathematician," *Balliol College Annual Record*, 1983, pp. 39–40.

    4. Richard Wagner (1813–1883), German opera composer, died in Venice on 13 February. Browning's attitude toward him can be summed up by the following comment in a letter to Hamilton Aidé, 30 May 1884: "I always recognised the high qualities of Wagner's genius, and appreciated adequately much of the music: but the ways of the man were never to my taste, and his admirers sounded his praise so loudly and—with respect to his predecessors—so (to my mind) invidiously, that I want the impulse to prolong the echoes just now when a little silence would seem fitting to help one to reconsider one's judgment of the past, whether favourable or adverse" (ABL).

    5. "I wish it were so!" Mrs. Bronson is trying to find suitable alternative accommodation for the Brownings when they have to leave Warwick Crescent.

Letter 13

ROBERT BROWNING TO KATHARINE BRONSON

19. Warwick Crescent, W.
March 6. '83.

Dear Friend, I must write *at once* about what frightens me somewhat in your kindest of letters—the allusion,—if I rightly understand it,—to my possible acceptance of your proffered generosity in the matter of the *Studio-house*:[1] no, no! Your presence in Venice will always be reason enough for my going there for as many weeks as I can manage,—but the necessities of my life—as they bind me now, at least—forbid any longer staying away than just *that*: so, if on account of your goodness to me & my Sister, you really were induced—apart from considerations of quite another kind—to involve yourself in a troublesome business . . Oh, how grieved and mortified should I be! Therefore I charge, on the feeling I so thoroughly value, that you put me and mine altogether out of the question in your negotiations with the *Proprietario*—which being done, I shall continue my old and true interest in them, as in whatever interests you. Do you understand? At all events, I could not rest easily for a moment until I had tried to keep myself free of the vexation of causing one trouble more to you whom I would be so glad and proud to help from the least touch of trouble. There! And you are evidently far from well, too: were I in Venice I should prove troublesome enough in one way, and plague you to death by way of saving your life—begging you to take exercise, and abjure company prolonged into the night. Such entreaties are generally urged on mistaken grounds and teaze rather than edify, but—all the same—if, at the end, they did an atom of good,—why, I would risk the being found an inveterate teazer. I myself have never been *quite* my old self since that foolish exposure to the open window and bitter cold at S.t Pierre,—accordingly, I shall not readily repeat the folly, but read Homer, while snow is on the mountains, with a proper guard of wraps and a cloak.

Will you please, Madam, to spare me one request for the future, and take it for granted that you will always find my "last book" go to you humbly for acceptance, without being bidden advance—as if it did not know its duty! I conclude that you mean the book that *will be* "the last" when once it gets published,—and you may have fancied, from the announcements in newspapers, that such is already the case: but the appearance, I find, is to take place on March 9.th[2]—and meanwhile I have not even a proof-sheet: when the book is a book indeed, and comes to hand—then, Madam, it will go to post—and, probably, "with my name on the title-page." Dear Friend, I have done—the writing: I go on—the thinking: and shall continue to be with you, so far as thoughts allow,

Yours affectionately ever
Robert Browning

My Sister's love goes with mine to you—and to dear Miss Bronson.

Publication: None traced.
Manuscript: Armstrong Browning Library.

1. The Palazzo Giustiniani-Recanati, next door to Ca Alvisi, which Mrs. Bronson had suggested the Brownings might like to rent if they chose to live permanently in Venice. Mrs. Bronson eventually rented the house herself for her guests, and the Brownings stayed there in 1883 and 1885.
2. *Jocoseria* was published on 9 March, and the 2,000 copies proved so popular that a second edition of 1,000 copies was printed on the same day.

Letter 14

KATHARINE BRONSON TO ROBERT BROWNING

Palazzino Alvisi, Venezia.
[ca. 1 December 1883]¹

Dearest Mr Browning

I think this is a dear letter from the bridegroom elect & I am so pleased to think that I knew slightly & admired greatly Miss Audrey Boyle.² Shall you send her a wedding present? & do you think *I* might do so? or w'd. it be too *empressé* on my part. If you will give away something that I give you—I will give you a little silver object wh̄ will please her from *you* far more than from me. Do, darling Mr Browning. I can give you something so very nice—and you will have inscribed on it something to please the father & children. Remember that your name on a piece of paper is dear, how much more on an object that perishes not! You cannot find anything at any of the shops that w'd be worth the sending—but I have a small thing in my locked treasure box wh̄ never has been seen by mortal eye but mine & a distant Teuton of whom I bought it—and so we will make several people happy. Only—only—tho' you say you will do any thing to please me—I know it is that you know I w'd never ask you to do anything against your own wish & judgment. I send a kiss for good morning to dear Miss Browning–

Your affectionate
KB

Publication: None traced.
Manuscript: Armstrong Browning Library.

1. Dated by reference to "bridegroom elect." Hallam Tennyson wrote of his forthcoming marriage in a letter dated 26 November 1883 to Browning. The letter was forwarded from London to Venice where Browning after reading it sent it to Mrs. Bronson because of her friendship with the future bride. Only the envelope has been preserved at the Armstrong Browning Library which bears a note in Mrs. Bronson's hand: "I find it quite natural that poets should be friends. Who if not they—superior to the foibles of every day life & intercourse?" In his reply to Hallam Tennyson on 1 December Browning said: "The news of the propitious event came here some days ago: and it happens that more than one friend at Venice was able to give me a very gratifying account of the Lady—while, for my part, I promptly matched it, as I well could, by my report of the qualities of the Lady's Lover" (Tennyson Centre).

2. Audrey Boyle was a beautiful but penniless Irish girl, whom Hallam had met when she was staying with relatives at Freshwater. They were married on 25 June 1884 in the Henry VII Chapel in Westminster Abbey, and Browning was among the guests.

Letter 15

KATHARINE BRONSON TO SARIANNA BROWNING

Venice.
Wednesday [12 December 1883]

Dearest Miss Browning

I suppose I will one day get used to your absence, but the time has not come yet, & I look with the same sadness across the lonely court every morn'g & evening. I have not yet had courage to go over to the P.º Giustinian, nor to arrange my studio there. The weather is disagreeable,—rain has washed away snow, & a cold mist has taken the place of both. Yesterday I had a tiring day with workpeople & "unfortunates"— in the afternoon Count Zorzi,[1] who told me his griefs with regard to *Ruskin*, who has *forgotten him* he says, & that the thought is a poniard in his heart! My youth of ambitions who was ill—is getting better, quite out of danger. He had typhoid fever.

The "little Munns"[2] as I call them are also better, & the Generale is very slowly improving. I send him a very good punch every day—w͞h you will find useful for some of your invalids if you ever have any. A tumbler of fresh milk—a wine glass of old Jamaica Rum—shake from glass to glass, add nutmeg lightly grated on top- The sugar must be put into the milk before adding the rum.- This w'd be good for your servant in his convalescence[3]—as it is easier to prepare than many other things- Don Carlos[4] is allowed to go out again—but he is so imprudent that he will have to *go in* again very soon. Princess Metternich[5] is coming to dine with me today—as her liege Lord has gone to Mogliano to stay with Csse[.] Marcello– Count & Countess Grüne were here yesterday– They are so very nice—that I am sorry I did not invite them while you were here—but truly in the last days of your stay I was so *discontented* because they were the *last* days that I could not think of new people– They made no impression on me[.]

Mr Furnivall sends me the Pall Mall Gazette with the sonnet to Goldoni[6]—w͞h laughs in the print, like its beloved author. Avignone[7] writes from Florence that he has dined with the Mackays to meet M. & Mrs Curtis—& that they all talked of Venice & of the Casa Alvisi & the Giustinian palace. In such a society we may be sure we were all well treated. Avignone says Florence is very cold & windy & he is not happy at all in his holiday & will come back soon to Venice– As I write the little Giuseppina[8] comes in with her head down in that queer way of hers. She throws it up as she shows me the gown that *angel* gave her—buona stofa Inglese she says it is, and just what she wanted for the cold weather. It is wonderful to hear her stream of talk about you. I wish I c'd transcribe it to make you smile. Her whole monologue may be summed up in the idea that no one has ever been seen to compare with either you or Mr Browning. She says she has a right to judge because she has seen so many forestieri[9] in her life– I will write no more—only to say how unhappy I am that I did not beg you to telegraph to me from Basle. I am haunted by the idea that you may have been cold en route—or that the sun bath w͞h made Mr Browning's head giddy should have had some after effect—always

Your loving
KB

Publication: None traced.
Manuscript: Armstrong Browning Library.

1. The Venetian Count A.P. Zorzi (1842–1921) was among the first to denounce the restoration of St. Mark's Basilica. He wrote a pamphlet of protest, which Ruskin, whom he met in 1876, arranged to have published with the addition of a Preface. For twenty years the Clerk of Works, G. B. Meduna, had been restoring St. Mark's by replacing the old marble facing with new material and destroying old mosaics in levelling the floor. Zorzi's pamphlet was successful, and by 1880 the combined efforts of Zorzi and Ruskin had brought an end to the barbarous restoration. The original marble that remained was replaced, and the restoration of the south front and the south-west portico, completed in 1886, was planned along different principles. Ruskin had not forgotten Zorzi in 1883, as Mrs. Bronson reports, but he was busy in England with his Oxford lectures. He was still vitally interested in St. Mark's, but, the battle won, he had left Zorzi to oversee the new restoration plans. Zorzi's account is given in his article, "Ruskin in Venice," *Cornhill*, August 1906. For a full discussion, see John Unrau, *Ruskin and St. Mark's*, London, 1984, pp. 191–210.
2. Probably Mrs. Bronson's affectionate name for the younger members of the Mundella family to whom Browning was introduced in 1873 and to whose daughter Maria Theresa he wrote on 10 November 1880: "How pleasant an interlude midst

troublous life was our meeting with you all in Venice" (Sheffield). Anthony J. Mundella (1825–1897) was an M.P.

3. The Brownings returned to London to find one of their servants dying from diphtheria. See letters 16 and 17.

4. Don Carlos Maria de Los Dolores (1848–1909), Prince of Bourbon, Duke of Madrid, claimant to the Spanish throne as Carlos VII, had retired to Venice after leading the unsuccessful risings in the Basque country in 1872–76. He was a member of Mrs. Bronson's circle of friends and had created a minor sensation in November by visiting the wife of Domenico Damian, Mrs. Bronson's second gondolier, to congratulate her on the birth of triplets and to give her some money—only to come under suspicion that he was the father of the children! Browning had sent him a signed photograph the same month and was told "Elle aura une place de choix dans ma collection." They also met on later visits. On 17 November 1885, for example, Don Carlos entertained the Brownings to dinner, "showed them his Indian curiosities, monkeys and dogs, and gave Browning his account of the Carlist War" (Appendix C, p. 175). Browning already knew something about the war from the Compte de Valras' book, *Don Carlos VII et l'Espagne Carliste*, a presentation copy of which was in his library (*Reconstruction*, A2373).

5. Princess Mélanie Metternich, the wife of Prince Paul (1834–1906), was a close friend of Mrs. Bronson. Browning had dined with the Metternich family during his stay and had written some verses in her daughter Lia's album (see following letters). Mogliano, where Prince Paul had gone to visit Contessa Andriana Marcello, is between Mestre and Treviso. Browning was particularly fond of the Contessa and visited her at Mogliano. See Appendix B, pp. 163–164.

6. Carlo Goldoni (1707–1793), major Italian comic dramatist, was born and lived in Venice for much of his life. The Venetians proposed to erect a statue to his memory in 1883, and Browning, together with the principal Italian men of letters, was asked to write something for a commemorative album. He quickly jotted down a sonnet, which was warmly welcomed. Mrs. Bronson sent a copy of this to Furnivall on 3 December for publication in the *Pall Mall Gazette*. See *BT*, p. 85. Daniel Curtis describes the occasion: "Yesterday afternoon (Nov 26th) he had in hand a Sonnet to Goldoni, composed in haste. ... This sonnet he read aloud with his hearty manner and emphasis which are habitual and genuine—although quite in contravention of that undemonstrative nonchalance and affected indifference which is now *bien vu*. ... The lines are in keeping with the subject—genial, affectionate and simple. I said, 'There are no big words in it.' Browning said—'I should think *not!*'" (Appendix C, p. 171).

7. Captain Antonio Marcello Avignone of the Italian Navy, stationed for a long time in Venice. He was a close acquaintance of Edith Bronson and her friend Zina Mazini (soon to marry the English painter Edward Hulton) and frequently brought them social news and gossip from Florence. A great favourite at Ca Alvisi, Avignone suffered from ill-health and depression; his many friends were therefore delighted when he married Teresina Spence in December 1887. Avignone and his wife then moved to Rome where he had a job at the Ministry of Marine, but after three months Teresina died of rheumatic fever and meningitis. Avignone, broken-hearted, resigned his commission and retired to Recco on the Riviera, where he lived a secluded life, corresponding only with those who had known his late wife. Among these was Henry James, who visited the Recco villa several times.

8. Giuseppina was Mrs. Bronson's long-serving "cameriera" or maid, and she sits in the centre of the photograph of the Ca Alvisi staff opposite p. xxxiii. Whenever the Brownings stayed with Mrs. Bronson, Giuseppina was specially employed to look after them.

9. Foreign guests.

Letter 16

ROBERT BROWNING TO KATHARINE BRONSON

19, Warwick Crescent, W.
Dec. 27. '83

My own dearest Friend, I got your letter last evening. S. and I have agreed to write alternately—so that each little quantity of news may not have been unconsciously skimmed of what may be there in the way of cream. Is it—can it be "news" to say that I think of you and all your goodness every day and—I do believe—every hour in the day? You well know how happy I was, those two full months, in the enjoyment of your presence: if I do not dwell more on the loss of those good days and afternoons and evenings, it is because I hold fast what I gained then, and feel sure that so long as you and I are on earth there will only be so much more or less earth and sea between us: and, for my part, be you as sure that whenever I can overpass these, in the body and not merely the soul, I will once—and if God please—many times again be with you. I wish there were so much obligation,—*just* so much conferred on you by this engagement as would justify me in claiming as a return that you care properly for your own health. It did really seem as if the little walks benefitted you—the keeping up that exercise is easily enjoined: but the innumerable apparently petty "taps," not blows, which do harm,—as the lapping wavelets of the Vaporetti are said to undermine your palaces,—oh, how better than "proud" I shall be if you mind my warning when tempted to submit to any of these you could avoid! I won't teaze, but my heart is in what I urge.

Well,—your Natale festival[1] went off as I *see*, (oh, the arch, and the garlanded picture frames!) and you dined with the Layards: I get into and out of the gondola with you, not unhelped by the fat Luigi,[2]—"Piano, Piano!",—and go through the same quiet delights back again,—and the end is Giuseppina's helpful tug at the Giustinian-Recanati door-bolt, and the lighted candles and bright fire, and—all under your—succession of roofs!

What can I tell you of my own doings? By our friend's hospitality we were spared much inconvenience as well as pain: I left on the 17.th and S. went resolutely home the next day.[3] Every sort of precaution was taken with our house-arrangements,—but it is clear to us *both* that the poor boy caught his terrible complaint elsewhere and, but for his refusal to get proper medical assistance in time, might be still alive. The other servants were admirable in their self-devotion to the sufferer—an awful

Courtyard of the Giustiniani-Recanati

19, Warwick Crescent

sufferer indeed. I stayed till the 21st at Hatfield:[4] beside our own Ball with its "thousand invited guests," there was another at Panshanger[5]—(my Balaustion Lady's place) which I also attended: our own party was very agreeable,—there being several of my friends there,—Ld Carnarvon[6] in chief: and the Royal folk were benignant and easily pleased. And I "contrasted Hatfield with Cà Alvise"—*yes, indeed!* No ingratitude being involved in simply saying that a dahlia is not a rose.

On the evening of the 22^d Robert arrived in good condition: he will only make a short stay here; but I understand that he too cannot be "in Venice"—figurative for "where one would always be." We have made up our minds to buy a house at once, not wait till they turn us out: I even believe that a house—much as the thing should be for our requirements— is within our reach: my Sister and Robert, on a very superficial examination, reporting very favorably of it: a house with a garden and even a small studio,—which may be replaced by a bigger one. I believe that, by some judicious chopping and changing of certain moneys, I shall gain instead of lose by the transfer: you shall be duly informed of the successive steps in the great event.[7]

Oh, and all Clerlé's cases have come,—the dishes and plates safely,— with one bit of exceptional breakage,—and the big "mobili" anything but safely, through the inveterately careless package: while my two choice pedestals,—the Marcato purchase,—cut indeed a piteous figure,—one of them being in perhaps a dozen pieces, and those pieces evidencing ancient damage and plenty of repairing. I have just conferred with a Cabinet-maker in whom I trust, and—with a sigh over the blind work of the screws—ineffective except where they go deep into the "mobile" itself—he believes he shall be able to set all right again,—and, after all, the very bits, and their breakage, is Venetian, and not otherwise than valuable!

I got all your newspapers, Roba Goldoniana, and only miss your own account of the affair. Were you present, after all? Thank M. Molmenti[8] for me,—do, pray, and warmly,—for the honor they have done me in various ways. I was much gratified by the notice of Enrico Castelnuovo,[9]—whose fame I have had at heart these five or six years. But an end must come—to all but what knows no end: so, I keep on loving you, Dearest Friend, and your Edith, and your Chapman,[10] and your Contenta[11] and everything that is yours. Bless you!

                                                                                    RB.

Address: Italia. / Mrs Bronson, / Cà Alvise, / Canal Grande, / *Venezia.*
Publication: None traced.
Manuscript: Armstrong Browning Library.

    1. Mrs. Bronson's saint's day—St. Katherine of Alexandria on 25 November—which she always celebrated.

2. Luigi Baffo, the chief of Mrs. Bronson's three gondoliers.

3. The Brownings arrived in London on 13 December to find that one of their servants, Edwin Guilliam, was dying of diphtheria. Because of the risk of infection, they stayed at Mrs. FitzGerald's London house (22 Portland Place) for a few days before Sarianna returned home and Browning went to Hatfield.

4. Hatfield House, the seat of Lord Salisbury, the Tory Prime Minister. Browning felt obliged to attend a ball at Hatfield, lest he give offence to Lady Salisbury, who wrongly thought he had refused a previous invitation on political grounds. See *LL*, p. 176. The main ball was in honour of Queen Victoria's youngest son, the Duke of Albany, and his wife.

5. Panshanger, the home of Francis Thomas de Gray Cowper, 7th Earl Cowper (1834–1905). Browning dedicated *Balaustion's Adventure* (1871) to Countess Cowper (1845–1913), after she had playfully asked him to "be her poet" and to translate something from Euripides for her.

6. Henry Howard Molyneux Herbert, 4th Earl of Carnarvon (1831–1890), Conservative statesman, held political office as Colonial Secretary under Derby and Disraeli, and as Lord-Lieutenant of Ireland under Salisbury. A man of learning and taste, he translated Æschylus's *Agamemnon* and the first twelve books of the *Odyssey*. Browning was a close friend and stayed at the Earl's home, Highclere, in 1873.

7. This was a false alarm: the first of several. Browning was prepared to give £6,000 for a freehold house, as an investment for Pen. Earlier in the year, he had written to George Smith: "I should prefer the house to be in South Kensington—such a house as he [Pen] could conveniently live in, let or sell" (Murray).

8. The unveiling of the Goldoni statue. Professor Pompeo Molmenti was on the committee and had written to Browning asking for a contribution. See Letter 15. He was a friend of Mrs. Bronson and a regular visitor to Ca Alvisi.

9. Enrico Castelnuovo, popular novelist, was highly regarded by Browning. He had first come to Browning's attention in 1878 in Asolo, where Browning and Sarianna found themselves with nothing to read in the albergo. They purchased Castelnuovo's *Alla Finestra*, which they enjoyed so much that they read all his later works as soon as they were published. Among the books in the 1913 Browning Sale were five of Castelnuovo's novels (see *Reconstruction*, A585–589).

10. Rose Chapman, known to the family as "Chappy," was the Bronsons' English housekeeper. She was with them before they came to Europe and had gone up the Nile with them in 1876. An educated woman, she kept the house accounts and supervised the servants at Ca Alvisi.

11. Contenta was Mrs. Bronson's favourite dog at this period. Writing about Contenta to Isabella Gardner in 1892, Mrs. Bronson said: "This reminds me of a Valentine which Pen Browning sent to my beautiful Contenta (who is now, alas, with the majority):

    'How could you be "Contenta" if you were not content?

    Things being as they are there's little to lament,

    But if, instead of being man, I were of race canine,

    I'd ask you for your pretty paw to be my Valentine.'

Do you find that silly or charming? I hope the latter" (IGM).

Letter 17

SARIANNA & ROBERT BROWNING TO KATHARINE BRONSON

[In Sarianna's hand.]   19, Warwick Crescent. W.
                                                         1ˢᵗ Janʸ 1884.

The very first word I write this year is to you, dearest Friend, wishing you every good gift that earth below, and Heaven above, can offer. If Robert does not write his own share in these kind feelings, it is only because we have agreed that we shall come more constantly before you if we keep our letters apart. You ought not to be weak and unwell—and it goes to my heart to hear that you cough. Put some sunshine into us by saying, with truth, that you are quite well. We need something to brighten us, for at this minute, though it professes to be nearly noonday, the air is so dark that I can scarcely see to guide my pen—and even this is an improvement on some days lately, when at the same hour we have required candles. There has been no rain.

Pen has been at home for a week, but will leave us to-morrow morning. I have not yet heard of a likely successor to the poor young man we lost, but I shall set myself in earnest to find one now that the holidays are over. We dined quite alone on Christmas day[1]—this New Year's evening we are to dine with a friend, (a batchelor [*sic*]) whose cook having suddenly left him will adjourn his dinner, which is to be small and friendly, to the Bristol Hôtel. By the bye, can you give me Mʳ Curtis's precise address at Rome. Robert unintentionally destroyed it, and though I think it is the Victoria, I am not sure. I hope Mʳˢ Eden's[2] indisposition has not proved serious, and that our other kind friends are well. Robert told you, no doubt, how badly the cases from Venice were packed. I shall be glad when we know where we shall be finally lodged, as we are unsettled in this house which is slipping away from us. However, I suppose we shall find some resting-place in due time. Is Miss Carr[3] still with you?

Remember us very kindly to Miss Chapman.

You cannot think how incessantly we dwell on the memories of the pleasant past. We are in Casa Alvisi in spirit daily, and I picture to myself all that is going on in the well-loved rooms. I hope Edith works at her guitar—she will find it repay the trouble.

Give our kindest love to her—and take yourself our loving hearts. God bless you this year.

                                        Ever yours affectionately,
                                        Sarianna Browning.

A faint gleam of light shows me what a blotted piece of paper I have taken in the dark.

[Continued by RB.]

I waylay the letter of S. to put in my word of love—love altogether—expressing itself in wishes for every good gift New Year can offer you—since I cannot embody itself in deeds. I have done with much work of various kinds, and feel at liberty to sit down and take my pleasure in talking to you,—so, talk there shall be soon enough. Meanwhile and ever keep me in mind as your affectionatest of friends

RB

Publication: Whiting, p. 248 (Sarianna's portion in part only).
Manuscript: Armstrong Browning Library.

1. This challenges the statement by Mrs. Bloomfield-Moore: "Christmas Day I was always to dine with them; and even when I had relatives stopping with me at Christmas, they were invited to the Christmas dinner, and met with a warm welcome from him and his sister" (Moore, p. 68). This seems to have been true of 1884 only.
2. Caroline Eden (1837–1928) and her husband Frederic (1828–1916) settled in Venice after an accident had disabled Mr. Eden and left him an invalid, unable to walk properly. They lived in the Palazzo Barbarigo and cultivated a particularly beautiful garden on the Giudecca which had flowers blooming all the year round—appropriately known as the Garden of Eden. Edith Bronson was a frequent visitor, and her photograph albums have many pictures of sunny afternoons spent there with the family. Frederic Eden describes the creation of the garden in his book, *A Garden in Venice*, London, 1903. Fannie Browning's copy of this volume, inscribed by Eden, is at the Library of Congress.
3. A mis-spelling for "Kerr." See Letter 2, n. 3.

Letter 18

ROBERT BROWNING TO KATHARINE BRONSON

19, Warwick Crescent, W.
Jan. 6. '84.

Oh, the dear, dear Friend,—will not she be glad to think how glad *I* am, who can tell her that my precious "Case" arrived, and all its precious packages came safely as safely could be,—so that my heart is no more broken than are her gifts: there they are ranged where my eyes may always reach and rest on them. Thank you all over again,—yet why now—or for these especially? Certain words and looks are just as present with me: "K. de K. B—I hear you speak!"

But indeed I was apprehensive about this particular consignment,—so badly had Clerlé and Marcato managed their packing: this, on the contrary, showed all possible care and contrivance; box within box: and I shall mention that the charge for all that was very moderate and subjoined to the general carriage-bill—thereby affording me a satisfaction, and denying you the wicked one of yourself going and paying it on the sly. I know you!

This morning there is—while I write, at least—a glint of sunshine,— the first visible this long fortnight. Such a fortnight of fog and dolefulness as we have had! Two Private Views of Pictures, at the Grosvenor Gallery and the Academy, by the Electric Light! Do you suppose Venice is out of mind as out of sight? Those two happy months!—and their good stays with me, the physical as well as the spiritual good, for, besides the memories, I seem to be living on the strength I stored up there [*sic* for then] and there: I swallow no end of fog and prove unchokable. Now, do pray contend with me in this matter,—try and tell me that if I hear "Anne Schreiber cough,"[1] it *is* Anne and not K. de K. B: and that to see the latter sitting on the low seat before the fire-place proper to Yaha-Bibi[2] (oh, the spelling!)—is mere hallucination! But one is never lectured into a rational care for oneself: still,—K. de K. B was so easy to be *hinted* into any amount of benevolence: let her be benevolent now! Even though benevolent to the selfish person who looks forward to more walks and talks.

I have gone out very little, and shall continue as quiet as may be,—till it may *not* be. Pen came, stayed a week and a day or so, then went back to his work. He, too, "wants to see Venice": I thought it would be so. What do you suppose I am going to do three hours hence? Keep an appointment with an architect and land-owner, who wants to build me a house! I am inclined to fancy that particular form of trouble may be the least,—since, if I buy a freehold, I can have a place made to suit my present need of few rooms but large ones,—and leave to Pen the pleasure of superimposing bed-rooms *ad libitum*, when his time succeeds mine. The objection to building instead of lease-holding was mainly the time building would take: but, observes my sagacious sister, "we could not get into any new house before the Autumn,—and that is just when we hope to be away: so that we can allow due time for the thorough drying." It may therefore be—and, not improbably, fail to be—for I am apprehensive. Have I any news, gossipry, to tell? Yesterday, at the Academy View, I met one of L.ᵞ Castletown's[3] daughters who said her mother was in the next room and would like to see me,—I was delayed by one acquaintance after another, and so missed her in the crowd. I saw Burton,[4] too. Did you eat mincepies with the kind Layards? All the names that occur in your letter to S. set the pleasant chime of memories ringing: there is no use in mentioning them particularly. Lowell[5] has resigned his office—for reasons which were apparent enough before he took it: and they now propose it to—you guess whom, in your goodness: but he will have no such bother, as he says in the letter just posted. Did you get my "Helen's Tower"?[6] I had forgotten all about it and supposed that its only publication would be on the wall where, I fancy, it is inscribed. I knew and much liked the lady—who was signally kind to a poor little Italian boy I introduced to her. Well,—did you ever see Chapman's Homer and how, in place of the orthodox *Finis*, he puts "The end of all the endless works of Homer?" This is the end of the endless thinking and loving of yours ever

                                                    RB.

My love to Edith—as if the words had never gone stiff into *formula*: my love to Miss Chapman too,—tell her how admirably the packing was done! S., as arranged between us, is always to speak for herself!

Address. Italy. / Mrs Bronson, / Cà Alvise / Canal Grande, / Venezia.
Publication: None traced.
Manuscript: Armstrong Browning Library.

1. Anne Schreiber was a relation of Sir Henry Layard's wife, Enid, whose mother, Lady Charlotte Guest (1812–1895), the Welsh scholar, had married Charles Schreiber as her second husband. Presumably Anne Schreiber was staying with the Layards at Ca Capello at this time.

2. Yahabibi was another of Mrs. Bronson's favourite dogs. The extraordinary name (understandably mis-spelled by Browning) is Arabic and was the title of a song, "Ya Habibi," taught to the Bronsons when they were in Algiers in 1879. Subsequently it became a favourite of Edith's, who sang it to her own accompaniment on the guitar.

3. Augusta Mary Douglas, Baroness Castletown (1810–1899), held a regular salon at her home in Portman Square, London. Browning was an occasional guest.

4. Frederic Burton (1816–1900), Director of the National Gallery, London, from 1874 to 1894. Browning probably knew him as early as 1839 when he exhibited two pictures of Helen Faucit at the Royal Academy. By 1870 he was well established as a portrait painter and water-colourist. Among his many successful drawings was one of Elizabeth Smith, wife of Browning's friend and publisher, George Smith. Burton was knighted on retiring from the National Gallery.

5. James Russell Lowell had resigned as Lord Rector of St. Andrew's University, and the students wrote to Browning on 3 January asking him to stand as the new Rector "on the ground of literary distinction." He declined.

6. Browning's sonnet "Helen's Tower" had been printed in the *Pall Mall Gazette* on 28 December 1883. Originally written for the Marquess of Dufferin and Ava in 1870, the sonnet was first printed in that year in a pamphlet commemorating the building of a tower on his estate at Clandeboye, Ireland, in honour of his mother, Helen, Countess of Dufferin. Very few copies of this pamphlet exist, and Browning offered the sonnet as a favour to F. J. Furnivall, who arranged for its publication in the *Pall Mall Gazette*. See *BT*, p. 87. The idea for the poem almost certainly came from Frederic Leighton's painting, "Helen of Troy," which Browning had seen in the artist's studio in 1865 and had described as "delicious" and "a lovely dreamlike picture" (*Checklist*, p. 122). Both painting and sonnet are based on the description of Helen in the *Iliad*, Book 3, 153–154.

Letter 19

ROBERT BROWNING TO KATHARINE BRONSON

19, Warwick Crescent, W.
Jan. 14. '84.

Oh, far from the hope of making you "ever so grateful," how glad I should be if I could succeed in never so little *satisfying* you! Would anything come out of what I am about to put down, as rapidly as I can, of what seems to me capable of being turned into a "comedietta for some three persons."[1] It is a reminiscence from a little sketch I read, years ago, in an Italian newspaper.

In the neighbourhood of—but some little distance from—any Capital you please—is an out-of-the-way Inn, near a Railway Station. A young gentleman arrives there by some accident—what you please—and will be kept there, against his will, till an evening train: expects to meet somebody,—quite a proper proceeding. He is shown into a room, however, by the experienced Landlord—or Landlady—who being exceedingly sagacious well knows the pretexts which gentleman [*sic*] come under when they visit out of the way inns: comments knowingly (aside) on the explanations of the visit, the mistake, the delay &c—has no doubt *somebody* will turn out to have made a similar mistake, and help to pass the afternoon!– Gentleman's surprise at the mysterious *knowingness*. Presently somebody *does* arrive, in consequence of some quite different but equally legitimate accident,—say, expecting to meet a relative— brother—who goes to the Station instead of the Inn: explanations to the Landlord, enquiries &c—which are just as he knew they would be,—of course, the "brother" is the young gentleman, and the "accident" an old contrivance he has known adopted fifty times. —Shows in the lady—who recognizes and is recognized by the gentleman as a slight acquaintance thro' an introduction some time ago. Chuckling (aside) of the Landlord at the bit of acting "Oh, yes—slight acquaintance,—quite an accidental meeting! &c." However, it is all for the good of the house, these accidental meetings being profitable. Being left by themselves, the situation explained, the parties less embarrassed, it comes out in conversation that each had been too much extolled by common friends who wished to bring about acquaintance between them, and each had consequently been disappointed in the other,—hence a polite coldness. They begin to discuss and account for this goodhumouredly, and, having no alternative[,] agree to order a dinner and wait till the time comes for getting away. Landlord's increase of knowingness and desire of helpfulness: has settled with himself that the lady is a wife—and the gentleman a husband: undertakes mysteriously to keep the coast clear,—let them know of any carriage arriving &c—to the bewilderment of the parties—who, at last, hit upon the secret of the man's nods and winks, as he goes in and out with the culinary cares—and their amusement is proportionate. "An idea! Suppose we act the parts he supposes we really play: I will be the run-away lady, and you the gay deceiver!" They rehearse rapidly—"You expect your wife every minute—I am full of anguish at what I have ventured,—may it not be too late!" &c. And, during the dinner, they do so, in an exaggerated fashion,—the lady caricaturing fear and remorse,—the gentleman full of passionate and chivalrous protestation,—all in hints and delicate touches meant for the Landlord—who interprets all in the (with *him*) customary way: but there keeps growing up, under the sham love-making, a real development of interest one in the other, which culminates just as the Landlord rushes in with the news that the Lady's Husband is come and will brook no delay in seeing her—and the gentleman's sister is downstairs and must come up too. Amazement as the farce breaks up in laughter, and the innocence of the parties becomes evident—to the Landlord's chagrin. "Well, here our acting ends: it is a pity your character, last May when we met, was not as well supported!"— "Nay,—was it not a pity that *you* did not help me out of my shyness,—could not be actually what you have played so well!["] "After all,—how much *has* been *acting*?" "Did you really *throw yourself into* your part?" *Eclaircissement*—the acting turns earnest—and the play ends by promising the disappointed Landlord amends in a wedding breakfast!!!

All this is scribbled even less hastily than thought-out—but the attempt has been made for your sake, my dearest friend!

                                RB.

Address: Italia / Mrs Bronson, / Cà Alvise, / Canal Grande, / Venezia.
Publication: None traced.
Manuscript: Armstrong Browning Library.

1. Mrs. Bronson's request for a plot of a "comedietta" was intended for a Venetian-dialect playlet she was planning to write for performance by Edith and her friends in Ca Alvisi. Five privately printed plays by Mrs. Bronson survive, the earliest dated 1883 and the latest 1894. One (*Un Inglese a Venezia*) is described as a "comedietta in due atti"; three are classed as "proverbio," and one (*Son Paron mi!*) is a "scherzo comico." It seems that Mrs. Bronson didn't take advantage of Browning's plot, but devised something simpler of her own for a performance six weeks later. See Letter 23.

Letter 20

ROBERT BROWNING TO KATHARINE BRONSON

19, Warwick Crescent, W.
Jan. 21. '84.

Dearest Friend,—if you only recognized—as you do so thoroughly—my good will to be of the least help in that little matter of the "Plot,"—*that* would be pleasure enough. I did the thing with more haste than was needed, probably,—and left out many minutenesses of possible amusement in the mistakings of the Landlord, confirmations of his suspicions, and so on,—and the more genuinely dramatic point of the sham love-making insensibly breaking down (or *up*?) into real sympathy. But I had you in my mind as picking up and polishing off the rough work I turned out. Next—as to that result of immense labour and stupendous excogitation from which I am scarcely recovered—the Rawdon Brown Sonnet[1]— conscious as I am of the load of obligation under which I laid you by the offering of that moment of Poetic Genius,—still, pray observe, the offering *was* absolutely an instance of generosity—yours to keep and yours to give again: therefore, much as I appreciate the Editor's gentleman-liness and liberality (for which return, please, my cordial thanks) I beg to put his remittance to a use that will most gratify us all,—as you may see recorded on the envelope.

I had the delight of hearing about you on Thursday from L? Castletown by whom I sat at dinner. She had just got "a long letter." I thought "*I* shall have my letter also before long!" and to-day it comes! I gather you are *well* on the whole, from what you report of yourself. Keep so,—for all our sakes—mine is not the least among them. For ourselves, S. and I continue perfectly well, and attribute that circumstance to our retention of the divine air, and the precious entertainment: physical and moral advantage of the highest value.

I am really in treaty—not too deeply *in* it for extrication at need— with the Landowner who proposes to *build* me the house I want—freehold, if you please!—so that it can be Pen's after me: my notion is to construct just what I & S. require *now*—leaving it in the said Pen's power to add and alter according to future advisability. As for the time the thing will take to get ready,—I say, "Can we not go abroad? Ay, can we not."[2] And very much "abroad" should I be if that did not mean dear Venice: and what would even dear Venice be without the dear friend of hers ever

R Browning.

Publication: Whiting, p. 248 (in part).
Manuscript: Armstrong Browning Library.

1. The historian Rawdon Brown (1806–1883), friend of John and Effie Ruskin, had come to Venice in 1833 to search for the tomb of the banished Thomas Mowbray, Duke of Norfolk, who had died in exile in 1399. Having achieved this objective, Brown stayed in Venice for the next fifty years, researching in the city archives until his death on 25 August 1883. Browning's witty sonnet, commemorating Rawdon Brown's love of the city, was written at Mrs. Bronson's request on 28 November 1883. Mrs. Bronson sent a copy to *The Century Magazine*, where it was published in February 1884. She then forwarded the editor's cheque to Browning, who returned it to her because the sonnet had been a gift and therefore was no longer his.

2. A possible reminiscence of line 2 of George Herbert's "The Collar": "No more. I will abroad."

Letter 21

ROBERT BROWNING TO KATHARINE BRONSON

19, Warwick Crescent, W.
Jan. 27. '84.

First and worst of all,—dear Friend,—how truly grieved I am to hear of the sad end of that poor little girl[1] I remember so well. Do not *you* remember how she with her sister walked before us on our way home from the Piazza on nearly our last evening? And how prettily she asked me, at her own house, to write in her Birthday Book! All this sudden extinction of light in that gay Cà Bembo[2] where I saw the silks bespread before your knowledge and my ignorance!

It is needless to say how much I pity the Princess—and her kindly husband too—and I am sorry, very sorry for *you* also, Dear Friend of mine,—well knowing how you must have suffered in your degree.

To go back to life—here is the Cheque properly countersigned: I might have guessed such a formality was requisite. "A Sonnet!" And you may have put the paper it was scribbled on among your precious things! Is there room for the original of that other one which they have been publishing of late and you may have seen—perhaps? I send the thing on the chance that it may slip into your Album,—no, not the chance,—but the dear certainty that you will be good and hospitable to even a fourteen-years-old paper of verse that has slept all that time in my desk. I knew the lady and have not flattered her.[3] By the way, you have probably received Furnivall's tribute to "Teena"[4]—a memory he is simply *mad* about. All I knew of the poor girl was that he brought her here twice—and that, failing to get a reading out of me on the first occasion, and being

Lia Metternich

Helen's Tower.   Ἑλένη ἐπὶ πύργῳ.

Who hears of Helen's Tower may dream perchance
　　How the Greek Beauty from the Scæan Gate
　　Gazed on old friends unanimous in hate,
Death-doomed because of her fair countenance.
Hearts would leap otherwise at thy advance,
　　Lady, to whom this Tower is consecrate!
　　Like hers, thy face once made all eyes elate,
Yet, unlike hers, was blessed by every glance.
The Tower of Hate is out-worn, far and strange;
　　A transitory shame of long ago,
　　It dies into the sand from which it sprang;
But thine, Love's rock-built Tower, shall fear no change;
God's self laid stable earth's foundations so,
When all the morning-stars together sang.

Apr. 26: 70.　　　　Robert Browning.

Draft Manuscript of "Helen's Tower"

put off with a promise that I would exert myself on some other day—presumably in the very far indeed Future—he claimed and obtained it soon after: out of which he makes the great affair he chronicles. Look at his portrait,—the whole man is there—whom yet I have a true regard for in spite of the most teazing tactlessness that ever plagued a man's would-be esteemers.

He is coming here this morning to try and coax out of me permission to print the Book[5]—whence came my long poem: as if it were expedient to pull up a shrub by the roots that every wiseacre might have his little speculation as to which fibre had done service and which had remained idle. I am making haste to get done before he arrives and turns my milk of human kindness sour—and I want all the cream of it, sweetest and thickest, for you,—dear friend—so take it (giving a lap to Edith) warm from the Robert Browning.

Address: Italy, Venice. / Mrs Bronson, / Cà Alvisi / Canal Grande, / Venezia.
Publication: Whiting, pp. 248–249 (in part).
Manuscript: Armstrong Browning Library.

1. Lia, Emilie-Marie-Félicie de Metternich, daughter of the Prince and Princess Paul Metternich, who died of scarlet fever, aged ten, on 20 January.

2. Some idea of the silken magnificence of Ca Bembo in the 1880's can be gleaned from this passage in Zina Hulton's "Memoirs": "The ballroom was hung with long panels of pale greenish-blue satin damask, each of which had a whole palm tree woven into it in soft natural colours with flowers and varied foliage growing round the bases of the trunks, and birds and butterflies fluttering above beneath the drooping fronds of the palm heads. This damask had been woven about a hundred years earlier—for this Bembo room" (Hulton, p. 20).

3. The manuscript of "Helen's Tower," to add to the manuscript of "Rawdon Brown" which Mrs. Bronson already possessed. Both manuscripts are now in the Armstrong Browning Library. There are four manuscripts of "Helen's Tower" extant: a) ABL—original draft with manuscript alteration in one line; b) Rosenbach Foundation, Philadelphia—a fair copy in a letter to Lord Dufferin, London, 27 April 1870; c) Newnham College, Cambridge—a fair copy sent to Furnivall for the *Pall Mall Gazette*; d) Houghton—a fair copy with a variant second line.

4. Mary Lilian ("Teena") Rochfort Smith (1861–1883), Furnivall's attractive young secretary and mistress, had died unexpectedly on 4 September 1883 after her dress had caught fire. Browning knew her only slightly and had no idea of the true nature of Furnivall's relationship with her. He was, therefore, surprised to find his own photograph, together with one of Furnivall, in the elaborate 16-page *Memoir* Furnivall edited and sent round to his friends in January 1884. Furnivall's photograph, taken by Lock and Whitfield, shows him at his impish best, with long beard carefully groomed and a roguish look in his eyes.

5. The Old Yellow Book, source of *The Ring and the Book*, which Furnivall wished to reprint or reproduce in facsimile for The Browning Society. After meeting Furnivall, Browning wrote to him firmly on 29 January explaining his reasons for not reprinting "the crabbed Latin document." See *B.T.*, p. 90.

$\mathcal{L}$*etter* 22

ROBERT BROWNING TO KATHARINE BRONSON

19, Warwick Crescent, W.
Feb. 9. '84.

Dear Friend, I kept your Comedietta[1] by me a whole week that I might taste of it again and again: how clever it is, who can know better than I who furnished the bare framework which your Virginian Creeper has overflourished so charmingly? It is all capitally done,—quite as much elaborated as the little conception was worth: but its great value to me is the proof it gives what really good work you might do on a larger scale could one take the cigarette out of the mouth (well,—I don't think I should like *that*, after all) and induce daily walkings (but—suppose there were no glad and proud companionship immediately available from Palazzo Giustiniani at signal of a whiteness at a window across the Court?) and .. and .. no end of "ands"—all to no purpose, because some things and persons are so entirely well as they are, and one hates to risk interference with them! So, things and the person being as they are and as I remember them, they shall stay so if they please, seeing that, even *so*, they can evolve a sparkling little play like "Chance and Change". No other Chance and Change therefore! Is it all unchanged with you? How of that horrible plague that was broken out in Venice? How is the poor Princess,[2] and did the calamity stop with the child I remember so well,— English-talking and all, I am sorry for them with all my heart.

The Layards are just arrived,—at least I have an invitation to meet them at the Higford Burrs'[3] next Wednesday. I dined last evening at John Murray's[4]—in the room where used to meet Byron, Scott, Moore, all those famous men of old, whose portraits still adorn the walls. M. told me he well remembered Byron and his ways,—could still in fancy see him and Scott,—and also *hear* them,—as they stumped heavily (lame as both were) down the somewhat narrow stairs. Sociality may well come to the relief of people who cannot amuse themselves at home—for the weather, mild and too mild, is grey, sunless and spiritless altogether: to-day it rains,—a rare occurrence. Did you notice—by an article in the good and friendly Daily News, which I believe you take in,—how the Pall Mall mishandled my Sonnett,[5]—mine own familiar Bookseller's print from which I had a right to expect a decent attention. This time I *was* angry, and cried aloud and spared not—extracting apology enough but missing any effectual redress. In consequence, I get cuttings from provincial newspapers—quoting the blunders, and adding that, *this* time,

Browning has exceeded himself, "and is Brown indeed!"[6] And then that sapient Cavendish Bentinck[7] with his assurance that Rawdon Brown,— "of whom I am sole executor and trustee,"—could not have had any interchange of speech with anybody but himself. "Trustee" indeed—as all the bric-à-brac shops told us, purchasers of the trusted-one's inherited chairs[,] tables, pictures, books and carpets. Let me but have an opportunity of telling him a piece of my mind!—and of telling you all my mind, if you don't know it.

Yours ever affectionately
RB.

Publication: Whiting, p. 249 (in part).
Manuscript: Armstrong Browning Library.

1. The Bronson-Browning comedietta has not survived. It may not have been performed at Ca Alvisi, because Mrs. Bronson later in the month wrote two shorter, simpler pieces for her tiny theatre. See Letter 24.
2. The Princess Metternich. See previous letter.
3. Mr. and Mrs. Daniel Higford Burr were great friends of the Layards and had travelled with them on expeditions abroad. Mrs. Burr (*née* Margaretta Scobell) was an artist, publishing *Sketches in Spain, The Holy Land, Egypt, Turkey and Greece* in 1841. Browning seems to have been introduced to the Burrs by the Layards. His ensuing friendship with Mrs. Burr survived her husband's death in 1885; when the Layards were in England in March 1889, she held a dinner for them to which Browning was invited. Margaretta Higford Burr died in Venice 22 January 1892.
4. John Murray III (1808–1892), whose father, John Murray II (1778–1843), had been Byron's, Scott's and Moore's publisher. The famous room in the firm's offices in Albemarle Street, mentioned by Browning, where Byron's manuscript memoirs were burned in 1824, still exists unchanged today.
5. Browning had allowed the *Pall Mall Gazette* to publish the Rawdon Brown sonnet, using *The Century Magazine* printing as copy. The botched result infuriated him, because his publishers—Smith, Elder and Co.—owned and printed the *Pall Mall Gazette*. Browning "cried aloud" to George Smith: "Will you kindly use any influence you may have with the printers of the Pall-Mall Gazette to intreat them not to cooperate with Mr. Liberal-Conservative Austin in making me ridiculous? They have left out a line (the 5th) bodily from the sonnet—besides printing the note of admiration after Toni, as *I* in the last verse but four ... So, I get my reputation of one hard to understand!" (Murray). Next day he returned to the attack in another letter: "I lost patience, earlier in the evening, over the treatment of that trifle of mine in the Pall-Mall Gazette,—and am far from having found it again this morning. Considering the reputation I have for writing nonsense, it is too bad to be made nonsensical indeed by a careless somebody whose only business is to transcribe fourteen plainly printed lines, and yet must needs leave out one of them, turn a mark of admiration into an article, and, in the next line to that, throw in a superfluous 'the' (*the* valise-straps). Three inexcusable blunders in a trifle,—hardly worth reproducing at all, but, if reproduced, surely not properly treated in this case" (Murray).
6. A reference to the final line of the sonnet: "Browning, next week, may find himself quite Brown!"
7. The Rt. Hon. George Cavendish Bentinck, an aggressive Conservative M.P. who contributed a number of peppery letters to *The Times*.

$\mathcal{L}etter$ 23

ROBERT BROWNING TO KATHARINE BRONSON

19, Warwick Crescent, W.
Feb. 21. '84.

One word, just one, shall go to my dearest Friend to say that the M.S. arrived safely last night:[1] I shall read it presently; but, lest *after* reading there should be no time, this much shall be scribbled now, and have a fair excuse for writing again more leisurely. But—where is Edith's piece,[2]—we broke out, S. & I, as we opened the roll this morning? Do find it! Give her all the love and congratulations in the world: she is "a dainty dish to set before the"—audience, and I should have dearly enjoyed making one of them. The Layards are here,—I wrung them dry of every drop of news about you,—and Venice afterward: they told me of that terrible fate of the poor child,[3]—about the most terrible that one can imagine,—for *somewhere* must have been negligence: a lady told me, a very few days ago, that the self-same accident happened to her little sister—who died in consequence. God keep us all, especially the little children!

Yes, best and kindest, the letter was *yours*, I divined,—but yours by instigation only, I thought: nothing could be better-timed, better-done, and I thanked Mr R. Walbran heartily.[4] Layard informs me that the necrological article in the "Times", whence I took the anecdote bodily,— only substituting Cà Pesaro—B's own Cà, for the Bevilacqua Palace opposite,—was written by Lady Eastlake[5]—probably a still older friend and certainly a more sagacious observer than Mr Bentinck who is always writing himself down "Ass" in some letter or other to the newspapers.

My time—my time! And I have said so little beyond the prescribed one word only! but here follows a weighty word—*How is Edith's throat?* That intelligence will get me a letter out of you, I feel sure. Both of us are anxious to know, and soon.

I dined last night at a house to meet Gladstone—who was in full force, and quite satisfied with his victory at 2. that morning.[6] His wife was going to another party—but, "being young",[7] as she said, he meant to walk home by himself some two miles.

Would I could fly to a home of mine and a housemate beyond the sea—"Wenn ich ein voglein wäre!"[8] But I must remain here, wingless except in fancy-flights to my own friend of whom I am the own friend while this machine is to him[9]— RB.

Publication: None traced.
Manuscript: Armstrong Browning Library.

1. These could be either more playlets by Mrs. Bronson or manuscript poems by Percy E. Pinkerton, both of which are mentioned in Letter 24.

2. Perhaps a play Edith acted in at Ca Alvisi.

3. Lia Metternich. See Letter 21.

4. Part of the correspondence over the Rawdon Brown sonnet in *The Times* and *The Daily News*. Browning's supporters rallied to his cause against Cavendish Bentinck, and Mrs. Bronson supplied Mr. Walbran with the substance of his letter, rather than write under her own name.

5. Elizabeth Eastlake (1810–1893), who in her younger days had savaged Charlotte Bronte's *Jane Eyre* in the pages of *The Quarterly*, was the widow of Sir Charles Loch Eastlake, President of The Royal Academy from 1850 to 1865. Her letter to *The Times* (8 September 1883, p. 6) about Rawdon Brown contained the following sentences: "Day after day and year after year . . . Rawdon Brown's truly English head, with his shrewd, shaven face and close-cut hair, would be seen poring over some dull and dusty delicacy; and equally day after day, year after year, did his tall, slim and well-knit figure, after his task was done, appear on the Grand Canal, rowing himself, gondolier fashion, to the Lido. It is long since he paid a visit to England. Some years ago he prepared to do so, but, stepping to the window, he looked down on the Grand Canal, all quivering and sparkling with the reflections from the Grand Bevilacqua Palace opposite, and, turning to his servant with a face of emotion, he said, 'Toni, unpack my things; I cannot go.' "

6. Gladstone's victory was on a censure motion "That this House . . . is of the opinion that the recent lamentable events in the Sudan are due, in great measure, to the vacillating and inconsistent policy pursued by Her Majesty's Government." It was defeated by 311 votes to 262.

7. Gladstone was in his seventy-fifth year.

8. *Wenn ich ein voglein wäre*—"If I were a little bird," the title of an Alsatian folk-song, first published in 1778 in J. G. Herder's *Volkslieder*. The sentimental words and melody were well known in the nineteenth century, and the song was later used as a motif by D. H. Lawrence in his short story "The Ladybird":

> Wenn ich ein Vöglein wäre
> Und auch zwei Flüglein hatt
> Flög ich zu dir . . .

> If I were a little bird
> And had two little wings
> I'd fly to thee . . .

Browning could have known the song from childhood, but his interest in it may have been rekindled by Mrs. Benzon, who taught him German in the 1870's.

9. An echo of the conclusion of Hamlet's love-letter to Ophelia, "thine evermore, dear lady, whilst this machine is to him . . ." (Shakespeare: *Hamlet*, II, ii, 122).

Letter 24

ROBERT BROWNING TO KATHARINE BRONSON

19, Warwick Crescent, W.
March 11. '84.

Dear Friend,—I ought to send back the two clever little pieces which I
have been keeping so long,—liking the outsides as well as insides, with
"K. de K. B. her mark" on paper and ink and a certain Venetian aroma
that comes from the roll, suggestive of two hands that tied it and directed
and sent it—all so kindly! I saw also (and, for the matter of *that*, shall
continue to see[)] the large long hall in the ever-dearly-remembered
Giustiniani,—where the stage must have been, how the actors must have
looked, and where the audience sat and laughed—and, among them, I
had most sight for—*not* never mind *who!* Both pieces, Charade and Play,
or Scene, as you prefer calling it, are superiorly funny,—only, in the
latter, more might be made of the situation,—if the Southern Lover were
given an opportunity (for instance) of showing his more generous quality
by being informed of the morgage-story [*sic*] by the Scheming gentleman,
and if, believing it, he made an offer which he had before hesitated to
make. Anyhow, with such acting as you described, the success was
assured. And now, having had my last little laugh in the present bit of
writing, I want to say how much touched I was by those dear innocencies
of the poor sweet child, [1]—"a week before the end"! The mother's discovery of that book,—those unsuspected yearnings in verse,—one cannot
venture to try and realize *that!* I like to think that when the kind little
creature asked me so prettily to write my name in her Birthday Book,
there went some sort of sympathy (in the asking) with a person she had
heard was "a poet"—not merely a stranger with a name other people told
her they had heard of: perhaps she was meaning to be herself "a poet":
well, she is passed into poetry—for all who knew her even so slightly as I!

The verses I return are picturesque:[2] I would see to the "lay" in the
3[d.] stanza, because though it may be meant for a past tense, it looks
terribly like the cockney *present!* "Late" might be substituted for the
epithet "deep". Another minute animadversion: I would make Armēnīans"
a trisyllable, and put in another foot: don't your ear like that better? It
is only in modern burlesque that "Sir Joseph Parker" can be told that he
might have been an "I-tal-i-an."[3] All the rest is very pretty,—tell Mr
Pinkerton, with my compliments!

Yes, the whole "White Mountain"[4] will be with you this Autumn—
and half of it, longer. I heard so at the Studio yesterday, which they cede
me for Pen's statue, busts, pictures, and belongings in general,—which

will abide there till distributed in the Galleries. His Statue[5] and Busts are in bronze now,—and his large "Idyl", three Landscapes, and what know I else? are to arrive soon: were you only here to see! Well, you can bear with the talking about them you shall undergo—for we two understand each other,—don't we—Dear,—dearest of friends? I know I am ever yours,—and your own Ediths,—affectionately

Robert Browning.

Address: Italia, Venezia. / Mrs Bronson, / Palazzino Alvisi, / Canal Grande, / Venezia.
Publication: Whiting, p. 252 (in part).
Manuscript: Armstrong Browning Library.

1. Mrs. Bronson, much affected by Lia Metternich's death, bound the little girl's letters in a leather album bearing the Metternich arms, and sent Browning the following childish verses which Lia had written when her brother Clement went away to college a few weeks before her death:

> Goodbye, Goodbye forever,
> See you again shall I never.
> To see you no more
> It makes my heart quite sore.
> O could you only stop here,
> You that I love so dear.
> And when you are on the wide sea
> Will you then think of me?
> O could I once more hear
> His voice so sweet and clear
> And when he sat in front of me
> We thought what our end would be,
> And now the end of both I know,
> For he is gone—& I will go.

The album is now in the Fossi collection.

2. The verses of Percy E. Pinkerton, who later became a friend of Pen's and shared an apartment with him in Venice. Browning is commenting on a poem "A sunset in Venice," published in 1886 by Pinkerton in his *Galeazzo, a Venetian Episode*. The third and fourth stanzas read:

> Now, with the sinking fires,
>> Yon train of spires
> Melts on its mirror in a mist of grey,
>> While an obscurer pall
>> Wraps the white wall
> Of lonely hills that deep in distance lay.
>
>> Swung high in convent-tower
>> Bells mark the hour
> For grave Armenian monks to bend in prayer;
>> They from their quiet isle
>> Watch the last smile
> Of sunset fade upon the golden air.

3. A reference to Gilbert and Sullivan's *H.M.S. Pinafore*, which had received its first performance at the Opéra Comique in London in May 1878. In the second act, the Boatswain and the Chorus celebrate the First Lord of the Admiralty, the Rt. Hon. Sir Joseph Porter K.C.B. with the following refrain:

> He might have been a Roosian,
> A French, or Turk, or Proosian,
> Or perhaps Itali-an.

But in spite of all temptations
To belong to other nations,
He remains an Englishman!

Browning, in recalling the song, mistakenly calls the First Lord Sir Joseph Parker, instead of Porter.

4. Browning rented Henrietta Montalba's London studio at 11, Campden House Road Mews for several months in 1884, and arranged an exhibition of Pen's latest work there from 29 March to 1 April. The reference to the "White Mountain" is, therefore, a pun on the name Montalba (Mont Alba), and means that the four artist sisters, Clara, Ellen, Hilda and Henrietta, accompanied by their mother, were to join their brother Augustus Montalba in Venice for the autumn, and that two of them would remain there longer.

5. The statue is "Dryope," which depicts a nude girl fascinated by Apollo in the form of a serpent, and which Pen later placed in the courtyard of the Palazzo Rezzonico. The only known bronze bust of the period is one of Adelia Abbruzzesi, a professional Parisian model used by Rodin for his statue of Eve, and by Pen for Dryope. The idyll is "A Faun playing the Pipe to two Nymphs by a River," and the landscapes are views near Dinant.

Letter 25

Robert Browning to Katharine Bronson

19, Warwick Crescent, W.
Apr. 13. '84.

Ah, dear Friend, with what a relief I take up this sheet of paper and say "my last letter of to-day, at least, shall be to Her!"—I kept it for *that*,—kept the comfort, I mean,—all these three weeks of busy idleness in the shape of—oh, no matter what, now it is over! My son has been and gone, his paintings and sculpture shewn, talked about and finally disposed of. I have toiled like a pack-horse,[1] and my rest is to be—another week of unremitting festivity at Edinburgh,[2] whither I betake my tired self to-morrow, when, instead of starting on a nine hours' journey northward, I should like to go to sleep even on the hardest of armchairs. Still, "Be the day never so long, at the end cometh even-song", and, if heaven please, "Be the next three months a game at Tennis—of which I am the ball—at the end comes Venice!"[3]

All the same, I am a fool for having myself put aside the letter or two I know your goodness would have refreshed my fatigue with had I simply given you occasion to write. Will you not give me a good camel-draught, a dear long letter to expect through the week and find at the week's end on returning here?

Among my distractions has been the search after, and negotiations about a plot of ground I am bent on securing if possible: the ground is

Manuscript Verses of Mrs. Bronson and Robert Browning

Robert Browning and Joseph Milsand

in my power, if I please, through the munificence of its owner, a man I have never seen in my life, who, on hearing that I was the applicant, at once offered it at half-price! Fact, I have it in writing. "Your friend, some Duke or other?" No, madam,—he is a tailor: and if nine tailors make a man, nine and ninety Dukes make such a tailor. My next attempt on generosity has been with the Crown,—seeing that my plot is adjoining to Royal Property, and I crave certain concessions—which may or may not be granted: yet hitherto the proposals have been treated with prompt and kind consideration, and I am assured that what can be done will be done: in which case, "I shall get" (quoth my intended architect) "the best piece of land in London, freehold, for nearly as good as nothing." Of course this is all for the son,—I myself, like Hamlet, "could live in a nutshell and count myself king of infinite space":[4] but I may as well invest thus profitably the little I have to leave him. This therefore lies, as Homer expresses it, on the knees of the gods:[5] but, for quiet me, the business has been a noisy one, and I wanted the main of it over before I breathed freely and took pen between thumb and finger.

Then Pen (call him so, you, please!)—he came over, and made a purely pleasant commotion, but still a commotion. He brought his Statue, two Busts (bronze all) and three ⟨no, *four*⟩[6] large pictures: one of these is (to the indulgent Paternal) a delicious Idyl,—two nymphs listening to a young Faun's flute-playing, in a rocky dell,—life-size figures: three landscapes: these are gone to the Academy and the Grosvenor, and someway or other will manage to give a sufficient notion of the artist's versatility as well as power. He is returned to Paris,—or rather to Dinant where he has work to do,—but will be back in a week or two. He speaks enthusiastically of a large picture by Julian Story,—did I tell you of it?—"Æsop relating his fables to a group of peasants." Pen maintains that nobody in England could paint the like.

Tell Edith I shook hands on a staircase, at a party given by Sir F. Leighton, with her friend Miss Kerr, who was in conversation with Mr Sartoris: she looked pretty, and that is all I can report, for we exchanged no words at all. My own heart's man-friend is here, in his usual yearly fashion, for a month or so,—Milsand,[7] I must have spoken to you about.

Also it was a delight to see again Salvini:[8] there was a vile "set" made against him by the Irvingites (Irving himself having no part nor lot in the matter, I can easily believe)—but his immense qualities took care of themselves. We are all in black,—and really in sorrow,—for the poor young man[9] I spent the week before Christmas with, at Hatfield: he was very amiable,—and if his "gifts", as the Queen styles them, were a little exaggerated, they were not altogether imaginary. He seemed so well, that I thought people had made more of his constitutional weakness than there was warrant for. He got into too good spirits, on being emancipated from supervision, broke some useful habits, and paid the price for them in his life which promised to be serviceable. I must end,—having hardly begun what I had in purpose to say: this however I will save and put down: I love you and Edith with all my heart. I hardly ever send a word to dear Miss Chapman,—as if her goodness were not always present with me!

Yours and yours and yours

ever yours—

R. Browning.

Publication: None traced.
Manuscript: Armstrong Browning Library.

1. Browning laid great store by these four-day exhibitions of Pen's work. He arranged similar occasions in 1881 and 1882, had special invitations printed and made every effort to cajole and implore his many friends in the art world to visit the exhibition, and to comment on his son's work. Millais and Leighton were two of many who pronounced favourably on Pen's painting and sculpture. All the tiring organization and administration was left to Browning, and it was only through his efforts that the exhibitions were well patronised.

2. Browning left London for Edinburgh on 14 April to receive an honorary degree from the university. He stayed there, as the guest of Professor David Masson, until 20 April. For an account of the festivities, see Rosaline Masson, "Robert Browning in Edinburgh," *Cornhill*, NS xxvi (February 1909), 226–240.

3. Browning's comic rhyme may well have been suggested by the more serious comment by Bosola in Webster's *Duchess of Malfi* (V, iv, 53): "We are merely the stars' tennis balls, struck and bandied which way please them."

4. Shakespeare: *Hamlet*, II, ii, 255–256.

5. The phrase "It rests in the lap of the gods" occurs in both *Iliad* and *Odyssey*. The origin is uncertain. Are the gods imagined as dispensing gifts from their knees, or is this a reference to sitting statues of gods on whose knees offerings were laid for acceptance? Browning uses the same expression in a letter two months later to Richard Congreve, 12 June 1884: "I wish it were in my power to bring out such an edition as you recommend,—but the determination about all such matters 'lies on the knees' of the Publisher" (BL).

6. Interpolated.

7. The French scholar, Joseph Milsand (1817–1886) was one of Browning's earliest admirers and helpful critics. His article on Browning's poetry in 1851 in a series called "La Poésie anglaise depuis Byron" in *La Revue des Deux Mondes* attempted to show the real importance and stature of the neglected poet. He later became a close friend and often stayed with Browning and his sister for a few weeks each Spring during the last thirty years of his life, and they visited him at Saint Aubin in Normandy. Browning dedicated the rewritten *Sordello* to him in 1863, as well as *Parleyings with Certain People of Importance in their Day*. With this letter Browning sent Mrs. Bronson a photograph of Milsand and himself looking at one of Pen's portraits, reproduced opposite p. 47.

8. Tommaso Salvini (1829–1916), Italy's leading tragedian, was a particular favourite of Browning, who considered him one of the greatest interpreters of Shakespeare. Browning first met Salvini in 1875 and praised his Hamlet; in the following year Salvini was Browning's guest at Warwick Crescent as well as a visiting member of the Athenaeum, Browning's favourite club. In 1884 Browning saw him play in *King Lear* and Soumet's *Gladiator*, both of which he enjoyed. The London press were not so kind. They saw Salvini challenging the supremacy of Henry Irving, England's finest Shakespearean actor, and gave both *King Lear* and *Othello* poor reviews. Browning realized

the partisan nature of such attacks and was delighted Salvini rose above them. Henry Irving was equally distressed and acknowledged Salvini's greatness, particularly as Othello.

9. Prince Leopold, Duke of Albany (1853–1884), youngest son of Queen Victoria, who died on 28 March. He suffered from haemophilia and the Queen was always over-protective towards him, believing that he would never live a normal life. Intelligent and affectionate, he surprised everyone by marrying Princess Helen of Waldeck in 1882. She bore him a daughter and was pregnant again in February 1884, when Leopold went to Cannes, ostensibly for health reasons. He injured a knee and soon afterwards died from a brain haemorrhage. His son, Leopold, was born on 19 July.

Letter 26

ROBERT BROWNING TO KATHARINE BRONSON

19, Warwick Crescent, W.
June 28. '84.

Do you know why I never wrote, my own Friend, when your letter reached me a month ago? I was going to Oxford,[1] as I told you, and supposed she was at least fairly out of danger: but on my return, two days after, there came a relapse, and the case was grave: enough that after five weeks' confinement to her bed,[2] she was only able to come down stairs, and get the air by a drive,—no other way of regaining strength being open to her. She is now far towards becoming her old self—walks and takes light food: but the surprise and alarm were perhaps felt unduly by me who never remember to have had any illness of the least importance before. Now, two days ago, somebody told me you must still be in Venice, because she (it was L.^y Alwyn Compton)[3] had seen—or heard of—Miss Bronson at the Edens': and that removes the last doubt as to whether I should seek you there or no. And, presently, I go again to Oxford, for a couple of days,[4] and I want to think that while I am away my present bit of writing will journey fast, and tell you that my long silence meant nothing but a trust that the next day, or at least the next week, would let me talk with you as nearly free from fear as the chances of this world allow. Only this! Which is only this—not the proper outpouring it might be if my minutes were not counted—and, just now, interrupted. Dear Friend, write and tell me all about yourself: where you are, if not in Venice. I am wearied out with this London season's hard work called amusement. The time is up! My Sister loves you, as you know. And I am as you know yours

R Browning

Address: ⟨Ital⟩y, Venice. / Mrs Bronson, / Palazzo Alvisi, / Canal Grande, / Venezia.
Publication: None traced.
Manuscript: Armstrong Browning Library.

    1. Browning was in Oxford for the weekend of Saturday 24 May to Monday 26 May. Soon after his return he called in a specialist to examine Sarianna and paid him £2.2.6 for the consultation.
    2. Sarianna's illness, described at first as "internal inflammation," turned out to be a severe attack of peritonitis. She was more seriously ill than Browning first realized and remained weak throughout the summer. The Swiss holiday at St. Moritz, therefore, was necessary to enable her to recuperate.
    3. Florence Alwyne Compton, wife of the Rt. Revd. Lord Alwyne Compton (1825–1906), Dean of Worcester, and from 1886 Bishop of Ely.
    4. Browning left for Oxford the day he wrote this letter, Saturday 28 June, returning the following Monday. He stayed at Balliol and discussed with Jowett his gift to the college of a portrait of himself painted by Pen. He had offered the painting early in May and Jowett had immediately accepted, but a year later the portrait hadn't been delivered, because it seemed to be permanently on exhibition in London galleries. Eventually it arrived at Balliol in March 1886 and was immediately placed in the Dining Hall. Jowett commented on 18 March: "Will you please thank your son and tell him that I think it a noble work which has an additional interest because it is painted by him: he has made you a trifle too stern and serious but this if it be an error is on the right side" (ABL). The picture now hangs in the Balliol College Library.

Letter 27

SARIANNA BROWNING TO KATHARINE BRONSON

Villa Berry. San Moritz. Engadin.
Friday, Sept. 5. [1884]

Dearest and best,

    I was on the point of writing to you when your letter to my brother came in, just now. So I go on, and he will write very soon. I was a little uncertain about our plans, which made me wait to say something definite. Our friend M.rs Bloomfield Moore is unexpectedly called away, on business, to America—much to her regret and ours for we are sorry to lose her, but her departure will not hasten ours, as the whole of the villa is hers till the end of December, and she has made every arrangement for our comfort.[1] We shall therefore follow our original intention of staying here, if the weather permits, during Sept. How fondly we had looked forward to October! hoping against hope. Our chief inducement in coming here, when debarred from Gressoney, was to be near our beloved Venice. But you will come to London, darling, and we shall see you again with delight. You have given me the hope—it would be too cruel to disappoint us.

Oh, *do* come! We will welcome you with our whole heart.

This place is exquisite with its bracing air and magnificent mountain scenery. We enjoy it so much, and are, both of us, so well. Never fear my walking too much. I never have been in the habit of fatiguing myself, though by nature and education I am a good walker. I am no climber, and do not attempt to get up any mountain that has not a gentle zig-zag ascent, like the one just opposite our house. I always avoid ascending even a mild campanile, or tower, or church—in fact, I am lazy by nature, though I enjoy exercise.

Is dear Edith with you? I count upon her as an ally in making you come to London. You *must*, or I will fret myself sick with disappointment. We shall be in London the beginning of October, at the latest—if we can count upon any thing in this mutable world. We shall look forward to meeting you there.

Write to us much of yourself—where you are, and whither you are going. God bless you, and give us to see you soon. Always remember us most kindly to Miss Chapman—and if Edith is with you, give her our dear love.

Ever your affectionate,
Sarianna Browning.

Publication: None traced.
Manuscript: Fossi.

1. When she heard that the Brownings were deterred by the cholera quarantine regulations from spending the autumn at Gressoney St. Jean in the Italian Alps, Clara Bloomfield-Moore offered to let them share her rented Villa Berry at St. Moritz with her. The Brownings happily accepted, arriving in mid-August, only to have their holiday interrupted by the summons which sent Mrs. Moore back to America on 3 September. The Brownings returned to England on 1 October.

Letter 28

ROBERT BROWNING TO KATHARINE BRONSON

Villa Berry, S! Moritz, Ober-Engadin, Sw.
Sept. 6. '84.

Yes, dearest friend, your pretty wreath came this morning, and opposite this table shall it hang till I leave the house, be it withered or no,—and at present it is fresh. Now, thank you—for what? for every thing, your love and thoughts and regrets too– Do not we two here regret that Italy is closed to us! But the comfort out of the vexation is that you will—will you not?—cross to London from Paris, [1] and so we shall see you for all the multiplied hindrances. Now, how do you suppose it is faring with us? We are alone. Our hostess was summoned to America last week to her extreme regret,—and, after a hot business of telegraphing and being telegraphed to, left last Wednesday. She had taken this comfortable Villa till the middle of December and would not hear of our quitting it: and, all things considered, we had little inclination to do so, for you were from home, and what would be the good of lingering out this month elsewhere,—the air and influences happening to suit us extremely. So, our plan is to stay out September here, and be content with at most two months' absence instead of the four we so utterly enjoyed last year. Mrs Moore was altogether as kind and considerate as possible, and has made every possible provision for our comfort after her departure. We are quite alone—friends are in the place, but we only get glimpses of them: the place is emptying fast, the pensions shut up, the walks on the mountain-side are wholly our own. Two days ago the snow fell thickly all day, and what a sight were the mountains next morning in a glaring sun! These changes I expect will diversify the whole month,—and inside this warm pleasant room I & S. read—and don't require "the devil to find some mischief still for idle hands to do."[2] You have much more to enjoy with all that good music thrown in,—and I am glad for you. We get books and papers enough, and I am correcting the proofs of the poem I was too negligent about in London:[3] many distractions stood in the way of that. After all, we have attained the main object of our journey—the complete re-establishment of the health of S., who walks twice a day just as of old. I am cheered to[o] by letters from Robert,—the last of which comes just now. He was anxious that his Statue of Dryope should be seen at the Brussels Exhibition,—a triennial one, and important from the concurrence of the best Foreign Artists: but the "Grosvenor," where it was shown, did not close till the first week in August, while the Brussels Gallery was closed to works on the 25.th of July. Robert sent his photographs with a petition for a "délai"—only exceptionally granted: the Committee conceded it "unanimement" and have given it a place where it stands by itself and is capitally seen:[4] he went to see it,—so did the King and Queen,—"to whom he would have been presented had he not been in morning-dress!" (The Father of *Robert* to the Mother of Edith!) (You see the slip of the pen,[5]—such is not my good fortune!)

You know very well how interested and delighted I shall be to read your German Translations if you send them: *do!* By the way, what is the most emphatic close of any verse I ever read, if not this which *you* shall read. It occurs at the end of the first of Quarles' Emblems[6]—a beloved book of my boyhood. There is a dialogue between the Serpent and Eve: arguments for plucking the apple and letting it alone: at last Eve decides—

Eve.   "I'll pluck, and taste, and tempt my Adam too
           To try the virtues of this apple."
Serpent. *"Do!"*

Now, my own friend, you once asked if I often thought of you: I could answer—by a mechanical contrivance, every five minutes at least. You gave me a dear coin, that issued by the Venetian Republic in '48: I had a ring affixed to it, and that again appended to my watch-chain,[7]—the only other token of love there being my wife's ring. But I think of you between whiles all the same. Bless you ever!

Ever your affectionate
Robert Browning.

S. wrote yesterday,—she is yours likewise.

Publication: Whiting, pp. 252–254 (in part).
Manuscript: Armstrong Browning Library.

    1. Mrs. Bronson's visit to Paris must have been occasioned by the increasing illness of her husband. In Letter 30 Sarianna describes it as an "errand of mercy."
    2. A reference to Isaac Watts's verse in *Divine Songs for Children*:
           In works of labour, or of skill,
           I would be busy too;
           For Satan finds some mischief still
           For idle hands to do.
    3. *Ferishtah's Fancies.*
    4. This statue had already caused Browning much heartache. Rejected by the Royal Academy, it had been accepted at the Grosvenor Gallery only at Browning's personal request. It was, therefore, unthinkable that it could be transported to Brussels before the Grosvenor exhibition closed.
    5. Browning had originally written: "The father of *Edith* . . ."
    6. Browning was given a copy of Quarles by his mother when he was a young boy. He later presented it to Mrs. Orr, who in turn gave it to Balliol College, Oxford. The book is annotated in Browning's juvenile hand.
    7. This was done in early August when Browning had his watch repaired. The watch itself, with the ring and the coin still attached, was sold by Sothebys at the 1913 sale for £270. It was later given to the British Museum, where it has since been lost, believed stolen.

Letter 29

ROBERT BROWNING TO KATHARINE BRONSON

Villa Berry, St Moritz, Engadin.
Sept. 16. '84.

Dearest Friend, your letters and all they enclosed or accompanied were so many delights to me: I think S. has spoken for herself. I have just

been securing places in the Diligence for departure, in a fortnight, for—
London!—and did not I think how differently I should have felt had it
been for Chiavenna and Venice! So it was last year, and the end of the
journey was at the Venice Station when the first blessing was that of
Luigi's fat face—lighting the way a few footsteps farther to the more
than Friend who had come in the rain to take us and keep us. Were you
at Venice now,—but you will be in London, and that is a compensation—
though the short time you will spend there will not bear comparison with
those golden afternoons and evenings through the long Autumn and even
longer. It is some years since I passed an October out of Italy: folks say
it is a good temperately warm month—which may it be!

I have read your verses and, for the love I bear their author, I try to
be of the least use, even though I may seem captious: I hardly can do
otherwise than try to treat them as if they were my own manufacture.
They are very good indeed, closely translated and yet limpid and musical
as if unprescribed by the originals.[1] I have scribbled my two or three
proposed corrections for you to adopt or not, with the reasons underneath
for what I venture to suggest. India rubber or bread-crumb will do away
with any alteration that does not seem for the better: but you will understand that. I return Mrs Eden's amusing letter—thanks for the sight of
it. Yes, the king is a fine fellow indeed,—"Avanti, Savoja!"[2]

While I write, I am keeping out of the sun: the weather is splendid:
I & S. have walked on the mountain-side for above two hours. We shall
perhaps never again breathe such delicious air,—and the colours today—
of all things, from the herbs to the mountain-snow, are wonderful.
Everybody is gone from the place, and we never meet a soul.

Very likely you may meet Robert if you stay long enough in London:
he is now in Dinant—but will probably be soon in Paris,—*there* you
may see him also, and with more likelihood. He always spends Christmas
with us. If you have an opportunity, do not let the kind people at Venice,
who treated us so kindly, suppose that we forget them,—especially
Avignone & the Edens—the Curtis family is away, I believe. I am really
delighted to gather from Mrs Eden's letter that Layard has been at last
awarded a pension:[3] but the Constantinople Embassy,—alas!

Dearest Friend, all love to you—and to Edith—from both of us here.
Remember we do not leave till October 1. Ever affectionately yours

RB.

Publication: None traced.
Manuscript: Armstrong Browning Library.

1. The translations from the German, mentioned in the previous letter, include poems
by Heine, Geikel, Lenau and Uhland. Mrs. Bronson preserved them and they are now
among the Fossi papers in Asolo. At the end of the manuscript Browning has written,
"All these are very good, and quite worthy of the originals."

2. Humbert (Umberto) I (1844–1900), who had succeeded his father Victor Emmanuel II in 1878, had achieved considerable popular support by visiting the cholera hospitals in Naples during the three-month epidemic which cost thousands of lives. He and his wife gave 300,000 lire to the relief fund, and their actions aroused much patriotic fervour. Mrs. Bronson was inspired to write a poem, "Avanti Savoja!," which exists in the following rough draft in the Fossi collection:

> O'er his young head his bright banner flying
> Humbert amid the plague-stricken is seen,
> Fearless he stands by the dead and the dying—
> Brother, and king, 'neath the Red White and Green.

> Red, for the glow of his mind's ardent dreaming;
> White, for his impulse, unsullied and keen;
> Green, for the hope in his honest eyes gleaming;
> Roses and laurels are red, white and green.

> Italy! Kingdom of Art, Love and Beauty,
> Pride is thy right in thy King and his Queen,
> True to traditions of honour and duty,
> Stainless they carry thy red, white and green.

3. Layard had been recalled as Ambassador to Turkey in 1880 but kept on full pay for twelve months. He had failed to establish good personal relations with the Turks and had become disillusioned with the Sultan and the Sublime Porte. In 1884 he was passed over for the Rome Embassy and his diplomatic career was at an end. Reluctantly Gladstone's government awarded him a pension of £1,700 a year—to which he was more than entitled.

Letter 30

SARIANNA BROWNING TO KATHARINE BRONSON

Villa Berry,
Saturday [20 September 1884]

Dearest and kindest of friends,

Robert is telling you of all the reasons which now make it better for him to return at once to London– His new book is coming out sooner than he expected, and it is too late to ask his publishers to delay it—and he must look out for a new home for Pen's paintings, and he *ought* to search seriously for a house.

I feel that your dear kindness is making you return before your work is done in Paris, and you are breaking off abruptly your errand of mercy. We must not be selfish, dearly as we should like a visit to you and Venice. I hope and trust that we shall meet at no very distant period and my love is durable to the end.

Consult your own taste and convenience for a visit to London: at all seasons (except August and September) there is much to be seen and done

in that vast human wilderness. Give my very best love to dear Edith—and
believe me ever,

Your most affectionate
Sarianna Browning

Publication: None traced.
Source: Transcript Rucellai.

Letter 31

ROBERT BROWNING TO KATHARINE BRONSON

Villa Berry, St Moritz, Engadin. S.
Sept. 23. '84.

For first thing, Dearest Friend, I am glad to know that my letter with the
Poems reached you before your departure: I had some fear that you might
miss it. It is like your goodness to care so much about what amounts to
so little,—I did what I could to be of use by amending—which perhaps
is a sort of fault-finding: I could certainly have done something more to
the purpose if the Poems were original,—but I knew your translations
were faithful—as they should be. When you write out of your own dear
head, let me see, and try hard to improve it never so little. I well remember
the whole book of verses you let me read at Venice:[1] I could not well
have helped you *there*. And now for a sorrow after the gladness: we do
not pass through Paris, this time, but take the direct and more convenient
route by Amiens and Calais. Last year, we wanted, or needed, to see
Pen, who was at his Paris Studio: but he is still in Dinant: I do not know
when he means to leave: if he finds you at Paris it will be a delight for
him to see you. Tell us when you propose going to London. We start—I
told you, I think—to-morrow week, the 1st October. The weather has
been magnificent—the last eight days a wonderful combination of sunshine and fresh air: but we have just returned from a walk in time—for
it rains! So, northward we go, as such things must be. You promise to
write from Paris: send us away rejoicing at least that we are not turning
our backs on you! Were you at Venice, how promptly would I convert
our places for Chür—and Bâle into corresponding ones for Chiavenna
and Milan! One dares not speculate on what a year may bring forth, but
I know whither my hopes go. Well,—yes, the King's behaviour has been
admirable: what a chance the poor Pope[2] has thrown away in not preceding
him! If the "Prisoner of the Vatican" had quietly walked out of his

confinement, with a cross before him and an attendant on each side, and passed on to Naples and the Hospitals, "braving all danger, in imitation of his Master,"—I verily believe there might have happened a revolution,—such events from much less causes being frequent enough. Where is the "wisdom of the serpent?"[3]

Dearest Friend, my Sister writes: all love to Edith,—all love to you from your ever affectionate

Robert Browning.

Who is Rawdon B's L. P.?[4]

Address: France. / Mrs Bronson, / Hôtel Meyerbeer, / Rond-Point, / Champs Elysées, / *Paris.*
Publication: Whiting, p. 254 (in part).
Manuscript: Armstrong Browning Library.

1. *Leaves from my Journal from Venice to Algiers* by K.C. de Kay Bronson, privately printed in Algiers in 1879. The poems commemorate a visit to Algiers and refer to places Mrs. Bronson visited en route. Thus the book begins at Como with a poem dated September, goes through Venice, Florence (October), Spezzia, Genoa, Marseilles, to Algiers (November). The book itself is a series of mimeographed sheets in Mrs. Bronson's hand, neatly bound.

2. Joachim Pecci (1810–1903), who became Pope Leo XIII in 1878, considered himself "the despoiled sovereign of Rome" and protested strongly about monarchist forces occupying the capital. His worldly power extended only to the few acres of the Vatican. Although Browning criticizes him for not taking the initiative by visiting the cholera hospitals in Naples, Leo had ordered the Cardinal of Naples to organize relief work.

3. "Be ye therefore wise as serpents, and harmless as doves" (Matthew 9:16).

4. This enigmatic question clearly refers to a comment Mrs. Bronson had made in a previous letter. It is probable she referred to Lord Palmerston as L.P., and Browning failed to make the connection. In 1862 Palmerston had commissioned Brown to calendar all the Venetian State Papers which mentioned England, a task which took Brown the rest of his life and resulted in eight published volumes. Alternatively the postscript might refer to legal matters about Rawdon Brown's estate, and return to the Cavendish Bentinck controversy of Letters 22 and 23.

Letter 32

Robert Browning to Katharine Bronson

Villa Berry, S.t Moritz.
Sept. 26. '84.

Dearest Friend, We have just received your telegrams—at too late an hour to answer them immediately, but you will hear to-morrow that all our arrangements are made for leaving next Wednesday, and we should cause great inconvenience in London by countermanding them. What we feel when—as we gather—you would really—in some measure for our sakes—return to Venice[1]—there is no way of telling you *that!* Now that you are in Paris, perhaps you may see reason to stay there, and to go on to London—so that we shall see you all the same. Who knows what a year may bring forth? If it bring forth no evil to any of us, we will hope to go to you—where else can we be so happy? I ought to explain a little better what are the reasons for making our return to London necessary: I have to find—at once—a place for Pen's Pictures now occupying Miss Montalba's Studio—which I cannot retain beyond this month: and, if possible, I would still try and get a Studio—*House and all*:—Of course, I might have tried to get somebody to act for me in these matters, had I been aware earlier that I could stay away the whole Autumn. Then my Book, I see, is advertised as in the Press—and I am desirous of arranging with my Publisher about matters connected with my whole works generally, which if done needs to be attended to at once.[2] And finally—*is*—or is it *not*—the case that your own change of plans is somewhat occasioned by your wish to gratify us? Nothing short of the goodness we have so thoroughly known you to be capable of, would inspire such a fancy, but—you are all goodness!

Write to us at at 19. Warwick Crescent. (where we count upon arriving on Friday E^g Oct. 3)[3] Here or there—at Venice or London, words cannot say how much I am yours

> affectionately ever
> Robert Browning.

S. is gone to bed: but I could not delay writing however hurriedly. I had forgotten about "the Cholera": no fear of it entered our thought at any time, though of the Quarantine,—extended, till a fortnight ago, to seven days,—we had fear decidedly. If the Cholera were actually raging in a town wherein my presence could be of no use I should be disinclined to play the mere indifferent visitor: otherwise, danger is everywhere, and people expect that we shall have the disease in London sooner or later.

Address: France. / Mrs Bronson, / Hôtel Meyerbeer, / Rond-Point, / Champs Elysées, / Paris.
Publication: None traced.
Manuscript: Armstrong Browning Library.

1. Hearing of the Brownings' thwarted holiday at St. Moritz, Mrs. Bronson proposed returning immediately from Paris to Ca Alvisi to entertain them there.
2. This is the first indication that Browning was thinking of reissuing his poems to replace the out-of-date 1868 edition. On his return to London he wrote to George Smith suggesting that he might bring out a new twelve-volume edition of the complete poems at 5/- a volume "or even more." Smith waited until January 1887 to produce specific plans, which led to the 1888–89 edition in sixteen volumes.
3. Parenthetical phrase interpolated.

Katharine Bronson, 1890

Letter 33

ROBERT BROWNING TO KATHARINE BRONSON

19, Warwick Crescent, W.
Oct. 7. '84.

Dearest Friend, we arrived here duly on Friday evening, having got your two letters just before we left S.ᵗ Moritz: ours—mine, at least—which reached you much about the same time, explained somewhat of the need there was for our return, and that fear of Cholera had no part in our decision to do so: a great part could not but be in our belief that you were making—or desirous of making—this immense sacrifice of your plans on our account. Well, "on our account,"—if no other cause were existing,—come to London and let us see you—with what delight!

I have got rid of my last Proof-sheets; and all of a sudden it occurs to me to ask—now that alteration is impossible, I suppose—whether I have offended in just dating the last poem[1] from the place where I wrote it—the Giustinian-R.ᵗⁱ The first poem was dated from the Inn at Gressoney—and the last seemed to belong to the beloved place where it was penned,—as I wanted to remember—or be remembered rather. Have I done wrong? (I hear at this moment my sister actually *singing* in the next room—so completely is she re-established in health!)

By letters, we find that the admirable weather at S.ᵗ Moritz was continued up to the end of the last week: here the weather is fine—finer than usual—but the sparkle is off the wine, the wonderful freshness of St. Moritz does not incline one to dance rather than walk. I am in absolute peace and quietude—and so thoroughly prepared to enjoy your coming—if that may be!

All love to both Edith and yourself: I thought not a little of Edith—deprived of Paris and London which she could not but have set her heart upon seeing. S. shall speak on her own account.

Ever affectionately yours
RB.

Address: France. / Mrs Bronson, / Hôtel Meyerbeer, / Rond-Point, / Champs Elyseés, / *Paris.*
Publication: Whiting, p. 255 (in part).
Manuscript: Armstrong Browning Library.

1. The "Epilogue" to *Ferishtah's Fancies.* For Browning's desire to link this poem with Venice and with Mrs. Bronson, see Introduction, pp. xlv–xlvii. Verses 3 to 6 were set to music in 1888 by John Farmer, organist of Balliol College, Oxford, and became the first of his series of *Balliol Songs.*

$\mathcal{L}$*etter* 34

ROBERT BROWNING TO KATHARINE BRONSON

19, Warwick Crescent, W.
Oct. 14. '84.

Dearest Friend,

I waited a little before replying to your letter, wanting to be sure when I could say that Robert would find himself in Paris: he proposed to go there yesterday, and you will certainly have a visit from him as soon as he can manage to do what I know he desires very much. Here are your verses, which I try to be as severe about as possible, with no success at all worth speaking of! You will take my corrections (infinitesimal, this time) for what they are worth, and continue to send me what you write, will you not?

I was surprised two days ago by a note from Mr Lowell inviting me, & my Sister, to meet the Storys at dinner to-morrow—they being his guests during a short stay in London: and, yesterday afternoon, they called on my sister,—the Ss. and Mrs Lowell: the former were flourishing, and go in a few days to Rome:—where they have passed the Summer we were not told. Last evening, at a dinner given by Sidney Colvin,[1] I met Mr James[2]—who showed great interest in hearing how near you were, and how much nearer you are like to be. On the other hand, there will be a sad visitor to Venice presently. Professor Huxley[3] in a deplorable state of health from over work. I hate to speak of what is only too present with me—your own health,—I trust you have got rid of that cough: all dreadful associations go with a "cough"—in my memory.[4] I suppose your D.[r] Herbert[5] is the brother of my friend L.[d] Carnarvon,—who was much confided in by the Curtis family among others.

My book—which you kindly enquire about—is out of my hands, and in print: but the publishing, its when and how, concern the Publisher: I do not expect to see the completed thing for another month. Yes,—I felt so lovingly to the Giustinian-Recanati, that I could not bear cutting the link allowed by the Place and Date which were appended to the M.S: and you permit, so all is well—if you remember me as ever affectionately yours

Robert Browning.

Address: France. / Mrs Bronson, / Hôtel Meyerbeer, / Rond-Point, / Champs Elysées, / Paris.
Publication: Whiting, pp. 255–256 (in part).
Manuscript: Armstrong Browning Library.

1. Sir Sidney Colvin (1845–1927), Fellow of Trinity College, Cambridge, and former Director of the Fitzwilliam Museum. In 1884 he became Keeper of the Department of Prints and Manuscripts at the British Museum. He wrote widely on literature and the arts, his life of Keats being a favourite of Mrs. Bronson's. He stayed with her whenever he visited Venice and also paid visits to La Mura. She described him as "somewhat dry but most intellectual" in a letter to Isabella Gardner in 1892 (IGM).

2. Henry James (1843–1916), novelist, became one of Mrs. Bronson's closest friends in Venice. He stayed with her a number of times but eventually preferred the more spacious accommodation at Palazzo Barbaro; even so, he was always a frequent dinner guest at Ca Alvisi. He wrote a sympathetic introduction which appeared with the English printing of her "Browning in Venice," and which he later incorporated into *Italian Hours* (1909) as "Casa Alvisi." Like so many of James's acquaintances, Mrs. Bronson became a character in one of his short stories, "The Aspern Papers," and was to have been the heroine of a projected but unfinished novel, "Mrs. Max." Browning is the subject of the well-known story, "The Private Life."

3. Thomas Huxley (1825–1895), one of England's leading evolutionists, was President of the Royal Society from 1881 to 1885. His biological research, his struggles for educational reform, and his service on numerous Royal Commissions undermined his health and he resigned from the Presidency. He suffered from chronic dyspepsia and increasing deafness which forced him in 1885 to give up all his official posts, although he continued to work until his death. Edward Clodd, in his biography of Huxley (1902), sums him up in Browning's words, "One who never turned his back, but marched breast forward."

4. A reference to his wife's ill-health and fatal last illness.

5. Dr. Alan Herbert (d. 1907) was indeed the brother of Lord Carnarvon. He received his medical training in Paris and stayed there all his life as physician to the Hertford British Hospital. He was decorated for his services during the Siege of Paris. As the best-known English doctor in Paris, it was appropriate that he should treat Mrs. Bronson for her cough.

Letter 35

ROBERT BROWNING TO KATHARINE BRONSON

19, Warwick Crescent, W.
Oct. 23. '84.

Dearest Friend,—be sure I know what you would do to gratify me were it possible—and would spare doing me such a wrong as to endanger your very life by coming to London when your doctor advises against it. "So gain we profit by losing of our prayers"[1]—and it will be profit indeed if I find that by foregoing a delight to me which, with such an apprehension attached to it, would prove the reverse of delight, you recover the health upon which I shall count as a source of enjoyment to me for what remains of my own life. Go to Venice—certain that I know you would give me the sight of you here were it really for my interest—as under the present circumstances it could not be. For me,—what may happen in a year?—but if nothing untoward does happen, I will gladly go to you in the Autumn and renew the enjoyment of last happy October and November. Pen tells me you have a bad cough: that is the only thing he tells which I would fain wish untold: he speaks of your great kindness to him—but I was prepared for *that*: still, the old kindness strikes as freshly as if it were a new experience. I must not dwell on this—in words,—at all events, written words. Here are your poems again—with my pencil-*pokes* at whatever looks like a little point in which I may be of use. I repeat,—I try to forget they are yours, and to be as slow in relaxing my brows over them as possible.

I saw Huxley's brother-in-law (Sir Robt Collier²) last evening at L.^y Granville's,³ and enquired about the stay in Venice: it will be a very short one, as he has to return almost immediately for the marriage of his daughter Rachel: I can hardly think he will *re-return*, the ceremony at an end, yet he may—and, in that case, he shall be informed of your goodness to-him-ward—in Apostolically appropriate language.⁴ He is a thoroughly admirable person,—in all but his inconsiderateness in this waste of a precious life. I duly told the Storys how much you wanted to see them—and they probably have seen you by this time. Mrs Story meant to rest at Paris, and forego the Amiens Route. She had been unwell, but I thought her appearance very satisfactory: I dined with them last week at Mr Lowell's—and called there on Sunday. I met Mr James the other day,—and surprised as well as inspirited him by the news that you were so near—and—as I believed—so soon to become nearer. Now, write to me, tell me all you are about to do: how is dear Edith? Oh no—Pen is none of mine to outward view, but wholly his Mother's⁵—in some respects, at least. At the same age, there was small difference between Pen's face and that of the brother she lost⁶—to judge by a drawing I possess. Dearest Friend, I am yours ever affectionately: so, I know, is my sister,—not at hand, nor is there need she should confirm my assurance. All love to you from us both!

Robert Browning.

Address: France. / Mrs Bronson, / Hôtel Meyerbeer, / Rond-Point, / *Paris.*
Publication: Whiting, p. 256 (in part).
Manuscript: Armstrong Browning Library.

1. "So find we profit by losing of our prayers," is spoken by Pompey in Shakespeare's *Antony and Cleopatra* (II, i, 7).
2. Sir Robert Porrett Collier, first Baron Monkswell (1817–1886), Solicitor-General, Attorney-General and later a judge. Browning knew him more as an artist, because he exhibited at the Royal Academy and Grosvenor Gallery with Pen. As a young man he had been a good caricaturist, but later he became an accomplished landscape painter, specializing in views of Switzerland.
3. Castalia Rosalind, Countess Granville (1847–1938), second wife of the 2nd Earl Granville (1815–1891), Foreign Secretary under Lord John Russell and Gladstone. Browning appears to have met her first in 1873.

4. A comic comment on Huxley's agnosticism. He had been described in *The Spectator* as "the Great Agnostic."

5. Like so many people who met Pen for the first time, Mrs. Bronson had been surprised by his balding, chubby appearance, and had remarked to Browning how unlike his father he was. Browning, in likening Pen to *Elizabeth*, had quite innocently misunderstood the comment. Typical of the many derogatory accounts of Pen, by those who knew parents and son, is this remark by Thomas Westwood to Lady Alwyne Compton in 1880: "There was but one novelty in Dinant, *Robert Browning, Jun.*, and he was a figure of fun, quite a droll little fellow in knickerbockers, with short, fat legs, and a ruddy countenance, the last man in all creation I should have chosen for Elizabeth Browning's son" (*LF*, p. 195).

6. Edward Barrett Moulton-Barrett (1807–1840), Bro, Elizabeth's eldest brother, who was drowned with two friends and a boatman when sailing in Babbacombe Bay on 11 July 1840. He had been staying with Elizabeth at Torquay.

Letter 36

ROBERT BROWNING TO KATHARINE BRONSON

19, Warwick Crescent, W.
Feb. 15. '85.

Dearest Mrs Bronson,—this dull morning grew too near blackness itself when, at breakfast, my Sister said, once again, "No news of her from Venice"—and I, once again, calculated and found, by this time, it was a month and a full half since we heard from you. Why should this be? If I had simply and rationally written a line, instead of thinking a thought, I should have known,—as your dear goodness will let me know, as soon as you receive this,—how you are, and how Edith is, now that the winter is over and gone with its incentives to that cough which was still vexatious when we had your last letter. Do not let us mind highdays and holidays,— be sure of this that every day will be truly festal that brings us a word from you: for other clouds than the material ones make us melancholy just now; and how this turbid element about us contrasts with the golden hours near the beloved friends—perhaps more vivid—certainly more realized as valuable than ever! I do not mean to write much, because what I want to impress on your generosity is just that a half-sheet with mere intelligence about you will be a true comfort and sustainment to me and to my Sister,—the barest account of yourself and what we associate with you: and, for our part, you shall hear at least that we are well or ailing, stationary or about to move—the former far the likelier case, for I get a little repugnant to the notion of moving—that is, travelling: probably "the grasshopper" is about to become "a burthen",[1] as Holy Writ declares will happen some day to all of us. In your last letter you enquired kindly concerning Pen: he was ill here, but, being properly cared for, got better sooner than we could expect, and returned to Paris and his work. This last fortnight he has again suffered from cold and sore-throat: but yesterday's account was more satisfactory, and he *may* be able to finish his picture for the "Salon," though the interruption has been considerable.

I need not tell you of the anxiety we are in: you have the newspapers, which give us all the little we can understand of the facts: I am glad you see the "Daily News" which perhaps is the best informed, through its communications with Government.[2] We hope still against hope that Gordon[3] lives: every hour may bring authentic news, but this Sunday morning is silent (in this part of the Town at least) up to noonday.[4]

Dearest Friend, I hold fast to your affection,—you know it, must know. Bless you and yours ever! My Sister is out,—but you know her feeling well enough. Give my true love to Edith,—my grateful regards to dear Miss Chapman. Cà Alvisi is a bit of blue indeed in the black heavens: so, I end with a prolonged "Magari"!—never to end as yours

affectionately

Robert Browning.

Address: Italy, Venice. / Mrs Bronson, / Cà Alvisi, / Canal Grande, / Venezia.
Publication: Whiting, pp. 257–258 (in part).
Manuscript: Armstrong Browning Library.

1. Ecclesiastes 12:5.
2. *The Daily News*, founded in 1846, was London's leading Liberal newspaper. Through its editor, F. H. Hill, it was in close contact with Gladstone's government and so would have the latest news of the Nile Relief expedition. In 1930 *The Daily News* merged with *The News Chronicle* and ceased to exist.
3. General Charles George Gordon (1833–1885) had been besieged in Khartoum by the forces of the Mahdi for five months. A relief expedition entered the Sudan in November and reached Khartoum on 28 January 1885, to discover that the city had fallen two days earlier and that Gordon was dead. Three weeks later the news had not yet reached London. Browning had "very deep and sincere feeling" for Gordon, but declined to contribute an appreciation of him for *The Contemporary Review* (see *N&Q*, 1956, pp. 539–541).
4. Browning lived in the residential area of Paddington, several miles away from the bustle of Fleet Street. There is also perhaps a reference to Sunday newspapers not being sold on the streets until after the morning services had finished at mid-day.

Letter 37

ROBERT BROWNING TO KATHARINE BRONSON

19, Warwick Crescent, W.
March 10. '85.

Dearest Mrs Bronson,—I had heard, with what mingled feelings you need not be told,—that you were in Paris and for what reason.[1] I do not venture to say a word: you know very well how any sorrow of yours must affect me: I refrain from even suggesting what may seem to be alleviations in this case: you will have resolved all the aspects of the case,—all I know is, I joy in your joy, grieve in your grief, accepting your estimate of both. I did not write to Venice at once, from my anxiety to give you some little time for the arrival of news from America,[2] either confirmatory of or in opposition to your apprehensions: I gather from the expressions in your letter that the news is favorable,—I trust so, at least. I shall hear from you when you feel able to gratify me, I know. Remember that Pen is at hand—Maison Lavenne, 1 rue du Départ, Gare Mont-Parnasse: if he can be of the least use to you, count upon him—I know he may be counted upon. He had information from a friend of yours, but desired me to say nothing about it—supposing that you might have reasons for wishing to remain undisturbed. But I shall leave off: no writing nor speaking, even, does justice to what I have in my heart to say—unless it is that I judge the event to have befallen happily for Edith,—whom I love, you know—as I love you, Dearest Mrs Bronson,

and ever shall be affectionately yours
Robert Browning.

Publication: None traced.
Manuscript: Armstrong Browning Library.

1. Arthur Bronson (1824–1885) had died on 2 March. He was buried in the cemetery of St. Germain-en-Laye, where Mrs. Bronson had the following lines inscribed on his tombstone:

> "His last conscious acts were those of loving kindness:
> His last conscious words were those of trust in God."

2. Presumably details concerning Mr. Bronson's will. As the event seems to have "befallen happily for Edith," one may assume she was a beneficiary.

Letter 38

ROBERT BROWNING TO KATHARINE BRONSON

19. Warwick Crescent, W
Apr. 8. '85.

Dearest Friend, this is not a letter, for I have this minute returned from a Funeral, in pitiless weather, and am unable either in body or soul, to write one such as I hope to do—with something of my warm self in it: but I find Burne Jones's pretty and touching letter, and want this leaf to serve as an envelope to what may please you—you who deserve so thoroughly that it should.[1] I will write in a day or two. I heard from Pen, poor fellow, this morning—he is at Dinant, being too ill to remain in Paris, but finds himself already better. He told me, and re-told me how good you had been to him. How I trust all is going well with you, certainly you need no assurance of. Enough that I love you with all my heart. Bless you and your Edith. It is an Edith—Procter's[2]—Barry Cornwall's daughter[3]—whom I have been following to her grave. Some fifty years ago, her father said to me, while caressing her, "Ah, Browning, *this* is the Poetry". "I know it"—"No, you know nothing about it." Well, if I was ignorant then, I am instructed now. So, dear Two Poems, long may I have you to "read" and to enjoy!

Yours affectionately ever
Robert Browning.

Address: Italy, Venice. / Mrs Bronson, / Cà Alvisi, / Canal Grande, / Venezia.
Publication: Whiting, p. 258.
Manuscript: Armstrong Browning Library.

1. On 6 April 1885 RB had written to Edward Burne-Jones and quoted from a letter from Mrs. Bronson about "his angels for the Church in Rome," a mosaic he had designed for the American church. Burne-Jones responded with the following letter which was enclosed in Browning's letter to Mrs. Bronson: "The Grange, West Kensington, W. / Very dear Browning / That was most kind of you to send me a comforting word about my mosaic—for indeed I designed it with a great deal of affection for it,—and when any one has asked me why I have no pictures to show this year, & I have answered 'because of my mosaic' they have all—all of them, said 'What a pity—what a waste' till I have grown abashed & silent about it—but I put the best that was in me into the design—for love of old mosaics, & pleasure at doing something to be set up in Italy—and hope that nice simple ignorant people might wander into the church and stare at it and ask questions and glee that for once a picture of mine would not have to listen to London gabble at a dinner party—so, see how welcome is this letter of yours—& thank that lady for me with all my heart for sending me such cheerful words, when no one else has cheered me—no, that isnt fair, the people who are executing it at Murano have comforted me mightily, but except for them I should be holding my head down. / I wont forget that you sent me this letter[.] / Your affe[ctiona]te. EB-J."

2. Bryan Waller Procter (1787–1874), who wrote under the name "Barry Cornwall," was a prolific poet, and later solicitor and barrister. Chiefly remembered today for a few songs and lyrics, he wrote longer poems which were successful in their time, such as *Dramatic Scenes* and *Marcian Colonna* (1820). Browning was a close friend from the 1830's and dedicated *Colombe's Birthday* to Procter in 1844 with the following words: "No one loves and honours Barry Cornwall more than does Robert Browning; who, having nothing better than this play to give him in proof of it, must say so." After Browning's marriage and departure for Italy, Procter looked after his financial affairs with Chapman and Hall, and with John Forster supervised the production of Browning's *Poems* of 1849 and chose the *Selections* of 1863. On his return to London in 1861, Browning became a regular visitor to Mrs. Procter's literary salon, held every Sunday at her apartment in Albert Mansions, 13 Upper Harley Street. The gatherings continued until her death in 1888.

3. Edythe Procter had been ill for some time, and, like her elder sister the poet Adelaide A. Procter, died of consumption. Three days earlier Browning had written to Mrs. Procter: "You may truly say 'I am sorry for you.' I can venture on no word of consolation your own good sense will not suggest: and what need is there to speak of the sympathy of us all? There is an end to great and hopeless suffering—that is our comfort" (Houghton). Edythe was buried at St.Mary's, Kensal Green, the Roman Catholic cemetery.

Letter 39

ROBERT & SARIANNA BROWNING TO KATHARINE BRONSON

[In RB's hand.]   Hôtel Delapierre, Gressoney St Jean,
                    Val d'Aosta, Italia.
                    Aug. [*sic* for September] 4. '85.

Dearest Friend, I write in the greatest haste so as to save a post, but I think I can put in this sheet all that you would not otherwise know: that I am incapable of one moment's forgetfulness of you—*that* you know sufficiently. My sister wrote to you just before we left London, more than a fortnight ago, and a few days after we arrived here—as we did on the 21.st You remember, this is the wild beautiful place whence we followed you to Venice two years ago,—as our hope was we should do once again. It will be heart-breaking if you are not in Venice, because we must go there even if you are absent: since Pen has arranged to precede us—in perhaps a fortnight—meaning to take a studio there and paint—a great object of his ambition—and we cannot disappoint the poor fellow: but what will Venice be without you!– All the same, don't fancy me so selfish that, if you needs must go, I and my sister will even wish to keep you from your duties—we thoroughly know how glad you would be to make us as happy as before:[1] still, but for Pen's mortification if we do not keep tryst with him, we should turn away our heads from the vacant shrine and departed glory—fine words but happening to be true. I believe Pen will be accompanied by a great friend of his, Peabody, who on returning to London a month ago, wrote to say that where Pen was, *he* would fain be,—and at once joined him at Dinant—whence I everyday expect to hear that they are leaving for Venice: of course their places of sojourn are altogether independent of our own,—but that we shall meet in the same place Pen counts upon—so go we must—but—

Well, dearest Friend, you will let us know as soon as you can what you determine upon,—and we will shape our course accordingly. The telegraph-wire connects us with the rest of the world,—a comfort which did not exist before. In the ordinary course of things we should leave here about the 1st of October—or even earlier: our mountain-tops—exclusive of Monte Rosa—are covered with snow this morning—rain in the valley, snow on the heights. Oh, I had so much to tell you! but "time is up." Still S., sitting by me, wants to put in a word. My last word can only be—God bless you, dearest Friend, and bless your Edith! I am ever your most affectionate

                                                            Robert Browning.

[Continued by Sarianna.]

Dearest Friend,   .

One line to add my special love—(I cannot say more with a dreadful steel pen)– I wrote to you just before leaving town—and again on arriving here. It will be a bitter disappointment to me if I do not see you in Venice. I have been longing so earnestly to see your darling face once more—but I know that we must all submit to what we cannot change. In any case our love and thoughts are always with you—Ever your affectionate,

                                                                            S.B.

Address: Austria / Mrs Bronson, / Bagni di Roncegno, / Trentino.
Publication: None traced.
Manuscript: Armstrong Browning Library.

1. Mrs. Bronson had gone to take the waters in Austria. Newly widowed, she did not wish to entertain in her usual style at Ca Alvisi that year. Browning's letter changed her mind, and she was back in Venice ready to receive him on 29 September.

Edith Bronson, 1880

Robert Browning, 1885

Letter 40

ROBERT BROWNING TO KATHARINE BRONSON

[Venice]
[ca. October 1885][1]

Dearest Friend, we are most anxious to know how Edith is this morning: we only have information at second or third hand from the servants. And we want also a word—just that—to tell us how yourself may be, after a night's watching: one word to

Yours affectionately ever
RB & S.B.

Publication: None traced.
Manuscript: Armstrong Browning Library.

1. This undated letter was written in late October 1885 when bad weather and illness had almost spoiled the Brownings' stay at the Palazzo Giustiniani-Recanati. Edith was ill first, followed by Sarianna, and finally Mrs. Bronson succumbed to a bad cold and cough. (Letter from RB to Miss Leigh Smith, 27 November 1885, ABL.) On 2 November Mrs. Bronson wrote to her friend Dr. Baldwin in Florence about Edith's illness which had almost passed (Morgan).

Letter 41

SARIANNA BROWNING TO KATHARINE BRONSON

19, Warwick Crescent, W.
[Late March-Early April 1886]

Dearest Mrs Bronson,

Robert has told you all about our Palace affairs,[1] and I turn to more cheering topics and say as well as I can, though not half strongly enough, how delighted we shall be to see you and dear Edith over here. I hope London will put off its fogs and do its best to give you a welcome.[2] I fear your Italian servants will not help you much, though on the other hand you are not used to English ones. We will do all we can—only too glad to be of any service.

Keep us apprized of your movements, and let us know when to look out for you.

I am glad to hear dear Mr. and Mrs. Curtis are looking so bright and well: they have been very kindly interested in our affairs.[3]

Pen, who has been working very hard in Paris, talked of going to Dinant for a little fresh air. He will be here some time in May.[4]

With true love to you both, I am always,

Your most affectionate,

Sarianna Browning.

Remember me to Giuseppina.

Publication: None traced.
Source: Transcript Rucellai.

1. Negotiations for buying the Palazzo Manzoni on the Grand Canal. Browning purchased the palace, which was situated next door to the former Albergo dell'Universo, in February 1886, and sent money to an Italian bank. The owner, the Marchese Montecuccoli, then refused to honour the agreement, so Browning was compelled to consider litigation.
2. The Spring of 1886 was unusually severe—"for five months not one wholly satisfactory day," wrote Browning to Mrs. FitzGerald on 10 April (*LL*, p. 190). For the Bronsons' visit to London, see Introduction, p. xxxiii.
3. The Curtises came to London in late June and kept Browning in touch with negotiations about the Palazzo Manzoni.
4. Pen arrived in London in May and returned to Dinant in mid-June, when Sarianna was recovering from a severe "inflammatory attack" which left her weak and exhausted.

Letter 42

ROBERT BROWNING TO KATHARINE BRONSON

19, Warwick Crescent, W.
Dec. 26. '86.

My dearest Friend,—if I have so long delayed writing, it was from believing in my heart that you would understand it was only because I hoped, week after week, to be in a condition to find myself as I ought to be when talking to you—quite happily removed from and forgetful of other cares. I expected Pen would leave Venice much earlier, and he kept promising "all the news" of the dear household: he only arrived on Christmas Eve. How I am brimful of gratitude to you for all the goodness he reports—and which needs not surprise me the thoroughly-experienced one—I cannot speak of properly,—though I thought to speak *somehow*. He brings your very charming present,—so unnecessary, so dear and precious! I have another reason for the putting off so long even this little sort of loving by letter. I had an attack, three weeks ago, which was more annoying in what it seemed to prognosticate than in its actual performance;[1]—and my poem, a more lengthy and elaborate affair than usual, had gone to the Publisher in a roughish state: I was apprehensive that I might be unable to correct the proofs properly—in which case, I should have destroyed the thing: but, by a good deal of resolute work—when work could be—I did all I thought wanting—and the last corrected proofs went off yesterday.[2] With this much writing to do,—and innumerable letters to answer,—which come thick and threefold in these latter days when I am least disposed to answer pleasant enquirers—the grasshopper is a burden,[3] and pen-and-ink a big grasshopper indeed. Dearest friend, you understand all this. I shall burn two thirds of my "correspondents" letters uncorresponded-to,—and make myself a breathing-space, wherein I can send my voice as I wish it to go—the heart behind it prompting—as now when it bids God bless you, my Dearest Friend—you and your Edith. I shall ever be your grateful and affectionate

Robert Browning.

Publication: None traced.
Manuscript: Armstrong Browning Library.

1. Diagnosed by his doctor as "Spasmodic Asthma," which could return every winter. In fact, it seems to have been little more than a bad wheezing cough and sore throat, and there is no evidence of its recurrence.

2. *Parleyings with Certain People of Importance in their Day*, published on 28 January 1887 in an edition of 2,500 copies, for which Browning was paid £250. The edition sold 2,064 copies in its first year.

3. Ecclesiastes 12:5.

Letter 43

ROBERT BROWNING TO KATHARINE BRONSON

19, Warwick Crescent, W.
Jan. 14. '87.

My own dearest friend, I am not going to let another gap deform our correspondence if I can help it: your letter comes this morning, and I say my little say about it at once. Goethe commends a wise somebody for never opening the letter just received, till he had opened desk, placed paper, and laid pen in readiness for a dip,—so as to begin his answer without a minute's delay: so one should do, perhaps: but there is a pleasant quiet "rumination" of the contents—lost by forthwith swallowing them. First, I want to reassure your goodness about the health of my Sister and myself: we are both ourselves again—*I*, alto[ge]ther,—she very nearly. There were some symptoms in my case that promised to develop into something ugly—but they are gone altogether. Possibly the abstention from a dose of the divine air, the whole long Autumn and early winter through, may have rendered each of us, in our respective ways, more sensitive with regard to this bitter season that began so early. The days lengthen, however; even brighten somewhat: and I daresay we shall come out like old snakes to feel the spring weather. Now for you: I don't call "trivialities" the constant business of happy-making which engages you, though it must be onerous enough. At this season, there is no harm in your needing to be punctually at home by 5.—but I grudge the summer afternoons which you cut short—and into which the occupied mornings extend perhaps. As for your "walking"—non é più come era prima![1] You ask if "I was disappointed by Pen's vain endeavour to find a palace": it was a strange misconception on his part that I wanted *any* abode in Venice, and not simply a palace for him which I could occasionally occupy. The first we thought to purchase would have answered our wishes in all respects: you know how our wishes came to nothing: *then*—the temptation of buying the other magnificent affair was entertained by Pen and only resisted by me (on his account) when I found the price would be far more than I could prudently pay. *That* renounced, I never thought that the enquiries he was making about other houses were other than a matter of mere curiosity. I am bound by too many ties to London, for such a complete disassociation from it as would be involved by constant residence anywhere else. I suppose that you made him too happy in Venice,—well for *him*, any how. He arrived on Christmas Eve, and left two days ago—having been far from well: indeed, the English climate has never suited him: but he has never been too long tried by it, and may choose his field of operation when I have done with mine. I heard from him satisfactorily this morning.

You know how we are affected here by the sudden death of L.[d] Iddesleigh[2]—one of the kind acquaintances whom I met but seldom; enjoyed meeting always: it stops—for the moment—the political noise all about.

The "dear book" (it reminds me of the beginning of a letter once reported to me—"Dere Tunnicliff—I calls you—'dere,' because you are so in your shop:") dear or cheap, it is out of my hands now, and only waits the expedition of your American printers, being bound to appear at the same time with their edition—for which they *pay*, properly.[3]

There is very various matter, and—with your divine indulgence,—it will go hard but something shall interest you: in any case, keep me in mind as ever your loving friend,—and Edith's too: I am happy in believing you will,—knowing myself to be ever affectionately

yours
Robert Browning

Publication: The Century Magazine, May 1912, 128–129.
Manuscript: Armstrong Browning Library.

1. It is not as it used to be.
2. Stafford Northcote, 1st Earl of Iddesleigh (1818–1887), Conservative statesman, was at the time of his death Foreign Secretary in Lord Salisbury's administration, having previously been Chancellor of the Exchequer and Leader of the Commons for Disraeli. Iddesleigh had collapsed suddenly in 10 Downing Street two days earlier. His unexpected death had temporarily quietened all political animosity while members of both parties paid him their respects.
3. *Parleyings* was published in America by Houghton, Mifflin and Company, who paid £100. From the contract submitted by Smith, Elder, now in the Houghton Library, it is clear that the American publishers considered this sum excessive and agreed reluctantly. One of the directors has written across it: "The amount seems too large, but to identify us as Browning's publisher and in view of the new edition, it seems best to accept the offer." On 15 January Browning signed a typed statement that Houghton, Mifflin were his authorized publishers in the U.S.A., which goes further than the statement printed in the first American edition that Houghton, Mifflin were merely the authorized publishers of *Parleyings*. Obviously the Americans wanted their money's worth!

Letter 44

ROBERT BROWNING TO KATHARINE BRONSON

19, Warwick Crescent, W.
Feb. 28. '87.

Dearest Mrs Bronson,—let us begin to talk together,—oh, that it could be *a quattr' occhi!*[1] I delayed answering at once, because there was another enterprise just engaging me, and so bent was I on not renewing the worry of last year by telling you of a purchase which proved no purchase at all, that I kept even Pen in ignorance of what I was busied about until I could inform him the thing was done and not simply dreamed about. The illness of my sister determined my laziness to act as it would have advantageously done so long ago: and I have bought a house—Oh, sad descent in dignity—not on *Canal Grande*—the beloved and ever to be regretted—but Kensington[2]– It is a nearly new one, and situated just where I wish: and in consequence of the temporary depreciation of that kind of property, I believe I have done very well. The search for the place was managed by my sister,—and the bargaining effected, with all zeal and abundant intelligence, by my kind and experienced Publisher— George Smith.[3] I was more than fearful that his diligent examinations, and the surveyor's lordly ideas of propriety from attic to basement would wreck the negotiation,—but all is concluded happily and I have just sent the specification of matters agreed upon to the Lawyer. All this, of course, is for Pen,—I should not have been at the trouble to secure a little more comfort merely for the remainder of my own life: so, I secure him a good freehold property which cannot well lose its value in time to come. He must himself look out for a Venetian Palazzo, "in other Summers which I shall not see." The work at the house will be begun at once—but there must follow no moving-in for some couple of months at earliest,—so pray do not direct a letter to me otherwise than heretofore, until I am fairly a resident at 29. De Vere Gardens. The street parallel with and next to that where Millais lives—you may know. As for the wretched Montecuccoli rascals, I have fortunately ended my struggle with the verminous family,—have paid their costs and my own,—strangely moderate, according to English notions—and am under great obligations to M.ʳ Bascheria [*sic*] for his conduct of the whole affair. [4] Therefore, dearest Friend, if my good fortune [*sic*] takes me again to Venice, I shall put myself under that warmest of motherly wings, the Giustinian-Recanati— How could I ever fancy it possible to wander elsewhere—forgetting La Fontaine and "les Deux Pigeons"! [5] All is for the best, I see. I leave myself little room for certain little bits of news I could wish to put down. The Layards are here, I have met them once—shall meet them to-morrow: they make no long stay here, I think. Pen is in Paris, working hard for both the "Salon" and our Grosvenor Gallery: he sees more of our Venetian acquaintances than I do—Forbes, Julian S[tory]., and others. Yesterday I met a young handsome man who spoke to me as having "met me at your house in *Venice*." I *think*: unluckily, I could not remember his name,—and how can one blurt out that fact in the face of somebody who seems to be intimate with every inch of you?

Be good and gladden me with an account of yourself,—and all that concerns you: how is Edith? Nay, how is poor Giovanni? [6] And his mother? And who are enjoying Venice,—this day of sunshine even here? Do you ever walk now? Not a word you can spare me but will go to my heart. God bless you, dearest Friend! I am ever affectionately yours

Robert Browning.

Publication: None traced.
Manuscript: Armstrong Browning Library.

1. Face to face.
2. 29 De Vere Gardens, opposite Kensington Gardens, near the Royal Albert Hall. Browning had Henry James as a neighbour; the American novelist rented No. 34 from 1886 to 1898.
3. George Murray Smith (1824–1901), Browning's successful and loyal publisher, not only helped to purchase the new house but was also responsible for some of the

interior decoration. For an account of Browning's relationship with Smith, see Michael Meredith, "Browning and the Prince of Publishers," *BIS*, 7, 1–19.

4. Browning gives the details of the low costs of withdrawing from the Manzoni Palace debacle in a letter to Mrs. Skirrow (*NL*, p. 340): "My own advocate had claims on me for previous and subsequent work. Adverse Party's charges 309 F[ran]cs, 55 cent[essime]—or £12.7s– My Lawyer's ditto—403 f[ran]cs—or £16.2.6d." On 8 February 1887 Browning paid his lawyer, Antonio Baschiera, £30.6.3d, which doesn't quite tally with the figures quoted above.

5. La Fontaine in his fable "The Two Pigeons" advocates the advantages of staying at home with one's loved one rather than wandering abroad. In the fable one of the pigeons decides it wants to broaden its experience, so flies away for three days, during which it is assailed by worldly dangers: the weather, nets, a vulture and stones from a catapult. Returning to its mate, it decides that travel is a mistake and that the nest is best.

6. Giovanni—unidentified.

Letter 45

ROBERT BROWNING TO KATHARINE BRONSON

29. De Vere Gardens. W.
June 20. '87.

Dearest Friend, we are at least partially installed in the new house[1]—as above. Few things have been more troublesome than the overlooking and underordering (S. having done the main business all along, and as well done as energetically.) There is plenty of work to get through still, but I believe the worst is over. We all—(Pen being here)—all like the place—and the situation could hardly be better. I daresay you associate a removal, from a house one has inhabited for twenty five years, with sad feelings—so much time ill-spent, opportunities neglected, hopes destroyed, and so forth: but I was supremely wretched when I entered into possession, and had no other hope than that of getting out of London as soon as possible: how time has slipt away! and but for the menaced invasion of the railroad I might be constant to the old place till I went elsewhere "for good" it is to be hoped: there[2]—here—and, I trust, elsewhere also, I shall be ever yours lovingly.

No words of mine can describe the crowds and noise to-day,[3]—and to-morrow will be more than its match. Your Fêtes, by all accounts, were charming—ours are going to be at least enormous: "The mountain sheep are sweeter—but the valley sheep are fatter."[4] I escape altogether by going to Oxford to-morrow for next day's "Commemoration": ah, last year![5] They make, among others, Story a D.C.L. I expected to hear that our Master,[6] who entertains me, could not undergo the fatigue,—he having been seriously ill: but he writes this morning a few kind words to say he "reminds me of my promise to come"—and go I will. The respected authorities who distribute the admissions to the Abbey "for the representatives of all classes",—not considering that Poets are of any importance as having done something towards the illustration of the last fifty years,—send none to the "likes of me"—whereupon the good Dean of Westminster wrote indignantly to say "*he* had a right to some places for his family, and meant to take me as his Grandson!"[7]—which pretty offer I declined with true thanks. And *at the same time* the Prince pleases to apply to me for "a poem to be set to music by Sullivan on the occasion of the Queen's laying the first stone of the Imperial Institute"—Tennyson having shirked Laureate-duty,—which I did not know, although in no case would I have written such a thing to order. After all,Tennyson,—goaded, I suppose,—tacked a couple of verses on to his "Secular Ode",—such as, it seems, even his name and fame could not help to acceptance: this comes of engaging to do what no true poet ought to attempt: so the Prince betakes himself to the proper person "of general utility" who will suit the occasion exactly—Mr Lewis Morris.[8] Tennyson is as able as ever to write transcendently when the mood is propitious: I could never understand how he came to wear the livery and take the wages.[9] If *he* had chosen to say "I am ill at these numbers,"[10]—"do *you* try and help me to get done," I would have *tried*, probably. Well,—Storys, both, are here—I met them at dinner on Saturday: and some sixty thousand Americans,—so affirms the Minister. Our weather is for once magnificent: and I hope they will enjoy the show as I shall the absence of it. And you—*not* here, nor dear Edith: in your letter to me there is no mention of her, but much in that to S. I do not even know if she was with you during that strange burst of storm,—comparable to an earthquake,—which you describe so graphically. Do not wait long to tell me—tell *all* here—how she is– I met Vernon Lee[11] yesterday at dinner, but could not get a word out of her across the table. I am up here, at the top of the house, alone—but I know Pen and S. love you heartily. And as for me—why say more than that I am yours—ever yours

RB.

While I write, two men are hammering—and otherwise confusing what of intelligence is left in me by household cares. Venice, Venice—and again Venice!

Address: Italy, Venice. / Mrs Bronson, / Casa Alvisi, / Canal Grande, / Venezia.
Publication: Ward, Vol. 2, pp. 287–288 (in part).
Manuscript: Armstrong Browning Library.

1. The Brownings moved into De Vere Gardens on 17 June, having paid the full purchase price of £5,000 on 3 June. Sarianna had supervised the redecoration and the

installation of furniture since early March. She had found a welcome friend in Anne Procter, then in her eighty-ninth year. On hearing that the Brownings were moving, Mrs. Procter had written to Sarianna on 5 March: "It is impossible to tell you how delighted I am to hear that you and your brother are coming to be neighbours. . . . Every day at half past one, I dine and I want you to do me the kindness to come and make your luncheon. . . . The work people are *never* punctual and you will be kept waiting. We are so near, that you can easily come. You will find a plain joint hot & a simple Pudding. . . . You will then return renovated for your business—having done me a great kindness" (ABL).

2. An anticipation of the last verse of "Epilogue" to *Asolando*.

3. The streets of London were decorated with flowers, flags and bunting for Queen Victoria's Golden Jubilee on Tuesday 21 June. In the evening there were illuminations and fireworks. Thousands of people came into the capital to join the celebrations, which included processions and the lighting of beacons on surrounding hills. A children's fête for 30,000 was held in Hyde Park on the 22nd, at which each child received a meat pie, a piece of cake, an orange and a mug.

4. Thomas Love Peacock: "The War-Song of Dinas Vawr."

5. Mrs. Bronson was present at the Oxford celebration in 1886. She stayed with Edith at the Randolph Hotel opposite Balliol College, where Browning had his own rooms and was the guest of the Master and Fellows.

6. Benjamin Jowett (1817–1893), acknowledged as the most influential Master of Balliol of the nineteenth century. Appointed Fellow in 1838 before completing Finals, he became Tutor in Classics in 1840 and Master in 1870. He was Vice-Chancellor of the University from 1882 to 1886, and Regius Professor of Greek from 1855 to his death. He and Browning were always on cordial terms, even though Jowett did not fully appreciate Browning's poetry and preferred Tennyson's. The illness from which he was suffering in 1887 was brought about by the extra work he had undertaken as Vice-Chancellor. It seemed at first merely a common cold but lingered for months and became an infection of the lungs.

7. Browning had not been invited to the Jubilee Thanksgiving Service in Westminster Abbey on 21 June. Dean Bradley had written to him on 2 June: "Is it conceivable that you have not had a ticket from the Lord Chamberlain? If he does not give you one you really must come as my *grandson!* Truly yours, G.G. Bradley. I have a right to take my family!" (Edward R. Moulton-Barrett.)

8. Lewis Morris (1833–1907), poetaster and barrister, wrote two books of popular poetry, *Songs of Two Worlds* (1871–75) and *The Epic of Hades* (1876). Their success led him to produce more books of optimistic and moralistic verse, almost all of which has now been forgotten. He befriended Tennyson and was disappointed not to succeed him as Poet Laureate. However, he was knighted in 1895, the Queen presumably appreciating his efforts at writing occasional verse, some of which dealt with her and members of her family.

9. Browning's criticism of Tennyson as Poet Laureate echoes that which he made of Wordsworth forty years previously in "The Lost Leader."

10. Shakespeare: *Hamlet*, II, ii, 119.

11. Vernon Lee, pen name of Violet Paget (1856–1935), a writer of culture and wide tastes. Her best books are those she wrote on the Italian Renaissance, but she also wrote delightful travel books, a novel and plays. She lived for most of her life in Florence in a villa on the hillside. She first met Browning in 1882 and corresponded with him, sending him a copy of one of her books. In return he mentions her in the poem "Inapprehensiveness" in *Asolando*. Miss Paget was also a friend of Mrs. Bronson. After Browning's death, Mrs. Bronson gave her a locket which had belonged to the poet, and Violet Paget was moved to write: "The thought of possessing anything which belonged to Mr. Browning is very sweet to me. I have always kept preciously some flowers he once gave me out of his buttonhole three or four years ago . . . I was so surprised and delighted to find my name in *Asolando*" (Meredith).

Letter 46

ROBERT BROWNING TO KATHARINE BRONSON

29. De Vere Gardens. W.
May 10. '88.

Dearest Friend, it was indeed a joy to hear directly from you, two days ago, and not merely through people more or less recently arrived from your Venice,—where you were *not* when the Layards, for instance, arrived last week. We got your letter from Amalfi,—the place I have never seen, though I looked hard in its direction from the Isles of the Siren,[1]—and my sister replied to it at once,—then—silence from you! which, it seems now, was imposed by the wretched Post Office there: nothing came—and, besides the lost letter, you speak of a photograph of Taormina: I had thought that these obliquities of the Post-office were things of the Past. But it never was, in the Past, never shall be, in the Future, the way of us your two lovers to receive a sign of reciprocated love in a letter, and put aside gratitude till a more convenient opportunity. S. must tell you of the visit of our Couple,[2]—how it came to an end in due time, how they went to Paris and stayed there till three days ago, and how we hear by Post-card that they are at Milan,—soon to be at Venice. So, you are to be parted from your and our dear Edith[3]—for her good, I am absolutely sure, or no parting would be. That she is quite well again is glad news indeed—but how will her sweet earnest face be detachable, in my mind, from the chair, and the sofa,—and, on festive occasions, from the recess I see so plainly—as I hear the soft Venetian trolled so archly and prettily from the pouting lips! Oh, give her my love—for what it is worth—to be remembered at least as very perfect in its kind. And you,—why am I to hear that the cough continues, perhaps increases? I sat by L.Y Layard last evening at dinner,—and enquired all I could: I gathered that you forget your promise to take exercise, or exercise enough. Where shall you go next? Shall you be in Venice later on? I carefully abstain from engaging to dispose of my time, but *if* we go to Venice may we hope to be be [*sic*] taken close to you as before? You may suppose what Pen and his wife desire and require of us: but *if* Venice is to be visited, and *if* the Palazzo is untenanted, and if .. but there is no other possible cause for fear: so I say, in these cases, we should go to you. But the going is altogether an unpledged affair: though while I write,—with all the pleasant days back again, it seems hardly realizable that another year should be added to the two that have passed away since I saw you with these eyes—not of the mind!

Seeing you thus,—or as I even now see you, I know I love you dearly and wish you all the good in the world and out of it—being ever yours affectionately

Robert Browning.

Publication: None traced.
Manuscript: Armstrong Browning Library.

1. Mrs. Bronson had been on holiday in Southern Italy and Sicily. The only time Browning could have looked in the direction of Amalfi was in late August 1844 when his boat docked at Naples. The Isles of the Siren are three rocky, uninhabited islands near the south side of Cape Misenum, off the coast of Campania. According to tradition, they were the home of the Sirens.
2. Pen and Fannie. Pen had married Fannie Coddington (1853–1935) on 4 October 1887.
3. Edith went to America to attend the wedding of her uncle Charles de Kay to Edwalyn Coffey in June 1888. She was particularly fond of this uncle, only a few years her senior, and the transatlantic holiday gave her a pleasant opportunity to visit family and friends in New York (where her grandmother Janet de Kay lived on Staten Island) and Newport.

Letter 47

ROBERT BROWNING TO KATHARINE BRONSON

29. De Vere Gardens. W.
Aug. 8. '88.

Oh, no, dearest friend, I am in no danger of your thinking that I forget you—much less of such a catastrophe's actual occurrence as that I myself can ever forget. The writing about what I feel has got, within this last year or two, to suffer sensibly from the daily dismal business of writing to everybody and nobody about matters which, at the best, do not interest me at all, and generally weary me past the saying with words. Books come with letters about them, rarely less than two daily, and it may seem an easy matter to dispose of a few goodnatured thanks and wishes, but the writers are shrewd, and sometimes will not be so put off. The other day a poetaster who, on the strength of having dedicated his book to me, has returned to the charge again and again,[1] "wanting definite opinions of its merit,"—this worthy on getting no satisfactory answer, reminded me that I had a different character for affability and sympathy with young attempters of verse from that of Tennyson "who has brought contempt and hatred on his white hairs by his callousness on the subject." This time he got an "opinion" so definite as to silence him altogether. So much for why, when I rise up after two hours exercise of the pen in this

unprofitable way, it seems to me that a single "Magari" sent over the sea
to you the beloved of Venice is worth whole reams of printed assurance
that if I had wings like a sea-gull I would fly thither and be at rest alongside
of Cà Alvisi. I write often enough to the Pens,—but that, not to speak
profanely, is as the Catholic does, who having taken and kept the pledge
generally to abstain from wine, takes a little regularly in the way of
religion.

Dearest, we have at last—only yesterday—*fully* determined on
joining the Couple at Primiero,[2] and, when the heats abate, going on to
Venice for a short stay. May the stay be with you as heretofore? I don't
feel as if I could go elsewhere or do otherwise: although in the case of
any arrangements having been made which stand in the way, there is the
obvious Hôtel Suisse. I suppose that at need there could be found a
successor to poor Giuseppina—whose misfortunes I commiserate[3]—You
know exactly how much and how little we want. But if I am to get any
good out of my visit I must lead the quietest of lives, and be lulled by
the cigarette-smoke of just my friend—not the *chiacchere*[4] of new acquaintance. We purpose setting out next Monday—the 13.th—Bâle,
Milan,—Padua, Trevigi,—Feltre,—Primiero:—by the week's end.

I have been nearly eleven months in Town,—with an exceptional
four days' visit to Oxford: and hard social work all the while, indeed up
to the latest when, three weeks ago, I found it impossible to keep going.
Don't think that the kindness which somewhat oppresses me while in
Town forgets me afterward—I have pressing invitations to the most
attractive places in England, Scotland, Ireland,—but "c'est admirable,
mais ce n'est pas la paix."[5] May I count on the "paix" where I so much
enjoyed it? I hear with delight that Edith will be with you again: *that*
completes the otherwise incompleteness.

Yes, the "Rezzonico"[6] is what you Americans call a "big thing"—and
I wish my Pen and his wife all successfull possession of it. But the interest
I take in the acquisition is different altogether from what accompanied
the earlier attempts at one: I have no responsability [*sic*],—look on
approvingly—as by all accounts I am warranted in doing—but there an
end. Perhaps something more may come,—if all goes well, who knows?

So, dearest friend, "*al rivederci*"! Give my love to Edith, and tell
her I hope in her keeping her kindness for me, spite of the claims on it
of all the others,—no end of others,—who must have gained a right to
it since I left her. And my Sister,—not one word of her! Somehow you
must know her more thoroughly than poor battered me, tugged at and
torn to pieces—metaphorically—by so many sympathizers real or pretended. She wants change—probably more than I do: and, but for her, I
believe I should continue here—with the Gardens[7] for my place of

healing. How she will enjoy the sight of you, if it may be! Tell me what is to be hoped, or feared, or despaired of—at Pen's address whatever it may be. And remember me ever as most affectionately yours

Robert Browning.

Publication: Whiting, pp. 271–272 (in part).
Manuscript: Armstrong Browning Library.

1. Browning echoes the sentiments of Alexander Pope in his *Epistle to Dr. Arbuthnot* (lines 7–10), who similarly protests about importunate poets:

> What Walls can guard me, or what Shades can hide?
> They pierce my Thickets, thro' my Grot they glide,
> By land, by water, they renew the charge,
> They stop the Chariot, and they board the Barge.

2. Primiero in the Austrian Tyrol, where Pen was painting.

3. Giuseppina, in spite of her misfortunes, looked after the Brownings later in the year as usual.

4. Idle chatter.

5. An adaptation of Maréchal Bosquet's words after the Charge of the Light Brigade, "C'est magnifique, mais ce n'est pas la Guerre."

6. Pen completed his purchase of the grandiose Palazzo Rezzonico on the Grand Canal on 3 September, and spent the next few years restoring and furnishing it successfully. The Palazzo was built in the seventeenth and eighteenth centuries, and was the home of Cardinal Carlo Rezzonico, later Pope Clement XIII.

7. Presumably Kensington Gardens in Hyde Park, which are situated at the end of De Vere Gardens. Here Browning could walk and sit by the Serpentine or the Round Pond in summer weather.

Letter 48

ROBERT BROWNING TO KATHARINE BRONSON

Albergo Gilli, Primiero.
Aug. 21. '88.

Dearest Friend, my arrival on Thursday evening was made happy by your letter. We had a painful journey, for I started anything but well, the passage was the roughest I remember, and the subsequent journey by day and night to Bâle, in the hottest of weather, an ugly business enough: at Milan I found myself better, and the next two days' journeyings to Vicenza and Feltre were easily managed. We found our Couple had done their utmost to make us comfortable,—and they—in combination with the pleasant place and satisfactory accomodations [*sic*] —have quite succeeded in doing so. I am convinced that in London I was slowly dying of asphyxia,—and the mere admittance of fresh air into my exhausted receiver set all to rights at once,—I am absolutely well again: and my Sister, who needed change as much as I did, feels the benefit equally. I heard, on arriving, that we were to be pitied for not going on to S. Martino,—"higher up and more picturesque": but I have no wish for any improvement in the present state of things: and here I hope to stay[1] till the proper time for a return to Venice—*when*—oh, what a Venice would it be if I went elsewhere than to the beloved Friend who calls me so kindly! My stay will be short—but *sweet* in every sense of the word, if I find her in good health, and, in all other respects, just as I left her:—"no change" meaning what it does to me who remember her goodness so well. It will be delightful to meet Edith again,—if only it may be that she arrives while we are yet with you,—even before, perhaps.

Can I tell you anything about our journey except that it was no agreeable one? On the first evening, as I stepped outside our carriage for a moment,—I caught sight of a well-known face. "Dr Butler, surely." (You have heard of his marriage the other day to a learnedst of young ladies, who beat all the men last year at Greek.) He insisted on introducing me to her,—I had seen her once before without undergoing that formality,—and accordingly I shook hands with a sprightly young person, pretty, and grand-daughterly: she is, however, only twenty-six years or so his junior.[2] Then, this happened: the little train from Monte Belluna to Feltre was crowded,—we could find no room except in a smoking carriage—wherein I observed a goodnatured elderly gentleman—an Italian, I took for granted. Presently he said "Can I offer you an English paper?"– "What, are you English?"– "Oh, yes—and I know *you*—who are going to see your son at Primiero".– "Why,—who can you be?"– "One who has seen *you* often." "Not—surely, Mr Malcolm?"[3]– "Well, nobody else." So ensued an affectionate greeting—he having been the guardian-angel of Pen in all his chafferings about the purchase of the palazzo. He gave me abundance of information, and satisfied me on many points. I had been anxious to write and thank him as he deserved,—but this proved an easier and more graceful way,—for a beginning at least.

Pen & his wife are as one could wish in every respect. He is at work on a pretty picture,[4] a peasant-girl whom he picked up in the neighbourhood; and his literal treatment stands him in good stead: he is reproducing her cleverly—at any rate, he takes pains enough.

How I must have tried your eyes with this "intimate" writing or scratching of mine: you know that, when so minded, I can manage better—and larger: but the desire of getting *close* spoils the intended calligraphy. Hear a conundrum to the point. "What is Freezing-point?— 32°. What is Squeezing-point? Two in the shade:" and this is the shade, and here are you and I,—and the squeezed writing follows of necessity—and desists through discretion.

Dearest Friend, shall I exact too much if I ask you to write again,—not immediately, but when you are generously disposed—no, that would be tantamount to asking you to write at once. Write when Edith is about to come, and the gladness of your heart will be wanting to communicate itself where it is sure to find a welcome. My Sister bade me just now give you her love—take mine (as if you had it not already!) and remember me

ever as affectionately yours

Robert Browning.

Publication: Whiting, pp. 272–273 (in part).
Manuscript: Armstrong Browning Library.

    1. The Brownings arrived at Primiero on 16 August and left for Venice on 12 September.
    2. The Revd. Henry Montagu Butler, D.D. (1833–1918), Master of Trinity College, Cambridge, from 1886, and previously Headmaster of Harrow School (1859–85). His second marriage, in 1888, was to Agnata Ramsay. In his youth he had been a good cricketer and a sturdy mountaineer, specializing in scaling mountain peaks which had a classical or religious significance. Since he was a vigorous man, tall and long-bearded, it was not surprising that he should choose an intelligent, younger woman as his second wife. Dr. Butler was a pall-bearer at Browning's funeral.
    3. Alexander Malcolm, an English solicitor living in Venice, who helped Pen negotiate the purchase of the Palazzo Rezzonico, and later became a friend. He was greatly interested in the history of Venice and helped Mrs. Bronson in the research for her article "Lost Islands of the Lagoon," which remains unpublished. Over 100 pages of manuscript remain at La Mura, some of it in Malcolm's hand. Malcolm died in Venice 22 January 1893 and was buried next to his father in the Protestant cemetery on the island of S. Michele.
    4. This picture has been lost and may never have been completed. A year later Sarianna was urging Pen to finish it, instead of continuing a portrait he was painting of her. See *Reconstruction*, K51.

Letter 49

ROBERT BROWNING TO KATHARINE BRONSON

Primiero,

Sept. 3. '88.

Dearest Friend, how good you have been with your telegram and letter![1] I waited till the arrangements of my Couple here should allow me to be tolerably sure of the day when we proceed to Venice—and, as it now appears, that day will be the 10th or 12th of the present month. Pen goes to complete his purchase, sign and seal &c, this afternoon, but will return in a day or two to finish a picture he has been employed upon: and we shall profit (physically) by a little more of this delightful air. We had torrents of rain for the last day and a half,—but the weather cleared up at noon: and this early morning is perfectly cloudless—showing a dazzling couch of snow on the mountain-peaks opposite my window: so that I hope my Sister and myself may complete—what indeed lacks little of completion—our cure of all London ailments. This will be given you by Pen in person,—and pray tell him what you can of yourself,—how you feel after what you call a fatiguing journey. I quite understand your interest in Ferrara: through circumstances, I was a long while before I could go there, although often tantalizingly near the place: and when I at last managed to fulfil my desires, my expectation was exceeded. [2]

Dearest friend, it is indeed a delight to expect a meeting so soon. Be good and mindful of how simple our tastes and wants are, and how they have been far more than satisfied by the half of what you provided to content them. I shall have nothing to do but to enjoy your company,— not even the little business of improving my health,—since *that* seems perfect. I hear you do not "walk," as in the old days,—I count upon setting that right again. O Venezia—benedetta.

I am in my room, have seen nobody, but everybody will ask me presently "Did you give our best love?"

Keep mine, Dearest friend,—for what can I give that you do not possess already?

Ever yours

Robert Browning.

Publication: Whiting, p. 286 (in part, as 1889).
Manuscript: Armstrong Browning Library.

1. Presumably these suggested arrangements for Browning's arrival in Venice, but one must almost certainly have acknowledged a present of "Love-in-the-Mist" flowers sent by Browning on 30 August.
2. Browning travelled extensively in Northern Italy, particularly in the years when he and Elizabeth were living in Florence, but somehow his excursions never brought him to Ferrara, a city which played an important part in *Sordello* and in which he set "My Last Duchess." It was not until 1880 that he visited Ferrara for the first time when he made a southern detour on his return to London from Venice.

Letter 50

ROBERT BROWNING TO KATHARINE BRONSON

Primiero,

Sept. 10. '88.

Dearest Friend,

We leave on Wednesday[1]—by the train from Feltre, which starts at 1. p.m. and arrives at Venice at 5.16.

How happy we shall be to see you again,—why attempt to say—
or why send love which is likely so soon to deliver itself?

Ever yours
Robert Browning.

Publication: None traced.
Manuscript: Armstrong Browning Library.

1. On 12 September. In her Diary-Calendar Mrs. Bronson entered their arrival in
Venice as on 5 September. Perhaps Browning and Sarianna lingered a week longer at
Primiero than she expected? She correctly marks their departure as 11 December. One
possible reason for delay was to wait until Pen had completed legal formalities to take
possession of the Palazzo Rezzonico.

Letter 51

ROBERT BROWNING TO KATHARINE BRONSON

[Venice]
Nov. 24 '88.

Dearest Friend, I shall not try for words to say what I feel. You know
how dearly I love and ever shall love you.

Here is a poor little token of an affection neither poor nor little: and
just as I found it impossible to complete the set by a sixth article,[1] so I
want the way of giving them value by anything I can write beyond a
simple—God bless you![2]

Yours, yours and yours again—
Robert Browning.

Publication: None traced.
Manuscript: Armstrong Browning Library.

1. This present is for Mrs. Bronson's Saint's Day, on 25 November (St. Katherine
of Alexandria). It is possible that Browning gave her the first five volumes of the
1888–89 collected edition of his poems, all of which had been printed before he left
England. The sixth and seventh were published while he was travelling. Mrs. Bronson's
complete set, however, is signed and dated 28 November 1889. This does not necessarily
rule out the theory, because the date could have been added later. There is nothing dated
25 November 1888, among the many mementoes Browning gave her.
2. Sarianna also sent a gift the following day. Her covering note reads: "To the
dearest and best of all Saint Katherine's—from her loving devotee / Sarianna."

Letter 52

ROBERT & SARIANNA BROWNING TO KATHARINE BRONSON

[In RB's hand.]   29. De Vere Gardens, W.
                                                   Dec. 15. '88.

Dearest friend,—I may just say *that*, and no more: for what can I say? I shall never have your kindness out of my thoughts,—and you never will forget me, I know. We shall please you by telling you our journey was quite prosperous,—wonderfully fine weather till it ended in grim London and its fog and cold: (at Bâle there was cold, but the sun made up for everything.) We altered our plans so far as to sleep and stay through the long day at Bâle,—visiting the museum, Cathedral &c,—and went on by nighttrain in a sleeping-car whereof we were the sole occupants—to Calais directly. At Dover, the Officials were prepared for us, would not look at the luggage (the bag & valise) and were very helpful as well as courteous,—and at London orders had been given to treat us with all possible good nature: they would not let us open any box but that where the Lamp was packed,[1]—offered to take our word for the weight,—and finally asked me "since there were three portions, would I accept the weight of the little vessel at bottom as that of the other two? "Rather"—as Pen says: so they declared it to weigh,—that is, the whole Lamp,—less than a quarter of what it does weigh—even then requiring assurance that I was "quite satisfied." We were to be looked after first of all the passengers, and so got away early enough, to find things at home in excellent order. The drawback to all this successful adventure was in my feeling unwell, besides suffering from a plague of a tooth—which, this morning, my capital Dentist,[2]—qualified by his American teaching,—has set nearly right already,—and is promised to begone in a day or two: the general feverishness (I can hardly see what I try to scribble) will soon vanish with it. Now, dearest, I have put down the main points,—in a fashion that surely will encourage you to "gossip" to my heart's content— sure as you must be, that I shall never see the word "Venice" without a rising of that heart at the memory of *you* there,—of the gondola, the Lido, the antichità-shops, all saturated with you. And my beloved Edie, the guitar, Ya-ha-bibi,—don't let me get foolish on paper about it. Let S. take up the tale, and do better. Yes, I forgot that poem in the drawer,[3]— will you either send it, or copy and send, for I have no other remains of it, on paper or memory. Dearest friends,—Edie my beloved being never disassociated from you,—bless you—I wish I could—love you—I know I do and shall ever.

                                                   Your RB.

29, De Vere Gardens

Drawing Room in the Palazzo Rezzonico, 1890

[Continued by Sarianna.]

Dearest Friend,

With scarcely a minute before post time, I send a hasty line to try to express the impossible—how much I love you, and how deeply I feel all your great kindness. Every hour of the day I miss you, and wish I were with you and dear Edith again in beloved Casa Alvisi. Robert will have told you, no doubt, all about our very successful journey, only damped by his suffering severely from tooth ache. The weather was glorious till we steamed into a dense fog as we approached black London. We breakfasted by gas light, and candles assisted the midday! I will write again very soon, more composedly. Meanwhile, give my best love to dear Edith, and remember me always to the good Giuseppina.

Ever your loving
S.B.

Publication: Whiting, pp. 277–278 (in part).
Manuscript: Armstrong Browning Library.

1. A silver Jewish "Sabbath Lamp" bought from Morchio, a Venetian antique dealer for 450 francs, and mentioned by Mrs. Orr (p. 377). After the poet's death it hung in Pen's dining room at Asolo, where it was sold in 1913.

2. Browning's dentist at this time was a Mr. Kluht. Browning had consulted him just before leaving for Italy, but broke a tooth at Primiero, which became infected a few days before he returned home.

3. "White Witchcraft," dated Primiero, 30 August 1888. Mrs. Bronson sent the original (now lost) back to Browning and kept a copy for herself. This has a number of textual variants and shows the poem at its earliest stage of composition. The copy remains in the Fossi collection and is reprinted on page 1 of the Introduction.

Letter 53

ROBERT BROWNING TO KATHARINE BRONSON

29. De Vere Gardens, W.
Jan. 4. '89.

Yes, dearest Friend, I can well believe you think of me sometimes, even ofttimes, for in what place or what hour, of the house or the day, can you fail to be reminded of some piece of kindness done by you and received by me during those memorable three months when you cared for me and my sister constantly, and were so successful in your endeavour to make us perfectly happy? Depend on it, neither I nor she move about this house (which has got to be less familiar to us through our intimate acquaintance with yours)—neither of us forget you for a moment—nor are we without your name on our lips much longer, when we sit quietly at home of an evening and talk over the pleasantest of pleasant days. But you know all this: And how good it is of you by yourself interposing in our talk, every now and then, by way of letter: our hearts leap when, by the last evening Post, your beloved hand writing is quickly discerned among whatever letters may accompany it: Do go on and gladden our hearts. We resolutely excuse ourselves from all out of door amusements this dismal weather: it is quite enough to manage living, without adding the wretchedness of being choked by the fog. The sole invitation I cannot but accept, this morning, is to the Farewell Dinner about to be given by the Ld Mayor to Mr Phelps, [1]—*that* I am bound to attend. I have not seen him, nor Mrs Phelps yet,—but they receive this afternoon for the first time, and,—if I am able,—I shall go. You will like to know that all our articles have arrived safely—and more expeditiously than we expected. The tables, lanterns &c are decidedly approved of, and fit into the proper corners very comfortably: so that everywhere will be an object reminding us,—however unnecessarily—of Venice. Your inkstand brightens the table by my chair, and the lamp will probably stand beside it: while Tassini tempts me to dip into him whenever I pass the bookcase. [2] I may never see the lovely City again,—but, where in the house will not some little incident of the three unparalelled [*sic*] months wake up memories of the gondola, and the stoppings here and there, and the fun at Morchio's, [3] the festive return home, behind broad-backed Luigi,—then the tea, and the dinner, and Gargarin's [*sic*][4] crusty-old-port flavour, and the Dyers, [5]—and Ralp[h] Curtis, and Forbes—oh, the delightful time! Of Edith, I say nothing, because she has herself,—the darling,—written to me,— the surprise and joy of *that!*—and I mean to have a talk with her,—on paper, alas!—my very self, and induce her not to let me have the last word. Oh, my two beloveds, I *must* see Venice again,—it would be heart-breaking to believe otherwise! Of course, I entered into all your doings—the pretty things you got, and prettier I am sure you gave: and I was sorry, so sorry to hear that naughty Edith,—no darling for half a second while I think of it,—did not figure in the Tableaux: I hope and believe she did, however, dance in the New Year. Bid her avoid this cold-catching and consequent headache! Do write, Dearest Friend, keep me *au courant* of everything—no minutest of your doings but is full of interest to me and to S. I heard yesterday from Curtis—at Rome, "where the sun was overpowering:" but I am at the paper's extreme edge. Were it elephant-folio[6] (is there not such a size?) it would not hold all I have in my heart and head too of love for you and "our" Edie—so simply, God bless you, my beloveds!

Robert Browning.

Princess Montenegro[7] sent me, by way of a New Year's Card, —what do you think? A pretty photograph of the Rezzonico. The young lady was equally mindful of S.

Publication: Whiting, pp. 278–280 (in part).
Manuscript: Armstrong Browning Library.

1. Edward John Phelps (1822–1900) had succeeded James Russell Lowell as American Ambassador to Great Britain in 1885. When Phelps retired, the Lord Mayor of London gave a banquet in his honour in the Egyptian Hall of the Mansion House on 24 January 1889. Browning had met Phelps and his wife on a number of occasions and had found himself staying at the same hotel in Llangollen in 1886.

2. A two-volume work on Venetian history by G. Tassini, *Curiosità Veneziane ovvero Origini delle denominazioni stradali di Venezia*, presented to Browning by Mrs. Bronson on 10 December 1888 with the following inscription: "For Mr. Browning, the lover of Venice, from his affectionate Katharine Bronson." Browning had read Mrs. Bronson's own copy of this book while staying at Ca Alvisi and had been particularly attracted by the story giving the origin of the name of Ponte dell'Angelo. Before he left Venice, he had asked to be rowed to the bridge to see the scene for himself, and on his return to England he wrote the poem "Ponte dell'Angelo, Venice" which he included in *Asolando*. The poem is dated 9 January 1889 in the manuscript, so it is likely that Browning was working on it when he wrote this letter. Mrs. Bronson's gift had kept the story fresh in his mind.

3. Bargaining for antiques at Morchio's shop.

4. Prince Léon Gagarin, a retired Russian diplomat, had been Ambassador at Athens, Turin and Constantinople, and was a friend of Mrs. Bronson's. She recounts an evening at Ca Alvisi when Browning and Gagarin were both guests: "To the great surprise of the prince, the poet recalled to his memory, and sang in a low, sweet voice, a number of folk-songs and national airs he had caught by ear during his short stay in Russia, more than fifty years before. First one would sing and then the other; if one hesitated for a note or phrase, the other could generally supply the deficiency, and with great spirit and mutual delight they continued this curious tournament for quite an hour" (Appendix B, p. 156).

5. Mr. and Mrs. Dyer were English friends of Mrs. Bronson. She may have met them at Hardwick Hall in 1886. Mrs. Dyer was the former Emily Haddon.

6. The term "elephant folio" was used in the printing and book trades, but has since been dispensed with. Its origin derived from a watermark rather than from its size.

7. Olga de Montenegro, daughter of the widowed Princess Darinka, whose husband, Danilo II of Montenegro, had been assassinated in 1860. Darinka had brought her family to Venice and become a friend of Mrs. Bronson, while Olga was friendly with Edith. The Bronsons sometimes went to visit the remnants of the Montenegro royal family (grandmother, mother, daughter and aunt) who lived simply and modestly in a small apartment near the Frari. Prince Gagarin used to say, "Dans cette maison il y a toujours plus d'amis que de chaises," and Browning on several occasions met the Princesses and had dinner with them at Ca Alvisi.

Letter 54

ROBERT BROWNING TO EDITH BRONSON

29, De Vere Gardens. W.
Feb. 7. '89.

Dearest Edie,

I did not reply to your letter at once, for this reason: an immediate answer might seem to imply I expected such a delightful surprise every day or week or even month: and it was wise economy to let you know that I can go on without a second piece of kindness till you again have such a good impulse and yield to it—by no means binding yourself to give me regularly such a pleasure. You shall owe me nothing, but be as generous as is consistent with justice to other people. All this means that I did greatly enjoy hearing directly from you. So with respect to letters from your beloved Mother,—but it is her way to make me happy and get so little or nothing in return. I hear of you—either or both—by almost every week's news-letter from Fannie or Pen: of you—how you did *not* "go to the Layards'" that evening of the day when you wrote, because of headache. But afterward I hear of your being well and gay—up to yesterday week when the party at your house was broken up (in some measure) by the bad news about the poor Crown-Prince,[1]—far worse have come since then, every day bringing an added horror, or truly or falsely reported,—all which comes of the silly attempt at concealment at first. Come, forget it.[2] I suppose you heard that our weather has been bad persistently: I "said in my haste"—not once in this month of January will I go out of an evening: nor did I, except to the complimentary farewell dinner our Lord Mayor gave Mr Phelps—which nobody could be excused from attending. We all grieve at the loss—more especially of Mrs Phelps who endeared herself to everybody: both of them were sorry to go from us.

"Going" suggests possible "coming": and you are to come here, you remember—at least I and my sister do, assuredly. I think we can make you something like comfortable,—in all but the stairs to climb: and even these are made more tolerable by our Venetian arrangement of lanterns which touch my heart, every step I take past them. Look where we will, there Venice suggests itself,—the curtains and tables and brackets and what not: all go in harmoniously, are fancy, and keep us from caring about the dismal fog outside—too often, not—I am bound to say—this morning. When you sit by us, and play the guitar,—the illusion will be too painful perhaps—for Mamma will be wanting, Yahabibi nowhere, Gargarin [*sic*]—ah, me!—and, worst of all, an end somewhere in the distance to your visit. I (seriously) believe I shall never have three such perfectly happy months as I had with you,—never again! How good it all was,—the tea and the music, the gondola, the exploration of the labyrinthine city![3]

I am suddenly called. No, I will not wait till to-morrow to finish this scribble: after all, I have said nothing you do not know already—how much I love you both with all my heart. Never mind the affected nonsense of my being resigned to getting only now and then a letter from either of you,—write and make my heart leap as it does when I think of you! All my love to you both: you have my sister's too, you well are assured. Bless you—

Ever affectionately yours
Robert Browning.

Address: Italy, Venice. / Miss Bronson, / Palazzino Alvisi, / S. Moisé, / Venezia.
Publication: Whiting, p. 280 (in part).
Manuscript: Armstrong Browning Library.

1. The Imperial Crown Prince Rudolph of Austria (1858–1889), only son of the Emperor Franz Josef and the Empress Elizabeth, shot himself and his young mistress Baroness Mary Vetsera at the royal hunting lodge at Mayerling in a suicide pact. Rudolph, undermined by venereal disease, dependent on morphine, trapped in a loveless marriage and embroiled in political intrigue, saw no point in continuing what was rapidly becoming a nightmare life. The news of his death shocked Europe, and at first the Austrian authorities declared that he had died from a heart attack. Later this was amended to shooting himself in a fit of insanity, but no mention was made of Mary Vetsera, whose body was secretly disposed of.

2. Browning had obviously received a very dramatic account of the upsetting scenes at Ca Alvisi which followed the disclosure of Rudolph's death. Zina Hulton, who was present, was equally affected and wrote a long description in her memoirs which begins: "On the 30th January there was an evening reception at Mrs. Bronson's and Monseigneur [Don Carlos] was also there. In the midst of this party Mr. Smart—known as 'le beau Smart,' a very handsome Englishman who had made his home chiefly in Austria—appeared and announced the death of the Archduke Rudolph. He had previously given the news privately to Monseigneur who had hurriedly left the party, and then told Mrs. Bronson and her guests. It fell like a thunderclap and a dead silence followed his abrupt disclosure. Then Countess Andreani, a daughter of Meyerbeer's, rushed to the front and placing herself before Mr. Smart vehemently denied the truth of his information" (Hulton, p. 56).

3. In his 1888 visit Browning explored much of Venice on foot, with Edith as his guide, making hundreds of new discoveries. Mrs. Bronson reported: "'Edith is the best *cicerone* in the world,' he said; 'she knows everything and teaches me all she knows. There never was such a guide'" (Appendix B, p. 153).

Letter 55

ROBERT BROWNING TO KATHARINE BRONSON

29. De Vere Gardens. W.
Apr. 9. '89.

So long since I have written to you,—so constantly that I have you, and your goodness, and your concerns and all connected with you in my mind! Dearest Friend, at last comes a respite, of a sort, from the plague of answering letters of no interest to me, and I can take up pen and paper without a weariness there is little to justify, perhaps in the circumstances of the case, but which is none the less real and oppressive: and the worst is, that by yielding to it, and letting alone the opportunity of obtaining—by one little exercise of the pen last of all—the remedy for all weariness and annoyance—a letter of yours, I go without the—I scratch out the true word I was about to put down. Soberly, dearest of friends, I know intimately, without need of talking about it, how much the misfortune of your friend must have grieved you[1]—grieves still, I am sure. You told me, it was on *her* love that you mainly relied, in Venice at least. How has it all ended? Has she left you altogether—or for a time? But say nothing about the circumstances, if it vexes you to do so. I hear of you—and of Edith—constantly, of course,—that you are both of you well. Pen and his wife are not so busy with their house-affairs as to omit mentioning when they have seen you—regretting when the days go by without the chance of giving me news they know I hunger and thirst after. Have you plans already for the summer,—and Edith's journey to Paris—is *that* certainly to be?—implying as it does her coming here?

There is arranged to be a sort of expedition of young Toynbee-Hall men, headed by Alberto Ball,[2] the son of our common friend,—for the purpose of *studying*—not merely amusing themselves with—the beloved city. Well as the Balls are entitled to say they know you, still the young and clever Ball chooses to wish me to beg your kind notice,—and, I suppose, that his companions are to be noticed also,—of what really appears to be a praiseworthy effort after self-instruction: will you smile on him when he calls on you?—for his father's sake, who is anxious about the scheme's success. I have bespoken Pen's assistance, and he will do the honors of the Rezzonico with alacrity, I have no doubt.[3] Dearest,—I scribble fast, this rainy and doleful morning: but at leisure how often do I think a slow thinking of all the wonderful three months I spent with you! Blessings on the House and its Inmates! Entire love to them from your ever affectionate

Robert Browning.

Mrs. Bronson and the Princess Mélanie Metternich

Robert Browning Sept. 5. Asolo. 1889.
written in great joy at finding himself there.

Publication: Whiting, pp. 280–281 (in part).
Manuscript: Armstrong Browning Library.

1. Princess Mélanie Metternich. The Metternichs had been forced to sell their home in Palazzo Bembo at the end of 1888. Presumably they were in financial difficulties because Mrs. Bronson did all she could to help them raise money at the sale. A letter she wrote to Zina Hulton at the time reveals clearly the Metternichs' need for money, and also something of her own personality: "You will be glad to hear that Mr. Peabody Russell has bought many of the unsaleable objects at the Palazzo Bembo. Please do me the favour when he goes to you tonight to *praise the objects*—an oak buffet, a gilded entoigneur, ditto long low armoire—and two oriental tables etc. etc.—I fear you may say if the subject is mentioned that you think the prices were very high—and I want you to be careful not to say so—as I don't want him to repent his bargain. You can say with truth that the Princess and all her friends are so pleased that *he* should have bought them for the beautiful Contarini. You see I am a *careful* friend am I not, and so you will like me to say that I am affectionately your friend, K.B." (Ashmolean). By March 1889 the Metternichs were on the point of leaving Venice. Browning wrote to Pen on 23 March: "Mrs. B. suffers much from the troubles of P P. Metternich,—'loses her best friend in her'—I should say, the loss is mutual" (Balliol).

2. Mrs. Bronson was friendly with John Ball (1818–1889) who owned a villa near Bassano in the Veneto. John Ball was a former politician, a botanist, mountaineer and traveller. The first President of the Alpine Club, he had written *The Alpine Guide* (1863–68). Earlier he had taken his seat in the House of Commons as an Irish Liberal M.P. and had been given office under Palmerston. Browning had met him in London in the 1860's and '70's, and was delighted to find he shared a mutual friend with Mrs. Bronson. John Ball had two sons by his Italian first wife, one of whom was Albert or Alberto.

3. Toynbee Hall is an institution for the education of the adult working-class near Aldgate in the East End of London. It was founded in 1884 by Canon Barnett, who brought Oxford and Cambridge graduates to the East End to learn about social conditions and to help in his teaching programme. Albert Ball was an early convert, and with his Venetian background brought a party of underprivileged young men on an educational visit to Italy in 1889. Browning was anxious to give the venture his support and wrote to Pen on 30 March and on 11 April (*LRB*, pp. 306–307) to remind him of his promise to show the group the Rezzonico.

Letter 56

ROBERT BROWNING TO KATHARINE BRONSON

29. De Vere Gardens. W.
June 10. '89.

Dearest Friend, it was indeed a joy to get your letter: I know you have been distressed of late, and that a change of place would be altogether desirable,—darling Edie told me so,—but I fancied you would not leave Venice so soon. I gather from what you say—and do not say—that even this brief absence has been of service,—and only am apprehensive that, if you return for July and August the heat may be as overpowering as S. and I found it when we spent a week there much later in the season. Why not try Primiero—a delightful retreat, quite as near Venice, and much more likely to invigorate you than Asolo[1]—besides being as lovely in its way. I have carefully guarded myself against making any engagements as to staying at Venice this year; but, should you be found somewhere in the immediate way to it, perhaps there would be no power of keeping away. Pen told my sister that if I did not leave England, he would come to me. One thing is certain: if I do go to Venice, and, as would seem to be inevitable, abide at the Rezzonico, it will only be on the understanding that, every day during the visit, I pass over to the beloved Alvisi and entirely beloved friends there, who are to me in Venice what S. Marco is to the Piazza. Enough of this now, and something about Asolo: I will answer your questions in detail. When I first found out Asolo,[2] I lodged at the main Hôtel in the square, an old large Inn of the most primitive kind. The cieling [*sic*] of my bedroom was traversed by a huge crack or rather cleft: "caused by the earthquake, last year: the sky was as blue as could be, and we were all praying in the fields, expecting the town to tumble in." On the morning after my arrival, I walked up to the Rocca;[3] and, on returning to breakfast, I mentioned it to the landlady—whereon a respectable middle-aged man, sitting by, said– "You have done what I, born here, never thought of doing." I took long walks every day,—and carried away a lively recollection of the general beauty,—but I did not write a word of "Pippa Passes"—the idea struck me when walking in an English wood,—and I made use of the Italian memories.[4] I used to dream of seeing Asolo in the distance and making vain attempts to reach it—re-peatedly dreamed this for many a year: and when I found myself once more in Italy, with S., I went there, straight from Verona. We found the old Inn lying in ruins—a new one being [built] to take its place: I suppose that which you see now. We went to a much inferior Albergo—the best then existing—and were roughly but pleasantly entertained for a week, as I say.[5] People told me the number of inhabitants had greatly increased, and things seemed generally more ordinary-life-like. I am happy that you like it so much: when I got my impression, Italy was new to me.

We had Pen and his wife here: the latter for a month—the former about half that time. Both seem just as I could wish—satisfied with each other and occupied with their household affairs. They left on June 2. for Southampton, where they met Marie,[6] the sister, in transit from New York, and all proceeded together to Bremen, Cologne—where I believe they are to-day—and will reach Wiesbaden to-morrow, where the sisters stay while Marie undergoes treatment from D.[r] Metzger—and Pen returns to Paris in order to finish work of various kinds. I left London for Cambridge the day before[7]—much out of health from the fatigues of London "pleasure"—and a cold besides—and failed to enjoy, as I otherwise should have done, the hospitalities of the "Lodge": a week's rest here has nearly restored me. I daresay I could interest you by an account of the folks I have met day after day—but to talk it all would be so much easier and better: Magari! I shall go to Oxford for Commemoration and stay a week, for another affair, a "Gaudy"-dinner given to the Magnates of Eton:[8] afterwards,—a little month,[9] and what? Nothing—no where— dearer intercourse than last year's memorable three months with you. Yet, something not unlike it may be again, if you will only be good and careful and not permit the naturally fine health to run to waste. Do, dearest friend, consider this, and profit by the coming autumn months,—walk, pray!—and otherwise care for ourselves *in yourself!* Shall I ever read to you again, keep the Sta Caterina again?

Here lie all your books, up to Vol XIV: two more volumes are wanting: but I don't know that your shelf will suffice for the six volumes of a corresponding edition of E.B.B[']s works, which you needs must house.[10] Well, you found room for two more troublesome occupants,— had not your goodness been blind.

My sister wrote to you the other day, she tells me—I think you will have found the letter at Venice: she sent a little book of poems by a great genius—a friend we know:[11] do you like it? She,—the sister, not the poetess,—is in her ordinary health, but a change of air must be managed for her, later on. Give Edith my true love—sorry I and S. are, from the bottom of our hearts, that she does not give us that visit we trusted for. Some other day, even next year, perhaps: but the chances and the changes, ahimé![12] By the way, the new little book of poems, that was to associate your name with mine, remains unprinted:[13] for why? The publisher thinks its announcement might panic-strike the purchasers of the new edition— who have nearly enough of me for some time to come! Never mind: we shall have our inning[s].

Give my kind remembrances to Giuseppina—indeed I remember all your household as if they were attached to poor me who have done nothing to deserve it but appreciate their kindness. As for you—but you want no telling. Bless you ever, and your Edith: keep me in mind as your very own—always affectionate

RB

Address: Italy, Venice. / Mrs Bronson, / Palazzino Alvisi, / S. Moisé, / Venezia.
Publication: Whiting, pp. 282–283 (in part).
Manuscript: Armstrong Browning Library.

1. Mrs. Bronson's brief holiday had been to Asolo and it is probable that she had already seen La Mura, the house that she was to buy later that month. She intended to return almost immediately to Asolo with Edith for a two-month stay. Browning felt this injudicious and wrote to Pen: "it is insufferably hot there, in spite of the hilly situation, and Mrs. B. wants a more bracing air" (*NL*, p. 381).

2. Browning discovered Asolo on his first visit to Italy in 1838. He stayed four days in the town, from 19–23 June, while on a walking tour of the Trevisan in search of local colour for *Sordello*, which he had half-completed.

3. The Rocca is a ruined castle, dominating Asolo from the top of the hill on which the town is built. Its high crenellated walls and its single fortified gateway made it almost impregnable. The present ruin dates back to the Guelf-Ghibelline feuds of the early thirteenth century, but there were fortifications on the summit of the hill from Roman times, when the town was called Acelum. When Browning first explored it in 1838, the Rocca was in much the same ruined state as it is today. Describing it as "that mossy lair of lizards," he made it the scene for the third part of *Pippa Passes*, where the young revolutionary Luigi is urged by his mother to give up his plans to assassinate the Austrian Emperor.

4. Browning is merely repeating the story he told Mrs. Orr and which she quoted in her *Handbook*, first published in 1885: "Mr. Browning was walking alone in a wood near Dulwich, when the image flashed upon him of someone walking thus alone through life; one apparently too obscure to leave a trace of his or her passage, yet exercising a lasting though unconscious influence at every step of it; and the image shaped itself into the little silk-winder of Asolo, Felippa, or Pippa." (*Handbook*, p. 54.)

5. This was in 1878 when Browning and Sarianna stayed at the *Stella d'Oro* from 26 September to 4 October. Writing from there to Mrs. FitzGerald, Browning had described the inn as: "much such an unperverted *locanda* as its predecessor—primitive indeed are the arrangements and unsophisticate the ways: but there is cleanliness, abundance of good will, and the sweet Italian smile at every mistake: we get on excellently" (*LL*, p. 69).

6. Marie Coddington (1856–1929), Fannie Barrett Browning's unmarried younger sister, was to prove one of the hindrances to Pen and Fannie's marriage. She was present at their wedding and several times stayed with them in Venice. There was an especially close relationship between the two sisters, and, when Marie was away in America, Fannie is said to have written to her every day. She is frequently described as an invalid, but her illness was probably a nervous complaint similar to that which was to affect Fannie. In 1888 she had intended to visit London and stay with Browning, but she suffered an accident which caused her to stay in America and which necessitated the treatment at Wiesbaden. She was in America when Browning died, but sent a wreath of pink and white dried flowers and immortelles which was placed on the coffin for the ceremony in Westminster Abbey. A few years later she was at the centre of an acrimonious dispute about the dispersal of furniture from the Palazzo Rezzonico, and was Fannie's chief supporter in the wearisome attacks on Pen and Sarianna, which resulted in a final separation at the turn of the century. For Marie, Fannie's marriage—coming soon after the loss of their father, mother and elder sister—was a considerable shock, as she felt it removed her remaining support. So, when Pen and Fannie experienced difficulties, Marie was content to exacerbate them.

7. Browning was at Cambridge from 1–4 June, as the guest of Dr. Butler of Trinity College. Although he was tired, he talked to Edmund Gosse for two hours in the Fellows' Garden at Trinity about his early life and aspirations, and Gosse noted his mental agility in developing an idea for a new poem. See *Personalia*, pp. 83–87.

8. Oxford provided Browning with a quieter time than Cambridge. After the Commemoration celebrations on 26 July, he was able to rest at Balliol, staying alone with Jowett (who was far from well) until the Eton dinner on 1 July. This celebration was a special occasion in honour of J. J. Hornby (1826–1909), the Provost and former Head Master of Eton, who was a member of the college.

9. A playful allusion to *Hamlet* I, ii, 147.

10. Volume XV of the *Poetical Works* was published on 18 June and Volume XVI on 17 July. Browning presumably sent one or two complete sets and a number of the latest volumes to Pen, because Mrs. Bronson's volumes were inscribed in Venice and not in Asolo. Elizabeth's poems were published in a matching binding in monthly volumes soon afterwards, but were not completed until January 1890—after Browning's death.

11. The friend is "Michael Field," pen-name of two women, Katherine Bradley (1846–1914) and her niece Edith Cooper (1862–1913), who lived and wrote together as one person in Richmond, Surrey. The book, as is shown in Letter 57, is *Long Ago*, a series of poems built around fragments of Sappho. Browning was genuinely impressed by their early work, but his description of Michael Field as "a great genius" is a surprising exaggeration, probably the result of Sarianna's temporary affection for both ladies. In fact, they wrote bitter memoirs in which they criticized Sarianna (to whom they always professed great friendship in their letters), Pen, and Browning (who had entertained them in De Vere Gardens). Mrs. Bronson also suffered their spleen, when she was described as having the eyes of a "hydrocephalic baby."

12. Alas.

13. Browning had assembled about three-quarters of the poems which were to comprise *Asolando* by June 1889. Three of the longest poems, "Ponte dell'Angelo," "Beatrice Signorini" and "Reverie" had been written in January and February, and so he felt he had almost completed the book. The delay, caused by the cautious George Smith, radically altered the structure and meaning of *Asolando*. The poems written in Asolo in September, and Browning's careful ordering of the earlier poems, make it one of Browning's most successful works.

Letter 57

Robert Browning to Katharine Bronson

29. De Vere Gardens. W.
July 17. '89.

Dearest Friend, I shall delight in fancying your life at Asolo, my very own of all Italian towns,—your house built into the wall,[1] and the neighbouring castle-ruins, and the wonderful outlook: on a clear day you can see much farther than Venice: I mentioned some of the dim spots pointed out to my faith as Towns—while what wants no faith at all, the green hills surrounding you, Possagno[2] close by,—how you will enjoy it! And *do*—go there and get all the good out of the beautiful place I used to dream about so often in old days—till at last I saw it again, and the dreams stopped—to begin again, I trust, with a figure there never associated with Asolo before. Shall I ever see you there in no dream? I cannot say: I feel disinclined to leave England this next Autumn that is so soon to overtake us.

Do you know about the Pens? Fannie has recovered from her illness, and has left (last Monday) for Innsbruck where she rejoins her sister: Pen stays a few days longer at Paris to finish his picture. He had declined to compete, at the Exhibition,[3] but has been awarded a medal,—3ᵈ Class,— which however enables him to dispense with the permission of the Salon that his works should be received. Julian S[tory]. gets also a medal of the same class. Pen is wanted at Venice, he says, and will go there first: then to Primiero, I believe. He reports stupendously of the Parisian

Show—but I am no way tempted to go there. And *how* can *I* go to Venice, with the certainty that, if I do so, there will be no more whole days and nights at the blessed Alvisi?

Well, you know how we have been entertaining and entertained by the Shah.[4] I met him at Ld Rosebery's and, before dinner, was presented to him—when he asked me, in French, "Êtes vous Poète?"– "On s'est permis de le dire quelque fois." "Et vous avez fait des livres?" "Plusieurs." "Plusieurs livres?" "Trop de livres!" "Voulez vous m'en faire le cadeau d'un de vos livres afin que je puisse me ressouvenir de vous?" "Avec plaisir." Accordingly I went next day to a shop where they keep them ready-bound, and chose a brightly-covered "Selection." He went to various places that I know, and preferred (so L^y Brownlow[5] tells me) Ashridge to Hatfield:[6] all the country looks lovely just now. All the "outing" I have accomplished was a week at Oxford—which was a quiet one,—Jowett's health, I fear, not allowing the usual invitation of guests to Balliol: I had all the more of him, to my great satisfaction.

So, that dear Edith is not with you—nor with *us*, as we hoped earlier in the year. Oh, it will be too hard to keep away from Venice always! Do write again, beloved friend, and be assured every stroke of every letter of every word you write is—what it is, and what I cannot well make you believe.

S. is quite in her ordinary health, but tired—as we cannot but be. She is away from the house—but I know how much she would have me put of love in what I say for her. Did you get a little book she sent by "Michael Field"—"Long Ago" a number of poems written to "innestare"[7] what fragmentary lines and words we have left of Sappho's poetry? I want to know particularly how they strike you—that's all.

Now, bless you, my own dear friend; I am ever yours affectionately

Robert Browning

Publication: Whiting, pp. 283–284 (in part).
Manuscript: Armstrong Browning Library.

1. Asolo is a walled town, and La Mura, Mrs. Bronson's house, is a narrow four-storeyed building, built along the line of the wall, next to one of the gateways into the town. It possesses a loggia with fine views of the surrounding countryside, which Mrs. Bronson had enclosed with tall windows to form a room rather like a summer-house, where she and Browning could watch the sunset. The house was later extended by joining it to its small neighbour along the street, which Mrs. Bronson had bought at the same time as the main building. Today La Mura remains substantially the same as it was at the end of the last century—with its stone staircase, old-fashioned wood stoves and much of Mrs. Bronson's furniture and decorations. In the dining-room is an old tin inn-sign in the shape of a pierced heart, bought by Mrs. Bronson, which can be clearly seen in her portrait by Ellen Montalba (frontispiece).

2. Possagno, the home of Antonio Canova (1757–1822), lies a few miles to the north of Asolo, and the Pantheon he designed and where he is buried is clearly visible from the top of the Rocca. Browning first visited Possagno in 1838. Inspired by the work of

Canova, some of whose statues and casts were in the museum formed in the sculptor's house and studio, Browning made this town the home of the sculptor Jules in Part 2 of *Pippa Passes*. Later visits in 1878 and 1889 reinforced his liking for Canova's work: "He would have been a greater man in a greater period," he told Mrs. Bronson (Appendix A, p. 132).

3. The Universal Exhibition, to commemorate the centenary of the French Revolution, opened in the early summer of 1889 on the Champ-de-Mars, Paris. Dominated by the controversial Eiffel Tower, the buildings and fairgrounds of the Exhibition demonstrated the latest French technology and taste, as well as displaying the art and culture of France's overseas colonies. There was a hall reserved exclusively for contemporary sculpture, in which Pen's mentor, Auguste Rodin, exhibited one of his "Burghers of Calais." In declining to submit work for the picture gallery, Pen probably felt that he had nothing new to offer, as he had been so busy restoring the interior of the Palazzo Rezzonico, and also that the Exhibition was intended to be an exclusively French occasion. He was persuaded to submit the bronze bust of his father, completed in 1886 and already exhibited at the Grosvenor Gallery in 1887 and the Paris Salon in 1888. This was awarded a bronze medal.

4. His Majesty Nasr-ed-din, Shah of Persia (1829–1896) spent the month of July in England as Queen Victoria's guest. He had formerly visited England in 1873, but his second visit was more elaborate and every effort was made to present him favourably to the public, presumably because it was thought Persia would have increasing political importance to the safety of India. After a week's entertainment in London, the Shah went north to Scotland, visiting Birmingham, Liverpool, Manchester and Bradford *en route*. After staying at Balmoral, he eventually completed his month's stay with a day at Osborne. Earlier, on July 5, during his week in London, he dined with the Earl of Rosebery in Berkeley Square, an entirely male occasion, at which the Shah sat between Gladstone and Lord Rosebery. Browning's presence at the dinner is explained partly by political sympathy with the Liberal party and partly by Rosebery's genuine liking for him. He wore his Oxford D. Litt gown, which the Shah told Rosebery was a decided success.

5. Earl Brownlow (1844–1921) was a landowner and Conservative politician (Paymaster-General 1888–89 and Under Secretary of State for War 1889–92). His wife Adelaide (1844–1917) was a fashionable hostess. At the beginning of her social career in 1876 she caught the eye of Lady Waterford: "I hear of Adelaide Brownlow dining at the Gladstones in red velvet up to her chin, and a row of pearls, looking beautiful—a beautiful woman, the girl gone" (*The Complete Peerage*, II, 350).

6. The Shah spent the night of 7 July at Hatfield with the Marquis of Salisbury, the Prime Minister, and attended a large Garden Party the following afternoon. This was a particularly grandiose occasion, and he may well have preferred the simpler pleasures of Ashridge House, Berkhamstead, the home of Earl and Countess Brownlow, his hosts for the following night. Here his official duties were merely to plant a tree in the garden. The Shah's friendly reception throughout his English tour was in marked contrast with political friction at home, and he fell—the victim of an assassin's bullet—near Teheran in 1896.

7. To graft onto.

Letter 58

Robert Browning to Katharine Bronson

29, De Vere Gardens. W.

Aug. 8. '89.

Dearest Friend,—there came to me, two days ago, a letter from Mrs Howe,[1]—all kindness, you may be sure: but it was supplemented on the outside by your addressing it to me,—and the magical stamp of Asolo crowned all. So, a fancy springs up which shall have utterance *as* just a fancy. The time is come for determining on some change of place, if change is ever to be—and,—I repeat, *just* a fancy,—if I were inclined to join you at Asolo—say, a fortnight hence,—could good rooms be procurable for S. and myself? Now, as you value—I won't say my love, but my respect and esteem,—understand me literally and give me *only* the precise information I want—not one half-syllable about all the accommodation in your own house! I ask because, when I and S. went there,— years ago—the old Locanda on the Square lay in ruins, and we put up at a rougher inn in the town's self: I daresay the principal Hôtel is rebuilt by this time or rather has grown somewhat old. Probably you are there, indeed. Just tell me exactly. Pen is trying his best to entice us his way—which means to Primiero and Venice: I suppose the latter is inevitable: but the laziness of age is subduing me, and how I shrink from the "middle passage"!—all that day-and-night whirling from London to Basle—with the eleven or twelve hours to Milan. Milan opens on Paradise,—but the getting to Milan!—perhaps I shall turn northward and go to Scotland, after all! Still, dear and good One, *tell* me what I ask. Meanwhile, here the weather is supremely good: it wants ten minutes of 1. p.m. I will look at the thermometer and report,—my window being wide. 66° exactly: Pen mentions, in a letter received yesterday, that the temperature "in the yard of the house" is only 80°

After the requisite information, you will please tell me accurately how you are, how that wicked gad-about Edith is, and where. And what else you can generously afford of news—news Venetian, I mean.

That poor Madame Acton![2] She is on my mind, with her face, and *manière d'être*—what was the dreadful cause of it all?

There comes the goodnatured gong to schreech [*sic*] me back from all but the thoughts of you—who are to take S's truest love, and mine as true—and always remember me as yours most affectionately

Robert Browning.

I received a week ago a pamphlet about *Christina of Sweden and Monaldeschi*—by G. Sommi Picenardi.[3] It interests me greatly and I am much obliged to him: have I met him at your house?

Publication: Whiting, p. 285 (in part).
Manuscript: Armstrong Browning Library.

1. Julia Howe, wife of the American painter William Henry Howe (1846–1929), who knew Pen in Paris. The Howes had been staying with Mrs. Bronson in Asolo, and Mrs. Howe had written to Browning, reminding him of a previous meeting and asking for autographs. His reply (printed in *NL*, pp. 382–383) refers to Mrs. Bronson as "the beloved woman whom we both know so well."
2. Madame Acton was an Austrian by birth and a widow of one of the Neapolitan Actons. She lived in Venice for a number of years and was considered charming, beautiful and elusive. She drowned in the Tegernsee in Bavaria, and her death is featured in Paul Bourget's novel *Cosmopolis*, where the heroine suffers the same fate. Bourget met her in Venice in 1887.
3. Browning's poem "Christina and Monaldeschi" had appeared in *Jocoseria* (1883). Browning was always interested in the latest historical research on subjects he had written about, although—in this particular case—he had used a great deal of poetic licence in dealing with the events of the story. Picenardi's article, "Di Cristina de Svezia," was published in *Giornale Araldico*, Vol. 16., pp. 5–24. Browning's copy is now in the Armstrong Browning Library.

Letter 59

ROBERT & SARIANNA BROWNING TO KATHARINE BRONSON

[In RB's hand.]   29, De Vere Gardens. W.
                                                              Aug. 24. '89.

Dearest Friend,

It is not in the nature of things that you should feel such pleasure in expecting our company as a long intimacy with you and your ways gives us a certainty of entirely enjoying. Indeed I only make sure of too much delight,—yet why? Knowing as I do what stores of goodness are in you. We shall set out as soon as we can next week and, once arrived at Milan, we will telegraph to you about the time of arrival at Castelfranco. Our weather has been exceptionally rainy and cold: today the glass stands, inside my room, at 64° and outside it at 59° So that, for the last fortnight and more I have been able to recover from the weariness of the season, and walk two hours daily; so that I hope to travel under better conditions by far than of late years.

Yes, I heard of poor Domenico's[1] dangerous illness from Pen, even before the news in your last letter—and I rejoice for your sake—and mine too—that his recovery is probable. I trust that as few clouds as may be will trouble the blue of our month at Asolo: I shall bring *your* bookful of verses for a final over-hauling on the spot where, when I first saw it, inspiration seemed to steam up from the very ground.[2] And so Edith is (I conjecture, I hope, rightly) to be with you: won't I show here [*sic*] the little ridge in the ruin whence one talks to the echo[3] to greatest advantage: and since she goes this year to Paris she is to remember that we exact the debt of a visit afterward, to the last minute—not to say, day and hour. My love to her,—my love to you, dearest friend, whose I ever am in all affection

Robert Browning.

I mean to make S. put a word or two at end of this.

[Continued by Sarianna.]

Dearest Friend, I can only repeat, with my whole heart, what I have said of the intense delight with which I look forward to meeting you and dear Edith. I hardly like to think of it too much for fear of being disappointed.

Ever your most affectionate,
Sarianna—

Publication: Whiting, p. 286 (in part).
Manuscript: Armstrong Browning Library.

1. Domenico Damian, Mrs. Bronson's second gondolier, the father of the prolific family mentioned in Letter 15, note 4. By 8 September he was out of danger.
2. An anticipation of the "Prologue" to *Asolando*, which wasn't written until 6 September.
3. The echo was discovered by Browning in 1838 and is mentioned in *Pippa Passes* (Part III, lines 1–4):

> Mother: If there blew wind, you'd hear a long sigh, easing
> The utmost heaviness of music's heart.
> Luigi: Here in the archway?
> Mother: Oh no, no—in farther
> Where the echo is made, on the ridge.

In 1878 Browning climbed up to the Rocca again: "... when we reached the ruined tower on the hill-top ... I said 'Let me try if the echo still exists which I discovered here' (you can produce it from only *one* particular spot on a remainder of brick-work)—and thereupon it answered me plainly as ever, after all the silence: for some children from the adjoining *podere*, happening to be outside, heard my voice and its result: and began trying to perform the feat—calling 'Yes, Yes'—all in vain: so, perhaps, the mighty secret will die with me!" (*LL*, pp. 68–69). By 1889 Browning found "the echo sadly curtailed of its replies" (Orr, p. 389) and was unable to demonstrate it to Mrs. Bronson: "'I should have thought an echo could never fade,' he said rather sadly" (Appendix A, p. 140).

Main Street of Asolo

The Loggia at La Mura

Letter 60

ROBERT & SARIANNA BROWNING TO KATHARINE BRONSON

[In RB's hand.]   Hôtel de France[,] Milan
Sunday, Sept. 1. '89

Dearest Friend, it is you who are thoughtful and over thoughtful by far for us. We shall have the most easy of journeys, and see you on your own appointed Wednesday at the end of all. We leave this afternoon for Brescia,—it being a holiday, and only an omnibus-train to Bergamo, we prefer going on by the *diretto*, and letting our first stay be at Brescia,— thence, on Monday afternoon, we shall go probably to Verona,—similarly on Tuesday to Castelfranco (passing Vicenza—having rather an untoward recollection of the Hôtel there[1]) and on Wednesday *evening*, as you suggest, we will proceed to Asolo—and be happy. This hôtel, excellent in all other respects, is very noisy—and last night the hubbub was incessant, so as to deprive S. of a moment's rest,—otherwise we might well continue here. I ought not to need say—if for any reason you feel it hard to be in Asolo by the time you mention,—assuredly we can wait, and wait patiently,—or *pleasantly* even if we know you are advantaged by it. So, may all be well! My dear love to Edie whom I long to see and walk with again. Ever yours and hers most affectionately

Robert Browning.

[Continued by Sarianna.]

Dearest Friend,

We long to be with you and dear Edith,—otherwise we are well contented to dawdle on the road. This hotel is extremely comfortable, only the bedroom windows face the street, and the inhabitants are addicted to singing in full chorus at two o'clock in the night—so we are going on to Brescia– Robert has told you all this—but neither he nor I can express how glad we shall be to see you.

Yours most affectionately
Sarianna—

Publication: None traced.
Manuscript: Armstrong Browning Library.

1. Browning spent two nights in Vicenza (2 and 3 October) on his way to Venice in 1883.

Letter 61

KATHARINE BRONSON TO SARIANNA BROWNING

La Mura
Asolo Veneto
8½ Evening
31 October. [1889]

My dearest friend,

Nothing can describe the loneliness of this tower!! Wordsworth says "lonely as a cloud," Shelley says the moon is "pale for loneliness"—*Our* great Poet may make some allussion [*sic*] to this uncomfortable sensation, but I do not call it to mind—(unless the Queen In a Balcony)[1] but certain it is that no-one describes the void you have both left in Asolo. Nina[2] says she is "persa"[3]—the little maids in my kitchen say tragically—"Pare una casa da morte"[4] and as for me I can't tell you what I feel, so you must imagine. By this hour I think of you as dining at the beautiful Palazzo Pen—and I hope & believe you are all well and happy. I am anxious to know if the journey was a good one—and if the rain held away until after you reached Venice. Here it ceased for some hours & then began again—and then ceased—and at this moment there is no rain, but no stars—and heavy clouds. The viper[5] proved a very eel for gentleness & amenabelness [*sic*] after you left, as he was indeed when you were here, & the 24 handkerchiefs may be his after all. They say, there's safety in numbers so I suppose the whole 24 will not be so compromising as Desdemona's *one*. I sent you, as I fondly suppose, by the 7. o'clock post a *fresh* woodcock w̄h I hope will arrive safely, and give your dearest Brother a few moments gastronomic pleasure. If the brave hunters bring me any more I will forward them—but you know the purveyors of Asolo are uncertain ministrants. The chimneys & fireplaces were begun to day. I am sitting in the Studio with more furniture in it from the other room than is comfortable, but I shall put up with any discomfort in order to get the work done, for many reasons. First, because no work can be done later in the season, second in order that Casanova may be free in the early spring to work on Pippa's Tower.[6] 3ᵈ if a thing *is* to be done let it be quickly.[7] I might add 4ᵗʰˡʸ The Asolan workmen conjugate the verb Asolare[8] as you would a charade—I, thou, he—you we they—all in eloquent actions–

I did not talk with Loredano after you left about the asilo, I thought I would say nothing lest the 'mieux' should be 'l'ennemi du bien'.

I send you my loving goodnight—(and the you is in the plural) and my love to dear Pen and Fanny.

> Always your devoted
> K C de K Bronson

If the great question is soon decided, as I think it will be, perhaps Pen will wish to come here again—as he can give many orders for works possible to do in the winter—I shall stay here until all is settled, and I may be able to be of some use to Pen when he comes—*if* he comes.

Address: Miss Browning / Palazzo Rezzonico / S. Barnaba / *Venezia.*
Publication: None traced.
Manuscript: Armstrong Browning Library.

1. The references to loneliness are from Wordsworth's "Daffodils" and Shelley's "To the Moon." Mrs. Bronson misquotes Shelley, whose lines should read:
    Art thou pale for weariness
    Of climbing heaven, and gazing on the earth . . .
Mrs. Bronson errs again in choosing Browning's "In a Balcony" as a third example. Loneliness features only in the Queen's situation in the poem, and not in the text; her unrequited passion for Norbert is skilfully portrayed in this short poetic drama, which Browning read aloud more than once at Palazzo Barbaro to the Curtises and their guests.

2. Nina Tabacchi at whose house, almost opposite La Mura, Browning and Sarianna lodged.

3. "I'm lost!"

4. "It seems like a house of the dead."

5. The viper is Count Loredano, an Asolan lawyer, who opposed Browning's wish to purchase a small piece of municipal land on which stood a derelict house, suitable for restoration and alteration. The two dozen embroidered handkerchiefs are presumably a present or bribe to make Loredano change his mind—hence the reference to the loss of Desdemona's handkerchief in *Othello*, which led to her being compromised and wrongly accused of infidelity.

6. The name chosen for the house Browning wanted to buy and convert.

7. A reminiscence of Shakespeare's *Macbeth*, I, vii, 1–2.

8. In his dedication to *Asolando*, Browning explains the title of the book as deriving from the verb "asolare," invented by Cardinal Bembo, meaning "to disport in the open air, amuse oneself at random." This is a romantic interpretation of a rare verb which usually means "to hang out (washing)," "to air," or, if referring to the wind, "to sough."

Letter 62

SARIANNA & ROBERT BROWNING TO KATHARINE BRONSON

[In Sarianna's hand.]　　　　　　　　　　　　　　　　Venice.
1ˢᵗ Novʳ [1889]

Here we are, dearest Friend, safely arrived in Venice,—thinking of and longing for, you and pleasant Asolo. Our days there passed pleasantly indeed! Thanks, chiefly, to your dear kindness. And now we want you in Venice. You must come back to us.

We found that the weather had been just as rainy here as at Asolo—and this morning is dull, and rather foggy. I have not yet been out. At the Treviso Station we met Nina's son, looking very well, and had a glimpse of Mʳ Malcolm in another carriage—he was returning to Venice.

Do pray come back—the chimneys do not need your presence as woefully as we. I am writing with horrid ink—and can only repeat come, come!

Remember us very kindly to our good Nina, and your own household.

Pat the kitten for me, and look out at the loggia at the house facing you, and fancy that we are there, and Asolo no longer "a nest of vipers" but a delightful set of friends.

Our best, truest love.

Your ever affectionate,
Sarianna—

[Continued by RB.]

Dearest Mrs Bronson,—I am away from you, in one sense—never to be away from the thought of you and your inexpressible kindness—I trust you will see your way to returning soon: Venice is not herself without you, in my eyes—I daresay this is a customary phrase—but you well know what reason I have to use it with a freshness as if it were inspired for the first time. Come, bringing news of Edith, and the doings in the House, and the sayings of the Sindaco,[1]—above all, of your own health and spirits—and so rejoice

Ever your affectionate
R Browning

Publication: Whiting, p. 291 (Browning's portion only).
Manuscript: Armstrong Browning Library.

1. The mayor of Asolo, Dr. Biadene, who had recently become one of Browning's supporters in the quest for Pippa's Tower (see *LRB*, pp. 319–320).

Letter 63

ROBERT BROWNING TO KATHARINE BRONSON

Venice,
Nov. 5. '89.

Dearest Friend,—a word to slip in the letter of S. which I cannot see go without a scrap of mine.[1] Come and see Pen and you will easily concert things with him. I have all confidence in his knowledge and power. I delight in hearing how comfortably all is proceeding with you at La Mura. I want to say that, having finished the first two volumes of Gozzi[2] I brought the third with me to finish at my leisure and return to you—and parenthetically I may mention that the edition is very rare and valuable. It appears that Symonds[3] has just thought it worth while to translate the work—(an insufferably tiresome and disgusting one, so far as I have read) and he was six months in finding a copy to translate from! Observe, I have not yet got to the apparently interesting part. But to-day is Tuesday, and soon you will be here, I trust; and we can talk. I do not trouble myself about Asolo—supposing that all will come right somehow.

I have got—since three or four days—the whole of my new volume in type[4]—and expect to send it back, corrections and all, tomorrow at latest: but I must continue at my work thereupon, for interruptions occur: so, bless you and goodbye in the truest sense, dear one! Ever yours affectionately

RB.

Depend on it, I remember dear Nina and all her goodness.

Is Loredano[5] proved the worst of vipers,
And is he still to get those broidered wipers?

Publication: Whiting, p. 292 (in part).
Manuscript: Armstrong Browning Library.

1. Sarianna's letter has not been preserved.
2. Carlo Gozzi (1720–1806), Venetian dramatist, who wrote fantasies and dramatized fairy tales in the tradition of the *commedia dell'arte*, the best known of which was *Turandot*. He was the leading opponent of the more famous Carlo Goldoni, whose comedies, with their emphasis on bourgeois realism, were firmly set in contemporary life. Gozzi's successful opposition led to Goldoni's leaving Venice for Paris. Gozzi's autobiography (*Memorie inutili*) was written in 1797–98, and explains his ideas on the function of dramatic art, as well as his arguments with Goldoni. One assumes that Mrs. Bronson owned a first edition of this work.
3. John Addington Symonds (1840–1893), scholar and poet. Apart from possessing a deep knowledge of Tudor and Jacobean drama, Symonds had a love for Italy and

Italian art and literature. He translated Cellini's *Autobiography* and wrote a life of Michelangelo, as well as a six-volume study of the Italian Renaissance. In 1890 he produced a version of *Memorie inutili*, called *The autobiography of Count Carlo Gozzi*, prefaced with his own essay on Italian impromptu comedy.

4. Browning sent the manuscript of *Asolando* to George Smith on 15 October, and received a set of page proofs almost as soon as he had returned to Venice and the Palazzo Rezzonico. His corrected set, now in the Pierpont Morgan Library, shows hundreds of small changes, mainly single words and punctuation, which help to make the meaning of the poems clearer. One or two poems, like "Rephan" and "The Bean-Feast," are more heavily corrected than others. Browning later received sets of "plate-proofs," one of which he gave to Mrs. Bronson and another he kept for reading aloud. A third was sent to Houghton, Mifflin for the American edition. These still contain about seven errors, all but one of which are corrected in the first edition.

5. See Letter 61, n. 5. After Browning's death, Sarianna and Pen became friendly with Count Loredano and in 1892 he agreed to judge the prizes in a window-box competition which Pen organized in Asolo.

Letter 64

KATHARINE BRONSON TO SARIANNA BROWNING

La Mura
Asolo Veneto
Thursday Evening [7 November 1889]

My dearest friend

I send one line tonight to ask if it be possible to send 3!!! photographs[1] of your dear brother to the 3 people who are *working* for the sale of the Asilo. There is always a little opposition on the part of people who wish to keep it as their pleasure ground (or for the purpose for wh̄ it was originally destined)—and the "Three" who are striving, have all expressed their great desire to have a portrait of the Great Poet— The names of these people are

Il Dottor Biadene.
          Sindaco di Asolo.

Conte Guido Loredano.
          Avocato–

Cavaliere Barea.
          Avocato–

The latter with all his pomposity & Latin quotations, is said to be no mean poet himself—& is filled with loyal reverence for the discoverer of Asolo. I do not mean to suggest that there is any doubt of the final happy issue of events—but it w̄d be so gracious if Mr Browning should send his portrait to these friends & admirers before the final decision[.] However that must be left to your *plural* judgment & that of Master Pen. I think a photograph of his portrait of his father would be the best thing possible—tho' the Sindaco & Loredano are both desirous of possessing one like one of the last he had taken, signed by him.

I have been very busy today painting & gilding & urging on the workmen—& will be ready to go to dear Venice on Saturday at half past twelve. So I shall see you on Sunday and this thought makes me very happy. Good night.

Ever your most loving
K C Br

I do not exaggerate when I say that I never saw such a moonlight as tonight. The light falls like snow on the castle walls—& the air is clear, & smells so clean & sweet!

The Sindaco & Loredano passed the evening with me, both intent on the sale of the Asilo—& sure of the happy end—but the question *cannot* be decided for 10 days yet—all on account of the re-elections & their subsequent formalities.

The drawing room![2] chimney place is finished today—and looks very well—Your pussy has disappeared—has she gone to Venice to find you?

Address: Miss Browning. / Palazzo Rezzonico / San Barnaba / *Venezia.*
Publication: None traced.
Manuscript: Armstrong Browning Library.

1. Oŋ his arrival at Asolo, Browning had given Mrs. Bronson one of a group of photographs taken by W. H. Grove earlier in the year, inscribed "Robert Browning, Sept. 5. Asolo 1889. Written in great joy at finding himself there." Mrs. Bronson had presumably shown this impressive photograph to friends in Asolo, and they had expressed a wish to have copies for themselves. See photograph opposite p. 93.
2. The punctuation indicates that Mrs. Bronson considers La Mura too humble a dwelling to possess a drawing room.

Letter 65

ROBERT BROWNING TO KATHARINE BRONSON

[Venice]
[ca. 23 November 1889][1]

Dearest Friend, I am much better, though not *quite* as I am accustomed to be. When your kind remedy came, I was in bed, with a strong lemon-lozenge in my mouth!—and I judged it inadvisable to subject your delicate remedy to such an adverse influence: besides the "shortness of breath" has left me. Whenever it recurs, I will follow your advice.

Ever yours

RB.

Address, on integral page: Mrs Bronson.
Publication: None traced.
Manuscript: Armstrong Browning Library.

1. Dated from internal evidence. Browning caught a cold on 21 November and started coughing badly. He met Mrs. Bronson on the 21st and 22nd. Concerned about his breathing, she sent him some medicine. He felt well enough to attend a tea party at the Hulton's on the 23rd.

Letter 66

ROBERT BROWNING TO KATHARINE BRONSON

Rezzonico:
Nov. 24. '89

Dearest Friend, to-morrow is your Birthday, or Name-day,—anyhow one giving me particular occasion to say or write what I feel everyday—how earnestly I wish you all happiness—you who have given me and my nearest belongings so much. Here is a little frame[1] for darling Edie's face, which you must accept for the sake of

Yours ever affectionately

Robert Browning.

Publication: None traced.
Manuscript: Armstrong Browning Library.

1. Mrs. Bronson has written the following comment on the album page beside the mounted letter: "My last note from my beloved Mr. Browning with a silver filagree frame—KB." The frame itself, purchased from Shorland Fooks, 16–17 East Street, Brighton, is in the Fossi Collection in Asolo. Mrs. Bronson has written on the back: "Given to me by my beloved Mr. Browning, 1889."

Letter 67

SARIANNA BROWNING TO KATHARINE BRONSON

[Venice]
25.th Nov.^r '89.

Dearest,

I send two small angels to pray for every blessing of health and happiness on you and yours on this sweet name-day. Give them shelter for the sake of your most loving friend

Sarianna—

Publication: None traced.
Manuscript: Armstrong Browning Library.

Letter 68

PEN BROWNING TO KATHARINE BRONSON

Palazzo Rezzonico.
9 o'clock. Thursday Morn.^g [12 December 1889][1]

Dearest Mrs Bronson,

The improvement of last night is scarcely maintained this morning. The action of the heart being weaker at moments. He is *quite* clear headed, and is never tired of saying he feels better:—"immensely better—I don't suppose I could get up and walk about—in fact I know I could not, but I have no aches or pains—quite comfortable—could not be more so"– This is what he said a moment ago.

I will let you know if there is any change as the day goes on. My love to you.

Yr Pen.

Publication: Whiting, p. 293 (as Monday evening).
Manuscript: Armstrong Browning Library.

1. Dated by content. This and the following letter were written on small note cards bearing Fannie Browning's monogram.

Letter 69

Pen Browning to Katharine Bronson

Palazzo Rezzonico.
10.30 [p.m.] [12 December 1889]

Dearest Friend,

Our Beloved breathed his last as St Marks struck ten—without pain—unconsciously– I was able to make him happy a little before he became unconscious by a telegram from Smith saying "reviews in all this day's papers most favourable. Edition nearly exhausted–"[1] He just murmured "How gratifying." Those were the last intelligible words.[2]

Yr Pen

Publication: Whiting, p. 294.
Manuscript: Armstrong Browning Library.

1. The first edition of *Asolando* appeared on 12 December and most of the 2,500 copies were sold immediately. The second and third editions were ready on 18 December. Smith eventually printed 14,000 copies of the book in ten editions in three years.

2. Miss Evelyn Barclay, who was staying at the Rezzonico and was present at Browning's death, gives a slightly different account of his last words. In her diary she notes: "A telegram came at that moment saying that the first edition of his book was all sold. Pen bent over him and he said, 'More than satisfied. I am dying. My dear boy. My dear boy'" (Barclay, p. 7).

Letter 70

Sarianna Browning to Katharine Bronson

29. De Vere Gardens.
Jan.ʸ 17. [1890]

My own darling,

I have already let a day pass without thanking you for the most beautiful locket, which I love more for your sake than his. I shall always think of you when I look on it,—of you so near, and good, and kind, and most dearly loved by him. Never dream that there was any other friend he loved better—or as well—as you.

All your kind, attentive care—how he felt it! All your watchfulness over our smallest comforts! God bless you for ever for all the joy you

1889

PALAZZO REZZONICO.

10 . 30

Dearest friend .

Our Beloved breathed
his last as St Marks
struck ten . — without
pain — unconsciously -
I was able to make
him happy a little

before he became unconscious
by a telegram from Smith
saying "reviews in all this
days' papers most favorable
Edith nearly exhausted —"
He just murmured "How gratifying,"
those were the last intelligible
words .

Jr Pen

Pen's Note Card to Mrs. Bronson Announcing His Father's Death

Robert Browning, 1889

gave him at Asolo—how happy he was! and how you were entwined in all our plans for the happy future we were to enjoy there! Think of him when you go back as loving the whole place, and yourself, the embodiment of its sweetness.

I hope dearest Edith has escaped this plague of influenza,—Venice seems to have been let off lightly, but at Athens the visitation has been severe.

I am getting better: this morning I have taken my first walk, and do not feel overtired, though weak. Fannie has been very unwell. She is improving now,—massage has done her much good. Next week, if we are all well enough, we are going into the country for a short time. The doctor says it will do us great good. We accept a kind invitation from one of Pen's uncles[1] to stay at his place near Sidmouth. The green lanes of Devonshire will be a change from dark London, though, just at present, the weather is good *for London*.

I have had the kindest of letters from Mrs Curtis, and want to write to her. How good and kind M^{r} & Mrs Curtis were!

Would you believe that I have never yet been to the Abbey? Yet I want to go there.[2]

Give my kind remembrance to Giuseppina, and, whenever you see her, to Nina of Asolo. We all join in love to you and dear Edith.

Ever yours lovingly,
S.B—

Publication: Whiting, p. 295 (in part).
Manuscript: Armstrong Browning Library.

1. George Goodin Barrett Moulton-Barrett (1817–1895), Elizabeth's fourth brother, who was the only male member of the family to correspond regularly with Browning after Elizabeth's death. A retired barrister of the Inner Temple, he was of a serious disposition, but Browning found him sympathetic and wrote his last letter to him from Asolo on 22 October 1889.

2. Sarianna was too ill to attend Browning's funeral in Westminster Abbey on 31 December.

Letter 71

SARIANNA BROWNING TO KATHARINE BRONSON

29. De Vere Gardens.
Ash Wednesday. [26 February 1890]

My dearest kind good Friend,

Your admirable piece of work came safely yesterday. It is beautiful, wonderfully warm, and the loving sweet words sent with it, are twined round my heart for ever.

I cannot thank you for your love, but I feel it like a blessing. Now that the world seems very dull to me, the thought of you who loved him, as he loved you, is inexpressibly soothing to me. Was it a spirit of prevision made you, my darling, provide for me this comfortable covering? I have been confined to my room for the last twelve days, and it may be as long again before I can get out. On my return from Sidmouth I felt so much stronger that I suppose I was careless, and foolishly got very wet one rainy morning—and had a severe chill on the facial nerve which brought on acute neuralgia, which relieved itself by a horrid rash on the side of the throat where the pain was. It is disappearing rapidly,— but my doctor persists in keeping me prisoner, because he opines that if I catch cold just now, the neuralgia will return and fix itself in the nerve. So here I am—much against my will as I miss fresh air: otherwise, I would just as soon stay at home.

Pen & Fannie have just been to Oxford for two days—and witnessed the performance of Strafford.[1] To-morrow they go to the Isle of Wight for a week.[2]

Dearest, it often comes over me, how beautiful Asolo must be now that "Year's at the spring."[3] I shall never see it, yet there it will be for others. Tell me any thing you hear of the place he loved so well.

I hope, in the Spring, I shall meet M![r] & M![rs] Curtis—they were to be in England early,—and he would have been looking out for them. How are your own people? Give my kind remembrance to Giuseppina. How are Luigi and Nadale?[4]   God bless you, dearest. I love you with all my heart, and dear Edith too.

Ever yours—
Sarianna—

Publication: None traced.
Manuscript: Fossi.

1. Fannie Browning records the event in *Memories* (pp. 33–34): "In January 1890, Jowett, the Master of Balliol, asked us to go to him for a weekend to see 'Strafford' given that year in honour of Browning by the Undergraduates' Theatrical Club, or

Union,—I forget just what it was called,— which we did. The play was very well done and I remember that Henry Irving's son, then at Oxford, acted in it." The play was, in fact, produced by the Oxford University Dramatic Society, and Mr. H.B. Irving, of New College, played Strafford. For an account of the production, see Laurence Irving, *The Successors*, London, 1967, pp. 144–147.

2. Presumably they went to stay with Octavius Butler Barrett Moulton-Barrett (1824–1910), Elizabeth's youngest brother "Occy," who lived with his second wife at Westover, near Calbourne, Isle of Wight.

3. From Pippa's song, *Pippa Passes*, Part 1, l. 221.

4. Natale Gavagnin. Nadale is the Venetian form of Natale.

Letter 72

KATHARINE BRONSON TO SARIANNA BROWNING

La Mura[,] Asolo[,] Veneto
28.th Nov: [1891]

My own darling.[1]

Asolo is in bright sunshine to day, & distant mountains are powdered with the lightest of snow. It is so enchanting to see *real* sun light again. The loggia is 65 when sun shines—60 when it does not. All the excitement of market day, pigs squealing worse than ever, & troups of youths conscripted singing all over the place each with a white handkerchief round his throat whatever that may mean. Letters tell two sad newses. One that M[me] Hurtado was *nearly* run down by a vaporetto. She was out for the first time in 3 weeks poor dear. Also the Brandolins thrown out of a dog cart, the Father & Mother were injured—but the children escaped unhurt. Edith[2] sent the last expression of cruelty in dog-whips to Tou Fou[3]– It is wonderfully made by "Tommy Briggs" but it is an evil looking instrument of torture. The Montalbas especially Ellen are enamoured of Tubby. He grows daily more comical, & now imitates everything he sees his pa do. I've just finished reading the book Charlie[4] sent me. "The Wages of Sin"—I find it an unpleasant but very clever book in its second rate way. I am amazed to hear that it is written by a daughter of Charles Kingsley who takes the nom de plume of Lucas Malet.[5] I think the lady must be very unlike her father. "A window in Thrums" by Barrie[6] you will be sure to like. It is not unlike—in sentiment—our favorite Miss Wilkins–[7]

This is only a trap to catch a letter from you dearest—so adieu

& believe me your ever
fond & faithful
K C Br[n]

The Layards say they will come to Asolo next week—Magari!

Publication: None traced.
Manuscript: Armstrong Browning Library.

1. Sarianna left England early in 1891 to live with Pen and Fannie in Venice. The following year she moved with Pen to his newly built house in Asolo. In 1893 the De Vere Gardens home was sold and the proceeds reinvested in the purchase of Casa Guidi.

2. Edith was on a visit to England and was to spend Christmas at Hardwick Hall, Bury St. Edmunds, Suffolk, the home of Gery Milner-Gibson-Cullum. Gery Cullum, whom she had met in Italy, was a great friend and introduced Edith to the pleasures of Scottish dancing. Mrs. Bronson stayed at Hardwick in 1886 as did Pen and Fannie in 1888. Gery Cullum later befriended the novelist Ouida in the unhappy final years of her life.

3. Tou Fou was the son of the favourite bitch Yahabibi. In his turn he sired Tubby who was to become the joy of Mrs. Bronson's final years. Many of the photographs and watercolours of her dogs still survive at Asolo. In a letter to Isabella Gardner on 16 August 1892, Katharine Bronson wrote: "Charlie Forbes took great care of us the week we were in Venice. He made a beautiful water colour portrait of my fetish Tou Fou and a still more perfect one of Don Carlos' pet bull-terrier Chollie. The King of Spain was moved to unwonted enthusiasm by it. What a frantic love some dogs inspire! They are good things to have if you are inclined to misanthropy. If you find people disappoint you you have but to turn to the grateful, tender, appealing eyes that love you, even if you beat their owner. ... A poet once told me to call my dog 'Rag-bag,' because it was the recipient of bits and scraps of affection 'left over,' but I thought this a disrespectful idea unworthy of canine bearing" (IGM).

4. Charles Forbes, the artist, see Letter 3, n. 1.

5. Mary St. Leger Kingsley (1852–1931), second daughter of Charles Kingsley, married the Rev. William Harrison, rector of Clovelly. She wrote a number of powerful novels, including *The Wages of Sin* (1890).

6. Sir James Barrie (1860–1937), Scottish novelist and playwright. *A Window in Thrums* (1890) is a sentimental early novel set in Barrie's birthplace, Kirriemuir, full of exaggerated local colour.

7. Mary Eleanor Wilkins (1852–1930), the New England regionalist writer. Miss Wilkins achieved an early success with her short stories of rural life in eastern Massachusetts, which she published in *A Humble Romance* (1887) and *A New England Nun* (1891). She later wrote a play about the Salem witch trials and a number of novels—those published after 1902 under her married name of Mary Wilkins Freeman.

Letter 73

KATHARINE BRONSON TO SARIANNA BROWNING

La Mura[,] Asolo[,] Veneto
Saturday 19.th [December 1891]

My own beloved.

Your little letter today was a great joy to me. I am so glad to know that the picture is finished.[1] I hope it will *half* convey the pleasure I have in looking at & being near the precious original.– No one seems to give me the same sense of peace & happiness as my darling S. does, for many & many a reason, indeed they are "too numerous to mention"——

The 3 Montalbas have departed & I am alone for the first time, & catch the occassion [*sic*] to make a fireplace in the dining-room[,] a new larder, where a refrigerator can be happy in hot weather, & a general reform in my kitchen chimney w̄h̄ if all accts be true has smoked persistently since the days of Catterina Cornaro. Everyone gave his or her opinion yesterday—so I telegraphed suddenly to my friend Michieli in Venice—who is a *once*[-]*er* for smoky chimneys, "Come at once." The poor man in his zeal rose at cockcrow—& arrived early this morning. He had a consultation with Casa Nova[2]—exactly like two doctors, & they agreed on the treatment—but nothing serious can be done until I go back to Venice, w̄h̄ will be about the 15 January,—always provided a too intense cold does not send me away sooner from my fireplaceless bedroom. I have made the sitting room very comfortable with warm curtains & many large fur rugs. The loggia is simply *intensely hot* when you sit with your back to the sun, but it is very chilly at morn & eve, especially late eve. I have a dear tame goldfinch who seems most happy, but I always bring him into the little anteroom at night. I have gone through intense anxiety since I wrote you last, my beloved Tou Fou has been very ill. He lost the use of his hind legs—whether from indigestion— or cold—or too long a walk up the hill with Nadal on a damp day—or more correctly a cold evening with *damp roads*, I do not know. The vet was kind but he gave me balls for TF as large as walnuts & no mortal power could make him take them. I wired Urbanetti who sent me Wax & Belladonna & the dear creature got better—whether by Nature's laws or Urban's skill I cannot say. He is still very weak in the hind quarters & cannot jump as he did, but his nose is cold & his eyes bright. Little Tub is always nicer & nicer. How delighted the poor beast w̄d̄ be if he c̄d̄ see you. He has had *no* sugar since you left—as it is fattening as you know, & he grows always more & more tub-like. A Miss Sharp has been here for a week past. She seems intelligent & kind—she "sketches in water-colours" & may or not be "first cousin to Lady Jones"—she is certainly "deeply religious" for she quotes Dr Watts & the Bible with great fluency—not in a sanctimonious way however, but with a light hand—only showing her familiarity with her subject. She has made a picture of Pen's house from the other side. The whole landscape including the Rocca is vermillion—I said you prepare your pictures carefully– This is finished she replied, so I remained mute. In her picture Pen's 'tower' rises far above Catterinas, so she must be subject to optical illussions [*sic*][.] She elected to paint what she calls the "House of the Siren"—w̄h̄ means that abnormal building made by two lunatic brothers on the road to Pagnano & Bassano, & I must say it is *excellently* well done– Do you know (apropos of Pagnano where he lived) that Pen's opponent the

Ingenico *Maran* died about 2 w. ago of pulmonite. His friends here seem very sad about it, as he left many debts & a family of 4.

I have very good news fr my ewe lamb[.] She was to go with M^r & Mrs Senior to Hardwick House to day– I am sure they will have a gay household & that Edith will greatly enjoy herself.

As for me I am very well & most contented here. The quiet & the beauty of the world can be enjoyed to the fullest—as there are no distractions. I have dined alone for several days while the chimney question in the dining room is being settled. If I had a good aide-de[-]camp I would like to make an Xmas tree for some of the small Asolani—but don't feel quite up to the struggle tho' after all Nina & Gilda & Nadale would all be good A.D.C's– My mind refuses to be a General that is the fact. Pss Metternich writes me "Nous arrangeons un grand arbre de Noël– Nous habillons 50 pauvres enfants de la tête aux pieds—cela nous donne tant à faire que la petite Titi se lève à 7 h du matin pour se mettre à l'ouvrage et le soir[,] lorsqu'elle dort[,] la gouvernante Anglaise, et moi, nous defaisons ce qu['Jel[le] a cousu car, dans sa hâte, elle le fait *trop* mal."– I shall have to content myself with giving away a few frocks—Tho' I *should like* to do more. If only dear Fannie were here we could join hands & do something cheery– Alone I find it difficult, not to say impossible.

Mr Young^3 seems delighted in finding himself alone. When he comes to see me we both avoid the subject of the B's, as by tacit consent. A letter fr H. James fr Dresden where he went to the deathbed of a friend^4— says "my poor dull play was withdrawn after 70 nights"^{5}– It seems to me long for a poor dull play. I am so sorry about his fiasco—he had so set his heart on success—and he is such a good true earnest man—his *friendship* when he gives it it [*sic*], literally[,] "à tout épreuve."

Please thank PP. (wh means precious Pen) for his nice letter. I must try to find a half hour in w$\overline{\text{h}}$ to answer it, for it was indeed a dear letter, but you see dearest I am more than busy—dashing about fr one set of workpeople to the other. Will not my PP come here before Jan 15. He shall have a warm little room & I will kill every fatted calf I can get hold of for him, & he can talk to Casa Nova, Coletta & Biadene to his heart's content. If he wants to come here in the spring *to live*, he really ought to come here now & give some especial orders as to things practical & important. It will be dull for him to come when I am not here—and much time will be lost if he waits until the Spring. The journey after all is nothing, think of the Curtis' & be courageous.

Goodnight dearest. Tell Charlie I will write to him very soon & that I would like him to send your picture here—as I've several frames waiting.

This is the address—care of *Capo della Posta* di Asolo. CORNUDA per TREVISO.

Much love to dears PP & F. & believe me,

Your faithful

K C de K Br:

Address: Miss Browning / No 2 Via Venezia / Firenze / Toscana.
Publication: None traced.
Manuscript: Armstrong Browning Library.

1. A painting of Sarianna by Charles Forbes, commissioned by Mrs. Bronson. This portrait and another, painted by Flora Stark in Asolo at the turn of the century, have disappeared. Photographs of Sarianna survive from this period.
2. A local builder.
3. Herbert Young (1855–1941), English painter and dilettante who discovered Asolo in 1890 through friendship with Pen, bought a house from an elderly curé and lived there for fifty years. His house was directly opposite La Mura, in the wall on the other side of the gateway, and so he became Mrs. Bronson's nearest neighbour. In 1925 he gave the house to Freya Stark, the traveller and writer. See Flora Stark: *An Italian Diary*, London, 1945.
4. A young American, Wolcott Balestier, who died of typhoid when visiting Dresden.
5. *The American*, which opened at the Opera Comique in the Strand, London, on 26 September 1891. Adapted from his novel, James's play was too melodramatic for popular taste, and, although a visit from the Prince of Wales gave it a temporary lease of life, it closed after seventy performances. See Edel, Vol. 2, pp. 29–31.

Letter 74

KATHARINE BRONSON TO SARIANNA BROWNING

[Asolo]
Xmas Day. [1891]

Only a word to my dear darling to say that I am thinking of her most of the time & that she is now most appropriately associated with angels, & such very beautiful ones too.[1] You know we always say that your wings spoil the set of your gowns at the back, despite your good dressmaker.

I gilded the fireplace as Pen suggested—but the gilding insists upon coming off in spots just above the shelf—so I tried to hide this by painting some pinks over the defective parts. Nina came in when this was done & her comment was after a very puzzled look—"Xe belo, *i par garofani* no xe vero."[2] as if she were by no means sure for what plant they were intended. You may fancy I did not find her hesitation very flattering. My very next letter shall be to my dear Charlie. I hope he is well of his cold, & that he has had a happy Xmas with you & dear P & F. Tell him I am longing to see the portrait. Edith went with Mr & Mrs Senior to Hardwick on Wednesday.[3] On Thursday they were to have a great Christmas tree.

I send you a loving kiss

Your own

K B.

Hilda M.[4] sent me a charming picture of the archway & Casa Novas house. Lady Enid[5] a bag embroidered in "up to date" jewels, & I have had cards & calendars ad infinitum—but nothing half so pretty as the envois of my trefolio di Firenze.[6]

Publication: None traced.
Manuscript: Armstrong Browning Library.

1. Presumably Sarianna had given Katharine Bronson some ornamental angels as a Christmas present, perhaps to complement those she had given her as a Saint's Day gift in 1889. See Letter 67.
2. "They are beautiful—*they're carnations*, aren't they?"
3. 23 December.
4. Hilda Montalba.
5. Lady Layard. Zina Hulton remembered her as "a very stately woman, tall and spare with a most dignified bearing. . . . The more one knew her, the more one appreciated her solid good qualities, but her manner was so aloof that many people never attempted to know her more" (Hulton, p. 53).
6. The trefoglio is the symbol of Florence—a lily with three petals, like the fleur-de-lis. As the Brownings were spending Christmas in Florence, Mrs. Bronson means "the gift of my three friends from Florence."

Letter 75

KATHARINE BRONSON TO SARIANNA BROWNING

38 Via Gregoriana[,] Roma.
Christmas day 1892.

My dearest & best.

This blessed day you may be sure brings you at every hour to my mind. How intensely I wish you were here, is my uppermost of all thoughts—a selfish one enough you will say—since it would separate you from those you love so dearly & who would be lost & lonely without you. I hope you received my letter from Florence, & that you will soon send me an answer to tell me how you are, if all trace of your cold has left you & if Pen and Fannie are all the better for their hygienic life at Asolo. The "Syrens of the Zattere" as Brabazon[1] & I always call Miss Leigh Smith & Miss Blythe,[2] had with their usual limitless kindness prepared everything most comfortably for us in this apartment. Cold bouillon[,] fires & flowers were ready for us on our arrival by the train from Florence the other night—a train due at midnight but which never arrives until past one! At first everything seemed very strange—but we have had time to see many friends—to receive many Xmas gifts & letters & cards—& to put familiar bits of silver & old stuffs about the red & gold drawing room & so force ourselves into feeling a little at home. We brought a misty air with us from Florence—though very mild, yesterday however was a perfect one, filled with birds song & flower odours—which made it a "pleasure to live" as people say—but today a fine rain is falling to dampen Christmas pleasures. The birds however are nothing daunted & are singing or rather chirping in myriads among the ilex trees of the garden across the street. Yesterday I saw the Roman ladies stepping to & fro shops & carriages in the Corso busily engaged in buying presents, wh made the street a most animated scene. The shops here are full of modern pretty things—I've not yet dared enter Segre's most tempting precincts.

Now I must wish you & Pen & Fannie my sincerest wishes for your health & happiness for the New Year.

Ever your loving
Katharina

Mrs Story[3] has just been to see me!! She is *wonderfully* well—quite herself again. She asked much about you all.

Publication: None traced.
Manuscript: Armstrong Browning Library.

1. Hercules Brabazon Brabazon (1821–1906), English artist. A gentleman of means and a bachelor, he spent a lifetime in painting, music and travel. Persuaded by his friend and fellow-artist Sargent, he held his first exhibition in London in 1891 at the age of 70. In spite of his contempt for the commercial aspects of art, his watercolours became very popular and his work was in great demand. He stayed with Mrs. Bronson in Asolo in October 1892 and wrote in her Birthday Book: "The poorest man may have a picture gallery in his memory which he would not exchange for the Louvre."

2. Miss Leigh Smith was an Englishwoman living in Rome who first met Browning in 1885 when she was on holiday in Venice with her friend Miss Blythe. She gave Browning a picture she had drawn of the Campo San Vio, and, on learning that she wished to rent an apartment in Venice, he suggested that she approach the Curtises at Palazzo Barbaro. In the event, she and Miss Blythe found something more suitable on the Zattere. Here they entertained the Brownings and Mrs. Bronson in the autumn of 1888. After Browning's death, they remained firm friends of Sarianna and Pen. Hearing of Mrs. Bronson's illness in 1891, they invited her and Edith to spend Christmas with them in the milder Roman climate in their house in Via Gregoriana.

3. Emelyn, wife of William Wetmore Story. She died in 1894 and Story created his masterpiece, *Angel of Grief*, to place over her grave in the Protestant Cemetery in Rome.

Letter 76

KATHARINE BRONSON TO SARIANNA BROWNING

38 Via Gregoriana
Sunday. [8 January 1893]

My very dearest!

I hope soon to have another little word from you to tell me how you all are. I cannot say how deeply sad I feel in the thought that the New Year brought you so much trouble & illness. I feel a sort of *personal* discouragement in seeing that all my prayers & wishes for your welfare are left unheard & unaccomplished. Even in sympathy comes in the everlasting Ego you see.

All the same I am disheartened– I see no prospect of your coming to Rome which is my great desire. Please tell me if there is any hope. I must not write you a long letter as I am much too gloomy to-day. Homesickness for Venice is a very bad malady, though I am most grateful to Cini[1] for sending me here because it has done my very "small health" as the French say so much good. I can walk up a stair now with comparative ease—though not yet M[rs] Story's Matterhorn of a climb.[2] You will be glad to know that she is seemingly quite restored to her usual health. She talks & laughs and makes amusing remarks as of old. Also Isabella Blythe is improving daily though she is still too weak to leave her room in the morning, or to go out of the house. I make herculean efforts to amuse Edith, & go out occasionally in the even'g. My hermit ways partly obligatory & partly forced upon me by lack of strength—do not make me a useful chaperone, & I have the painful consciousness of being rather useless to her[,] poor darling. However she has a sweet happy nature easily pleased & always contented.

We went to the new American Minister's first reception yesterday. He has M[r] Wurts'[3] wonderful apartment. It seemed like another world,— so ancient is the palace,—so marvellous the collection of antiquities of every kind within its walls, yet withal so warm & cozy & thoroughly comfortable. M[r] Wurts was there, & the contrast between his own insignificant appearance & the great work he has done, was most curious & interesting, teaching one never to judge of people by their outward & visible man,—but to seek out the inward & spiritual.

We have seen many people—old & new friends– The Princess Salm & Rosa arrived yesterday—& we expect the Hurtados tomorrow. Did you hear that poor M. de Hurtado lost his beautiful favorite horse on the voyage fr America. His coachman telegraphed from Gibraltar that the poor beast had perished in a heavy sea off that port. Ida writes that he Hurtado is quite crushed by the news. It was a horse he had *trained* & loved only too dearly. So must perish idols of clay. You will let me have a word from you dearest will you not? Has the worst happened—& could you not save poor old Ferdinando?[4]–

Edith sends her love to you & Pen & Fannie to wh please add mine.

I embrace you tenderly

Your most loving

Katharina Br

Publication: None traced.
Manuscript: Armstrong Browning Library.

1. Dr. Cini was the physician to the English and American colony in Venice. He was present at Browning's deathbed.
2. The Storys lived on the top floor of the Palazzo Barberini, which was itself on the side of a hill.
3. George Washington Wurts, career diplomat from Philadelphia, came to Italy in 1865 and acted as unpaid attaché until promoted to Secretary of Legation. He was abruptly dismissed from this office in 1882 by a controversial administrative decision which was said to have hastened the death of the United States Minister to Italy, George Perkins Marsh (see *BAF*, pp. 328–332). It seems from Mrs. Bronson's comments in this letter that Wurts may have succeeded Marsh and acted as American Minister until late 1892.
4. Ferdinando Romagnoli, Robert and Elizabeth Barrett Browning's manservant at Casa Guidi during the 1850's. He married Elizabeth's maid, Elizabeth Wilson, and they lived a stormy, eventful life together for nearly forty years. When Browning left Florence in 1861, Ferdinando helped Wilson run a boarding-house in the city; in 1864 they tried a similar venture in England at the Yorkshire seaside resort of Scarborough. When this failed, they returned to Italy, where, destitute, they appealed to Browning for help. He allowed Wilson £10 a year in 1872 but lost touch and heard no more from them until, to his surprise, he rediscovered them cooking for a friend in Venice in 1885. In 1890 Pen took the elderly couple into the Palazzo Rezzonico and gave them a good home until Ferdinando died in 1893. Elizabeth Wilson survived until 1902. Pen buried her in the cemetery of Santa Anna in Asolo, where her tombstone may still be seen, next to the grave of Eleonora Duse. See *DI*, pp. 9–10.

Letter 77

SARIANNA BROWNING TO KATHARINE BRONSON

Asolo[,] Veneto
24 Nov. 1900.

Dearest Friend,

Your festa day comes round bringing with it all kind thoughts and dear memories and heartfelt good wishes for your health and happiness. We remember you affectionately, and wish you were with us again.

I send you a queer little box in which you can put sugar for Tou-Fou, and sometimes remember me in your drives.[1]

Always, dearest Friend,
your loving
Sarianna Browning

Publication: None traced.
Source: Transcript Rucellai.

1. Mrs. Bronson was living in Florence and was within three months of her death. She would not see Asolo again. Sarianna lived until 1903, Pen until 1912.

Letter 78

PEN BROWNING TO KATHARINE BRONSON

Asolo[,] Veneto
Nov. 24 1900.

Dearest Mrs Bronson

My heartiest good wishes go to you for your Festa together with my true love.

I sent you yesterday two little boxes of the fruit you used to like, planted, picked, and packed in Asolo by your

always affectionate
Pen.

I hope to see you soon.

Publication: None traced.
Source: Transcript Rucellai.

Appendices

APPENDIX A

Browning in Asolo

By Katharine C. de Kay Bronson

with Sketches by Clara Montalba[†]

"To live in hearts we leave behind is not to die."

THE POET'S LOVE OF ASOLO

TOWARD THE END of his life Robert Browning turned with ever greater pleasure to the places which had delighted him in youth. Venice, and, for a change to upland air, Asolo in the Veneto, drew him from his London home and the gaiety of the great city; but especially Asolo, where the scene of "Pippa Passes" was laid, seemed on each visit more delightful, so that when his only son married and settled in Venice, Browning went about with a fine scheme to raise a tower like Pippa's near a certain property in Asolo, where he and Miss Browning might pass at least some months of every year. He did not live to see the tower built.

Neither he nor those who loved him imagined for a moment that a visit he made to Asolo mainly for the purpose of concluding the purchase of this property would be his last. In answer to a letter written in the spring of 1889, from "La Mura," at Asolo, inquiring what his early impressions of Asolo were, he replied in a letter from London, dated "De Vere Gardens, June 10, 1889":

> I will answer your questions in detail. When I first found out Asolo I lodged at the main Hotel in the square, an old, large Inn of the most primitive kind. The ceiling of my bedroom was traversed by a huge crack or rather cleft; "caused by the earthquake last year; the sky was as blue as could be, and we were all praying in the fields, expecting the town to tumble in." On the morning of my arrival I walked up to the Rocca; and, on returning to breakfast, I mentioned it to the landlady, whereon a respectable, middle-aged man, sitting by, said, "You have done what I, born here, never thought of doing." ... I took long walks every day,—and carried away a lively recollection of the general beauty,—but I did not write a word of "Pippa Passes." The idea struck me when walking in an English wood, and I made use of the Italian memories. I used to dream of seeing Asolo in the distance and making vain attempts to reach it, repeatedly dreamed

†Reprinted from *The Century Magazine*, 59 (April 1900), 920–931.

this for many a year, and when I found myself once more in Italy with my sister, I went there straight from Verona. We found the old inn lying in ruins, a new one about to take its place; I suppose that which you see now. We went to a much inferior albergo, the best then existing, and were roughly but pleasantly entertained for a wcck, as I say. People told me the number of inhabitants had greatly increased, and things seemed generally more ordinary-life-like. I am happy that you like it so much. When I got my impression Italy was new to me.

The oft-recurring dream here referred to is spoken of in a letter written some years before: "the beautiful place I used to dream about so often in the old days, till at last I saw it again and the dreams stopped."

He remarked one day: "I never heard of any one dreaming even twice on the same subject, yet my Asolo vision came to me many and many a time. Just ask my sister how often I have said to her at breakfast, 'I had my old dream again about Asolo last night.'"

LA ROCCA, ASOLO.

Answering my curiosity as to the points of the dream, he said: "It is simply this. I am traveling with a friend, sometimes with one person, sometimes with another, oftenest with one I do not recognize. Suddenly I see the town I love sparkling in the sun on the hillside. I cry to my companion, 'Look! look! there is Asolo! Oh, do let us go there!' The friend invariably answers, 'Impossible; we cannot stop.' 'Pray, pray let us go there!' I entreat. 'No,' persists the friend, 'we cannot; we must go on and leave Asolo for another day,' and so I am hurried away, and wake to know that I have been dreaming it all, both pleasure and disappointment."

One day Mr. Browning related an incident of a visit to Asolo when Austria was in possession of Venetian territory. He was asked by the chief dignitary of the town, "What have you come here for?" "To see the place." "Do you intend to stay?" "Yes; I hope to remain a few days." "But you have seen the place already; how can you possibly wish to stay longer?" "Because I find it so very beautiful." The Austrian looked at him in puzzled amazement, and then, after a moment's pause, signed the "permit of sojourn" required.

So far as I can judge, I believe that Browning's last visit to "Asolo, my very own of all Italian cities," as he calls it in one of his letters, was one of unalloyed pleasure. He seemed to enjoy every hour and every moment. "To think that I should be here again!" he would say reflectively, as though he felt that a mysterious destiny had conducted him hither, independent of his own plans or will.

He never wearied of gazing from the loggia of La Mura at the view over the plain, and of pointing out sites he had kept clear in his mind while writing "Sordello" and "Pippa Passes."

"See!" he would say to each newcomer, "there is Romano, cradle of the Eccelini, those cruel twelfth-century tyrants, you know. The tower stands there, to the right of those trees and walls. That is Bassano; it had a wonderful history in the middle ages, and there Napoleon fought; he created one of his generals Duke of Bassano, you remember? On this nearer hill is San Zenone, scene of the most fearful tragedy in all history."

If his listener seemed interested he would relate in a few fiery sentences the story of Alberico, betrayed in his last stronghold; how the Trevisani determined to extirpate the race of Eccelini from the earth, and how, to this end, they destroyed Alberico, his wife, and five children, by tortures too terrible to describe. At another time the poet would put aside the tragic medieval memories, and looking toward the tower on the opposite side of the ravine, standing bold and high against the western sky, would talk of Queen Caterina Cornaro, and of her graceful, poetic little court, as it was held during twenty years within those yellow-gray, flower-covered walls. Snapdragons, rose and mauve, and white ferns and grasses and stonecrops grow out of every crevice between the stones, and replace with their tender tints the bright frescos that once covered the walls. Of these only a frieze under the slanting roof of the tower, a simple arabesque, remains, with one red base of Grecian form, which has outlived its fellows. Within one of the windows of the tower is a sun-dial, which once marked the hours of the widowed queen.

Browning said: "People always speak of Caterina with compassion because she lost Cyprus; but surely this is a better place, far more beautiful than the distant island, where she was a stranger. I am sure the happiest years of her life were those when she was queen of Asolo."

It was her secretary, Cardinal Bembo, who, as Browning tells us in print, suggested the name "Asolando" for his last volume of verse.

At times forgetting all else, Browning rejoiced with keen artistic sense in the beauty of nature in this favored spot, noting the ever-changing cloud-shadows on the plain, the ranges of many-tinted mountains in the west and southwest, and the fairy-like outline of the blue Euganean Hills, which partly form the southern boundary of the vast Campagna. He spoke of the indelible association which these hills bear with the names of Shelley and Byron, as being a grand monument to their memory. His face always lighted with pleasure when he spoke of a poet's undying fame, or heard of honors, even if only in the form of a tablet on a wall, to prove that the great dead are not forgotten. Looking out upon the wondrous beauty of the varied landscape before him, he said:

"I was right to fall in love with this place fifty years ago, was I not? We outlive some places, people, and things that charmed us in our youth, but the loveliness of this is no disappointment; it is even more beautiful to me now than then."

BROWNING'S ROUTINE

The great poet, perhaps because he was so great, ruled his days with a precision and regularity such as one would more naturally attribute to a mathematician. At Asolo he began his day at the early hour of seven, took his cold bath, scarcely tempered even in chilly weather, then his simple breakfast, served punctually at eight of the clock, then with his sister—here, as elsewhere, his inseparable companion—he wandered over the hills, seeking and finding such points of view and interest as he had known in his first youth. He recognized a bit of old fresco still left on a house wall, a Gothic window here, a doorway there, the palace where Napoleon slept before the battle of Bassano, the graveled bit of square above the market-place, which in his time was the site of a bowling-alley, where from his hotel windows he could see the Asolani playing their favorite game at odd hours of the day. After their long walks the brother and sister returned to the morning readings and writings; the former were alternately English newspapers, the memoirs in Italian of Carlo Gozzi,—a book which he said he continued to read to the end "out of sheer obstinacy," but which he did not find to his taste "in the very least,"—and the reading, entirely to his mind, of various Greek plays. About midday luncheon was served with much the same menu as he was wont to choose in Venice in previous years, namely, local Italian dishes and native wines. He wrote and read again after this light repast, and at three o'clock appeared on the loggia of La Mura, his favorite place in Asolo.

"Here you can see all this beauty without fatigue, and here we are protected from sun or wind or rain. Blessings on the one who built this!" he said more than once, in his happy, enthusiastic way. Its charm made him break through his abstemious, self-imposed rule of refusing any refreshment in the afternoon. He liked to see and hear the hissing urn on a table in the middle of the loggia, and would accept a cup of tea and a biscuit with the greatest pleasure, as he did so saying, "I think I'm all the better for this delicious drink, after all."

Soon after three o'clock we went to drive, and explored the country for miles around. He seemed to take the same unfailing delight in the daily drive at Asolo as in the daily row in Venice. Neither carriage nor gondola was ever kept one moment waiting, such was the poet's punctuality, and such the punctuality of those who wished to please him.

Summer was nearly over when he took the long, delightful excursions he so greatly enjoyed. He rebelled at first against the numerous wraps piled up in the carriage, which prudence suggested as a precaution against change of weather or autumnal air. "One would think we were going to Siberia," he said; but he relented as the afternoon grew chill, and accepted the Siberian rugs with

GATEWAY ADJOINING "LA MURA."

words of approbation. He observed everything observable by the way—the thick hedges that border all the roads and fields, the great chestnut-trees and apple-orchards, which give an English character to the landscape, unknown in other parts of Italy already familiar to him. He remarked upon the vivacity of the clear, running brooks between hedges and highroads, the charm of the little river Musone, with its borders of alders and willows and shivering aspens, the perfumed wains of autumn hay, the great *carri* piled high with white or purple grapes, which he said "might serve as models in a procession to Bacchus." He uncovered his head in returning the salutation of a priest, and touched his hat to the meanest peasant, who, after the manner of the country, lifted his own to greet the passing stranger.

"I always salute the church," he said to me in an aside; "I respect it."

Sometimes the people he thus greeted smiled in surprise, but all admired and honored his never-failing courtesy.

At Possagno, the birthplace of Canova, he looked carefully at every object in the museum, where casts of all the works of that sculptor, together with several originals in marble,—tombs, groups, and statues,—are preserved, the whole forming a very large collection. "Pen must see this," he said, for the thought of what would please his son was never far from his mind.

"He would have been a greater man in a greater period," was his verdict on Canova. Such was his interest in art in all its branches that he had patience to examine the uninteresting collection of Canova's drawings in water-color, which present the appearance of very early attempts of a not very promising aspirant to fame.

One day, on returning from a drive to Bassano, the poet was unusually silent; no one spoke. I felt anxious lest he should not feel quite well, but forbore to question him, and consoled myself by thinking, "He is tired; perhaps he is resting his brain." We had nearly reached home when he said:

"I have written a poem since we left Bassano."

"A poem! How? When?"

"Oh, it is all in my head. I shall write it out presently, as soon as I can find a bit of paper."

"The subject? Please tell."

"No, not now; you will see it quite soon enough when it is printed."

"Will you not even say what inspired it?"

Then, smiling: "Well, since you are so inquisitive, the birds twittering in the trees have suggested it to me. You know I don't like women to wear those wings in their bonnets." It was "The Lady and the Painter."

This drive to Bassano was, I think, his favorite. We passed, in going and in returning, the tower of Romano, which he never could see too often, and our road came within close sight of tragic San Zenone. We generally started on this expedition in the morning at ten o'clock, reaching Bassano at twelve, and took our luncheon at the little inn of Sant' Antonio. The simple food pleased the poet and his sister. Both were always in the highest delight because it was "Italianissimo." After luncheon we went to an old book-shop, where Browning's quick eye and exceeding erudition discovered such books as properly illustrate the history of the surrounding country. His choice was of great assistance to me in the formation of a collection of works on local subjects. His "Take this," "Not that," was unerring, and sufficient to insure a wise selection. The small Bassano museum, where relics of every kind connected with the ancient place and its story are carefully collected and cared for, interested him exceedingly. A valuable collection of Venetian coins, beautifully arranged in a glass case, met with his keen approval, and he was exceedingly pleased to see me take a list of the missing ones in the hope of being able to fill up the blanks at some later day in Venice. To my great delight, he said: "Quite right! I am glad you think of it; they deserve it: this museum is kept up in the true spirit."

ON THE LOGGIA AT ASOLO

On one occasion we drove some miles beyond Bassano, thereby adding an hour or more to our return journey. We visited the majolica factory at Nove, an ancient industry modernly renewed. Then another half-hour's drive took us through Marostica, a wonderful little fortified town; its castles and walls of bright-red brick were built by the Scaligers, and retain their ancient outline nearly perfect. Again he repeated, "Pen must see this. Dear Pen!" His whole affectionate nature was bound up in his son—that great nature in which the sister took a second place, perhaps, though in its way an equally intense one.

If we were ever late in returning to Asolo, he would say, "Tell Vittorio to drive quickly; we must not lose the sunset from the loggia." So the horses made their best speed, and we generally arrived in time for the spectacle he so delighted in; if we chanced to be late he was always disappointed. Often, after a storm, the effects of sun breaking through clouds before its setting, combined with the scenery of plain and mountain, were such as to rouse the poet to the greatest enthusiasm. Heedless of cold or damp, forgetting himself completely, though warmly wrapped to please others, he would gaze on the changing aspects of earth and sky until darkness covered everything from his sight.

A SHRINE TO ST. ANTHONY, ASOLO.

VIEW OF ASOLO FROM THE LOGGIA OF "LA MURA."

On this protected loggia he took his walk when bad weather made roads impassable, pacing up and down like an officer on a quarter-deck, but never uttering a word of impatience or complaint, such as less self-controlled people so often do, because the elements had thwarted him in his program for the day. As he walked he measured the distance by consulting his watch and his memory, and would come into the tiny drawing-room rosy and triumphant, saying, "I have walked so many miles, and have seen such a beautiful country!"

THE NEW "PIPPA'S TOWER"

Here, too, he received the syndic and other dignitaries of the town when they came to call upon him, and here held long conversations on the subject of a bit of municipal property, a small piece of ground on which stood an unfurnished building commanding the finest view in Asolo. Many obstacles stood in the way of the purchase, but the poet determined to buy it if possible, and make an Italian *pied-à-terre* for himself and his sister. It is a part of the pleasure-garden of Queen Caterina Cornaro, and separated from the castle at the present time by a high wall. It is divided from La Mura by a deep ravine with precipitous sides, covered with olive-, fig-, and nut-trees, interspersed with vineyards. At the bottom of the ravine runs a stream of water, the overflow of the fountain in the market-place. With the poet's accustomed impulsive ardor he talked constantly of this new scheme for making a temporary home in the land he loved so dearly. He planned how the house should be altered and built, and how it should have a loggia even larger than that of La Mura, where he could take still longer walks in bad weather.

"It shall have a tower," he said, "whence I can see Venice at every hour of the day, and I shall call it 'Pippa's Tower.' We will have flag-signals," he went on. "When I ask you to dine, the flag shall be blue—it is your favorite color; and remember, if the answer is 'Yes,' you float a blue flag; if 'No,' it must be a red one. We will throw a rustic bridge across the streamlet in the ravine. It will be easier for us than the long walk round by the town and the castle. The telephone is too modern; don't you think so?"

And so on and on, beguiling the time with playful plans to amuse himself and his hearers. Sometimes, turning very grave, he would say:

"It may not be for me to enjoy it long—who can say? But it will always be useful for Pen and his family. They can come here so easily from Venice whenever they need rest or change of air." Then, with his old courage, faith, and fire: "But I am good for ten years yet. I am perfectly well."

And so, indeed, he seemed, apparently quite his old self, so gay, so strong, so wondrously youthful in mind and sentiment. True, on his arrival in Asolo a difficulty in his breathing was very apparent, especially after mounting steep stairs or a hill; but this annoying symptom disappeared after a few weeks, either under the influence of the pure, invigorating air, or the small globules of arsenicum which he took daily to please those who recommended them; perhaps through the effects of the two precious remedies combined.

He was overjoyed when his son came to make him a few days' visit, and wanted to show him everything at once, and especially the site he had chosen for Pippa's Tower. After this project had been well discussed, and, to the poet's delight, greatly approved of by his son, he took him to see the Villa Maser, about six miles distant, a villa built by the Barbaros of Venice, and decorated by Paul Veronese. A rapid tour of inspection was scarcely over when we observed from the windows of the *sala* a storm approaching over the place, and heavy black clouds hung ominously near the castle.

"PIPPA'S TOWER."

"TEMPESTA"

We drove away, hoping rather against hope to reach home before the clouds could break or fall. Only a few moments proved that to be impossible, and Vittorio was ordered to find shelter. By great good luck he was able to drive under a covered entrance to a farm-yard, a place already half taken up by a huge carro filled with golden grapes. The storm beat wildly around and above us, hail falling on the roof of the portico with a sound like the rattle of musketry. Peasant boys with dark-brown eyes climbed on the high wheels of the carro, and leaning across, offered bunches of sun-kissed grapes to the occupants of the carriage. Cool and delicious they were, and served to make the long half-hour pass less tediously, for the air was hot and heavy in that crowded haven. The size of the hailstones was something extraordinary. Barefooted children brought us specimens as large as walnuts. As we drove back to Asolo, after the storm had abated, we found the road quite white and slippery, while in corners and ditches the hail lay piled some inches high. The poet had never before seen the dire effects of a fierce Venetian *tempesta*, and his kind heart was moved to great pity for the unlucky tillers of the ground.

"How fortunate we were to have found a safe retreat so quickly!" he said. "Horses are so terrified by hail; they think the stings of ice are those of the driver's whip, and often lose their heads from fright and get quite beyond control." So all was well for us, as it ended well, and we were none the worse for the escapade.

THE GRAY FEATHER

Another day, a bright and beautiful one, we drove to "El Barco," on the plain, some four miles distant from Asolo. It is a place little known and seldom visited—once a pleasance of Queen Caterina, and now used as a common farm-house, inhabited only by peasants and their families, and many varieties of marketable beasts and birds. The latter are better tended than the former, notably a breed of ducks which would take a prize, or honorable mention at least, at any exhibition of feathered tribes. Browning was much impressed by the strange contrast between the grand building, bright with frescos, and the neglected and untidy barn-yard around it. The wall-paintings are of Giorgione's time; they cover the whole façade, are singularly well preserved, and have certain intrinsic merit. The poet remarked: "How curious to see that great doorway with St. Jerome on one side and Neptune on the other—paganism and Christianity! The artist must have been a *libre-penseur*."

The whole place is exceedingly interesting and suggestive. The chapel interior has lost its wall-frescos, the combined effects of neglect and damp, but the ovals of the frieze are nearly intact. They represent the apostles and the evangelists. Rushing through the grounds are streams of clear water, which once fed miniature lakes and marble fountains, and paused to freshen the queen's flower-beds. Where care and beauty once reigned supreme, all is now unkempt and squalid. One tried to imagine bygone scenes, for history recounts many an episode of royal pomp and hospitality. A certain princess of Mantua is described as arriving here to visit the queen, "accompanied by her knights," and followed by "a train of no less than two hundred servants." She was surely a somewhat indiscreet guest, even for that extravagant time.

As we left the grounds the poet picked up a gray feather, not more nor less than that of a domestic turkey. Giving it to me, he said, "I don't object to this in a woman's bonnet; surely it is pretty enough," referring, of course, to his horror of the sacrifice of wild song-birds for decorative purposes.

ALBERICO'S TOWER

Browning having expressed the desire to revisit Alberico's tower, we drove there one sunny day by the highroad to Bassano. A circuitous turn about midway between Asolo and that town brought us to the hamlet of San Zenone. The horses with heavy carriage could only make a partial ascent of the hill, through a road bordered by acacias, whose fallen and falling yellow leaves perfumed the air with the sweet, pungent odor peculiar to that tree in autumn. At a sort of memorial chapel we descended from the carriage, and continued the steep ascent on foot; we passed great rock walls and blocks of stone, foundations of the once impregnable stronghold. It held out long and fell at last by treachery, after which the wretched holders were put to death, and the whole fortress and its dependencies razed to the ground. Nothing now remains but the table-land with ruined walls about it, and a tower built from the debris of the castle to preserve that memory of tyranny and bloodshed. A small modern church and

IN THE COUNTRY NEAR ASOLO.

a cemetery cover a part of the ancient ramparts, and as the author of "Sordello" looked thence upon the wild land at the foot of the eminence, he said: "Just think of Alberico tied to the heels of his horse, dragged to death over those sharp rocks and stones!"

Vainly we tried to persuade him not to climb the insecure wooden staircase within the tower. It seemed a dark and perilous place, I thought. My mind was filled with dreadful memories of the past, so much so as to make me doubt the honest intent of the poor and surely innocent custodian who accompanied us. It was evident that the poet had set his mind upon looking out from the very top of the tower, and entreaties to the contrary were useless. I well remember waiting in terror for the return, and that my excited imagination played me cruel tricks on the occasion. From the top he could scan the whole Venetian plain from north to south in its bright autumn tints under a declining sun. He remained there some time in contemplation; what were his thoughts, who can say? We may be sure they were great and far-reaching ones, passing over six hundred years of time, from the darkness and ferocity of the middle ages to the sunny, peaceful landscape of to-day. He had studied so closely the history of this part of Italy that personages connected with it were to him living people, and he would speak of them as such. I am sure he saw quite clearly all their forms and faces, the fierce knights and lovely ladies, the innocent children massacred before the eyes of their parents; everything, whether fair or terrible, was mirrored on his mind. Truly a great imagination has its joys, but it has also its tortures.

We retraced our steps seriously, if not sadly, from the gruesome place, which might illustrate in its strange position and outline the "dark tower" of Childe Roland. At the carriage door stood a peasant in a picturesque costume, consisting of a pointed hat, tight stockings, short breeches, and a jacket of velveteen, such as has been worn by the rustics of the region for hundreds of years. He held in his hand something wrapped in a bit of crumpled paper. Opening it, he showed the poet some rusty spear-tips he had found in tilling the ground near Alberico's tower.

"They are not rare," he said naïvely; "the whole place is sown with them half a meter below the surface; but the larger ones we must send to the museum at Bassano. Will the signore buy these?"

Browning took them at once at the man's own price, a trifling sum, and said to me, with a smile, "One's pleasures cost little in this favored land."

He wrapped the relics carefully in their paper, and turning, placed a large piece of silver in the man's hand. The poor fellow's delight was so evident, and the poet's pleasure in the relics so apparent, that the two impressions served to dispel all terrible medieval memories, and we drove cheerily away. He looked and relooked at the lance-tips, and said to me:

"If you will promise not to interfere with me I will tell you what I am going to do with these."

"Do I ever interfere?"

"Yes; if I tell you my idea you will want to save me trouble and have it executed for me. I do not wish it. Have I your promise?"

A STREET IN ASOLO.

That given, he proceeded to explain that he would have a small box made for his treasures, with an inscription describing their origin on the cover. Some days later I suggested that a deft young Asolan carpenter whose shop we passed nearly every day could be trusted to make a "treasure-box," but he said:

"No; I want it of fine wood and lined with cloth. I think I can get it better done elsewhere."

THE SEARCH FOR THE ECHO

The "Rocca" of Asolo is a ruined fortress of prehistoric foundation which crowns the hill above the town. The poet always enjoyed the steep and slippery walk, or rather climb, which leads to it. The views by the way are very striking, and from the summit the little town may be seen lying at one's feet, the immense stretch of plain before it bounded by the sea. He remembered an echo he had discovered within the fortress walls fifty years before, to which he alludes in "Pippa Passes," and so anxious was he to refind it that he could scarcely be persuaded to wait until the fatigue of his journey from England should be dispelled before seeking to hear it again. More than a week elapsed before a suitable day could be agreed upon for the rough excursion. He specially wished that the horizon should be clear of mist, that he might plainly see the Adriatic and the campanile of St. Mark's. We reached the wretched hut near the top of the hill, where the keys of the one portal of the strange old fortress are kept, and chairs were brought out for us by a peasant woman that we might rest before attempting the sharp finish. A number of small, bare-footed children were to be seen idly sprawling on the ground, interspersed among cats and hungry-looking fowls. At one side of the house a rustic, with a heavy hammer in his hand, was engaged in building a wooden partition in what seemed to be a cow-shed. He explained that, as the family grew larger every year, new rooms were required, and that he always built them himself.

Browning's face and voice expressed the tenderest pity at the sight of this discomfort. It moved him to such compassion that I am fain to think that a rest on a rush-bottomed chair was never before paid for so generously.

He asked sympathetically, "Do you find it hard to live up here so far from the town?"

"We get on pretty well in summer, but oh, signore, the winters are long and cold."

"They must be," he said tenderly. "*Ci vuol pazienza.*"

Suddenly the woman addressed him with, "I know who you are."

"Who am I?" he inquired.

"You are a great English poet."

"How do you know that?"

"Because I see your shirt; one of my friends ironed it last week, and no one else has one like it down in Asolo."

This appealed to Browning's sense of humor. The garment in question was of a very simple pattern, white with fine blue lines. He laughed aloud, and said, "Well, upon my word, this is the very first time I was ever recognized by my shirt!" and he told the story to others afterward with great glee.

Once within the Rocca fortress we could find no echo, though small boys were easily persuaded to shout for it. "I should have thought an echo could never fade," he said rather sadly; but she was there, after all, his nymph Echo, only she proved for some reason coy on that occasion.

It is only within the last few years that the commune of Asolo has taken proper care of this unique monument. Until lately any person in the neighborhood who happened to require building-materials was at least not prevented from carrying them away in requisite quantities. A master builder in the town assured me that in his youth the top of the fortress was crenelated, and that ever since he can remember stones of every size have been rolled down the hill and removed to other sites.

Our view was unobscured by the lightest cloud; the campanile of Venice and the domes of Padua were distinctly visible, the clear air perfumed by wild thyme and other herbs crushed under our feet. Everything was perfect in the poet's eyes. Even the boy guides he thought "such handsome, spirited little fellows," so much so that his generosity must have led them to fancy him a *principe reale* instead of, or as well as, a *sommo poeta*. We descended the hill on the opposite side from the one by which we mounted, with smoother paths, and through the charming gardens of a beautiful private villa, and so out upon the highroad leading to the chief street of the little town.

THE SPINET

The evenings at Asolo were spent very quietly, and with no visits to interrupt the agreeable monotony. Immediately after dinner Browning played on the spinet, the same one he had used in Venice in other years. It is a curious instrument, not only for its tone, which is like a mandolin in some notes, in others like a guitar, but also because it bears the maker's name, "Ferdinando Ferrari, Ravenna, 1522," inside the sounding-board. Browning played in a dreamy manner, generally recalling old music he had heard in early youth, English ballads and Russian folk-songs, the airs always melodious, often melancholy; and he would occasionally sing his favorite "Chanson de Roland," and seemed troubled because he could remember only one or two verses.

"I will write them all for you when I get back to London, Edith dear," he said to his young friend, of whom he was fond, and whom he always wished to please, little thinking that the time would never come when he could fulfil his promise or see his beloved England again.

To his sister he said one evening: "I must have a small piano in my study in London. I like to play when no one can hear me," to which she assented, as was her wont when he expressed any desire she knew was for his good. Then he added: "But those London houses! You can hear the piano-fortes from one to another. It would annoy me to think that I was disturbing a neighbor. I know by experience how vexing it is."

A STREET IN ASOLO.

I suddenly remembered having read of a new invention in Boston of soft-pedal pianos, which cannot be heard even in an adjoining room. I told him of this, and he seemed much interested.

"Delightful!" he said. "Why was it never thought of before?"

I was happy to hear him say this, and ventured to ask timidly,—for he did not like to have gifts thrust upon him,—"Would you accept one from me? I can so easily send for it."

He looked at me gravely for one moment, and then said, "From so dear a friend I would accept anything," and I felt supremely honored and happy. Alas! my project was never fulfilled; it was the last week of his last visit to Asolo.

READING ALOUD

After playing for some time on the spinet, his fingers, so long out of practice, would get tired, and he would leave the instrument, saying, "Now I will read to you. What would you like?" "Any poem signed 'R. B.'" "No, no; no R. B. to-night." Then, with a smile, "Let us have some real poetry." So saying, he would take Shelley or Keats, Coleridge or Tennyson, from the book-shelves, read aloud some of his favorite poems, and say:

"This is poetry; don't you know it is?"

Once, on his first arrival at La Mura, he said of his own accord, "I will read Shakspere to you to-night."

I was silent, conscience-stricken, and watched him run his eyes quickly along the book-shelves. All his own volumes were there, the works of the poets above mentioned, and many others; but they were not what he sought.

"What! No Shakspere?" he exclaimed. "I would never have believed it! Now, to punish you, I will read one of my toughest poems—at least, so the critics say."

It was far from being the punishment he pretended I deserved, for when he read a difficult poem, giving his own emphasis and punctuation, it seemed to be revealed in a new light, and to become as clear and comprehensible as one could possibly desire.

Though one would have supposed his morning hours to be more than occupied with the preparation of "Asolando" for the press, together with his walks and his correspondence, yet he always found time for his favorite Greek plays, which he read from a small edition, the fine print of which would have wearied any eyes less remarkable than his own. He said to me one day, speaking of his delight in such reading:

"Shall I whisper to you my ambition and my hope? It is to write a tragedy better than anything I have done yet. I think of it constantly."

THE THEATER AT ASOLO

During Browning's last sojourn a good theatrical company arrived at Asolo. There were fifteen representations, if my memory serves me, and he never failed to go to them, except when the night was absolutely stormy. Even then it was with a protest that he was not so decrepit that a little rain could hurt him. "But you will not like to go alone, and we ladies dare not venture in such weather." That was enough.

A COUNTRY HOUSE NEAR ASOLO.

"True, true, I never thought of that. Well, I am sure we can make ourselves quite happy at home." And the evening was spent as usual, with books and quaint music, and the dear sister busy with her netting in the corner of the little drawing-room.

The theater of Asolo had an interest for the poet apart from the stage and its actors. It is built in the castle, precisely where, in the days long past, stood the banqueting-hall of Queen Caterina Cornaro, while beneath it are the local prisons. When Browning inquired how many malefactors were confined there, he was told that there were never more than three or four at one time, and that their crimes consisted in thefts of grapes or fowls, or the sale of contraband tobacco. He smiled benevolently on hearing this, just as he did when reading a similar account in the Venetian newspapers—as one would say, "If other prisons had no worse tale to tell."

This combination of theater and prison is surely unique, for the criminals can hear the orchestra distinctly from their cells. The entrance is the same as that used in old days by the queen. You pass through the same arched gateway, walk—you cannot drive—over the same steep road, paved with cobblestones, that existed in her day, and if you are inclined to be lazy, you will long for the sedan-chair of past generations. It was a curious experience for the poet, on leaving his house each evening, to pass through the lofty line of dim arcades, with here and there a twinkling light before a madonna's shrine, cross the market-place with its flashing fountain under a great expanse of starry sky, go up the toilsome, dusky street, through the arched gateway and green inclosure, then mount a neat stair, and find himself at last in a brilliantly lighted theater, fitted up in perfect taste, all white and red and gold—in fact, a playhouse of which any populous city might well be proud.

"This is all very extraordinary," he would sometimes say; "something I could never have imagined. And such acting—so good to its smallest detail! They are born actors, these Italians." He seemed really disappointed when the bad weather prevented him from being present at the last three representations, and pleased to hear that the company was going on to Venice. "We can see them again there," he said; "it is a pleasure deferred."

THE POET'S CONVERSATION AND CHARACTER

If I try to recall Robert Browning's words it is as though I had talked to a being apart from other men. My feeling may seem exaggerated, but it was only natural when one considers my vivid sense of his moral and intellectual superiority, and connects that with his kindness to me and mine. It has been observed that his conversation so fascinated the listener that if one tried to recall it an hour afterward the very subjects seemed to elude one's memory. Or was this an uncommon experience, more an idiosyncrasy of my own, rarely shared by others? I cannot surely say.

Not that his talk was abstruse and intricate, like some of his writings. Far from it. Perhaps an instinct told him that it was kind to others to bring himself down to the ordinary hearer's level, or he may have needed that repose to the mind which easy talk brings to those who think intensely. As a rule, he seemed purposely to avoid deep and serious topics. If such were broached in his presence he dismissed them with one strong, convincing sentence, and adroitly turned the current of conversation into a shallower channel. This was no loss, for everything he chose to say was well said. A familiar story, grave or gay, when clothed in his words and accentuated by his expressive gestures and the mobility of his countenance, had all the charm of novelty, while a comic anecdote, the very same that from another might seem trite or spiritless, from his lips actually sparkled with wit, born of his own keen sense of humor. I found in him also that most rare instance of a powerful personality united to a nature tenderly sympathetic. When I saw him daily I felt constrained to conceal the very slightest contretemps or a commonplace household annoyance. Such trivial matters as the shortcomings of a servant or the exaggerations of a chef were no despised trifles to him. His knowledge of the importance of detail made him take even minor occurrences quickly and acutely to heart.

During his sojourns in Venice he had his own apartments, whence he was free to come and go as he wished, where no one ever presumed to disturb him, where, with his beloved sister, he could always find peace, privacy, and repose. The thought deeply impressed me that one who had lifted so many souls above the mere necessity for living in a troublesome world deserved from those permitted to approach him their best efforts to brighten his personal life; that each one should be, so to say, a mouthpiece for the world's gratitude. The ephemeral studies for his comfort, the small cares entailed upon me during the brief days and weeks when his precious life was partly intrusted to my care, might seem to count for little in an existence far removed from that of an ordinary man; yet, as a fact, he was glad and grateful for the very smallest attention. He was pleased, thankful, and appreciative of all things. He never regarded the sentiment of gratitude as a burden, as less generous minds are apt to do. His elevated nature accepted frankly any sign of friendly feeling or affection from all who genuinely offered it. He read the human heart as few have read it, nor did he, as the common saying is, "judge others by himself"; yet the result was that he was the most unsuspicious of men. He never attributed evil or interested motives to any one. He seemed to ignore human weaknesses, unless they were absolutely forced upon his notice. We all carry about with us a parcel of the divinity, the so-called "divine spark." In him it appeared as a great flame. An interpreter of the secrets of heaven, one who looked with inspired "second sight" into the life to come, he was at the same time completely in touch with the living present. His was a duality equally powerful in both its phases.

The delight he took in everything connected with Venice is well known. For Italy in general he retained, undimmed by time, the affection expressed so many years ago in his well-known lines:

> Italy, my Italy!
> Queen Mary's saying serves for me—
> .   .   .   .
> Open my heart and you will see
> Graved inside of it, "Italy."
> Such lovers old are I and she:
> So it always was, so shall ever be!

APPENDIX B

Browning in Venice

By Katharine C. de Kay Bronson

with Sketches by Clara Montalba[†]

IN A LETTER from Browning dated in London, speaking of a pleasant experience in Venice, he says: "It has given an association which will live in my mind with every delight of that dearest place in the world." Again, in allusion to an album of carefully chosen Venetian photographs received as a Christmas gift, he says: "What a book of memories, and instigations to yet still more memories, does that most beautiful book prove to me! I never supposed that photographers would have the good sense to use their art on so many out-of-the-way scenes and sights, just those I love most."

Nevertheless, he did not acquiesce when people suggested that he should leave England and take up his permanent abode in Venice. His answer was: "Impossible! I have too many friends in London. I would never forsake them. Still, I admit that for three or four months in the year I should like nothing half so well as Venice."

To this end he once made all arrangements for the purchase of an ancient Venetian palace. Everything seemed propitious. He was charmed with the early fifteenth-century construction, with the arched windows and exquisite façade covered with medallions of many-colored marbles, and pleased himself with plans and fancies of how, with certain alterations, it could easily be made a perfect summer and autumn residence. All was decided, the law formalities were nearly complete, and the purchase-money was ready, when, at the last hour, a flaw in the title became apparent, partly owing to the fact that the property belonged to absentees. So, to the poet's intense chagrin, he was obliged to give up his darling scheme. Perhaps he had never, in his long lifetime, been so thoroughly annoyed by a thwarted project as by the failure of this one. There came a day, some years later, when he saw that all had been ordained for his good. As a matter of fact the foundations of the palace were as insecure as the title, there were many sunless rooms, some of the floors were sunken badly, and an enormous outlay of money would have been required to make the place habitable.

[†]Reprinted from *The Century Magazine*, 63 (February, 1902), 572–584. This article was printed simultaneously in the *Cornhill*, 68 (February, 1902), 145–171 in which version there is a prefatory note by Henry James.

These drawbacks the poet at first refused to consider. He thought only of the beauty and the archæological interest; he doubted that the façade was in a perilous condition; pleased himself by fancying how many windows he could open to the morning sun on the garden, how many balconies could be added toward the south; in fact he may be said to have passed a month, not in building, but in restoring a "castle in the air" hanging over the waters of the Grand Canal. Even when he became convinced that Fate had kept a kindly hand over him, and that the purchase, had it been concluded, would have proved a source of endless trouble and perhaps regret, he still remained offended with the unseen and unknown owners of the palazzo. It was only after his son had bought the Palazzo Rezzonico that the father was really reconciled to the loss of the Manzoni.

The poet's nature was so essentially joyous that one was at a loss to decide where he took the keenest pleasure, whether in his daily walks or his afternoon rows in the gondola. He seemed never to weary of either, but my personal experience of his delight was in the latter, when we floated over the still lagoons. The view of the rose-colored city rising from the pale-green waters, of the golden light of sunset on the distant Alps, of the day as it turned to evening behind the Euganean Hills, never seemed to pall upon his sense.

"Only Shelley has given us an idea of this," he would say, and quote lines from "Julian and Maddalo." "Never say Eugánean," he corrected me; "many people make that mistake, but if you keep in mind that the poet makes the word rhyme to 'pæan,' you will remember to pronounce it Eugané-an."

His memory for the poems he had read in his youth was extraordinary. If one quoted a line from Byron, who, he said, was the singer of his first enthusiasm, he would continue the quotation, never hesitating for a word, and then interrupt himself, saying, "I think you have had enough of this," to which his dear sister and I would give silent consent, lest the effort of memory should tire him. He was very proud of his retentive memory and of his well-preserved sight; the latter he attributed to his practice of bathing his eyes in cold water every morning. He was proud, too, of his strength, of his power of walking for hours without fatigue, of the few requirements of his Spartan-like daily life, and above all he was proud of his son, who was his idol.

Yes, that was his vulnerable point, the heel of Achilles. People who praised or loved or noticed his only child found the direct road to his heart. Even those who only spoke with him of "Pen" were at once his friends and worthy of attention and interest. He said to me many years ago, while awaiting anxiously the result of his son's earnest art studies:

"Do you know, dear friend, if the thing were possible, I would renounce all personal ambition and would destroy every line I ever wrote, if by so doing I could see fame and honor heaped on my Robert's head."

What a proof are these words of an intense nature devoid of all egotism! In his boy he saw the image of the wife whom he adored, literally adored; for, as I felt, the thought of her, as an angel in heaven, was never out of his mind. He wore a small gold ring on his watch-chain. "This was hers," he said. "Can you fancy that tiny finger? Can you believe that a woman could wear such a circlet as this? It is a child's."

The only other souvenir on his chain was a coin placed there years ago, the date 1848, a piece of the first money struck by Manin in Venice to record the freedom from Austrian dominion. "I love this coin," he said, "as she would have loved it. You know what she felt and wrote about United Italy."

He had no personal vanity: it never occurred to him to admire himself in any way, to call attention to the beauty of his hand, which in old age was the hand of youth, nor did he seem to be aware of the perfect outline of his head, the color and brightness of his eyes, or the fairness of his skin, which, with his snow-white hair, made him look as if carved in old Greek marble.

After his disappointment with regard to the Palazzo Manzoni he cherished a momentary—idea, may I call it?—perhaps fancy is the better word—of buying an unfinished villa on the Lido, the sand-strip toward the Adriatic, begun in years gone by for Victor Emmanuel. He would talk of this with great zest, saying, "Thence one could see every day the divine sunsets," and continue with a list of the charms and advantages of the really beautiful place, then pause and wait for the assent and approbation of his sister or some listening friend. He seemed annoyed when no such word was spoken. He could not bring those who loved him quite to agree with so unpractical a scheme, yet all contrary arguments of distance from town and markets, exposure to storms, and so on, seemed to annoy him, until at last every one ended by listening to his enthusiastic plans, while offering no direct opposition to them. After a time, finding that in this case silence meant the reverse of consent, he ceased to talk and dream of a "villa on the Lido."

He expressed one day a wish to go to the Church of San Niccolò to find the tomb of his hero Salinguerra. On the way he talked of the character and deeds of this soldier prince, who plays so important a part in the poem of "Sordello";

A VENETIAN GONDOLA.

how he was taken by the Venetians at Ferrara, and kept for years an honored prisoner by the republic, and how he died in Casa Bosco at San Tomà, and was buried with great pomp at San Niccolò al Lido. After searching vainly for some time through the lonely church, where no sacristan was to be found, he discovered or rediscovered the memorial tablet in a sort of corridor attached to the east side of the church. It bears in Gothic characters the name and date of death of the renowned Salinguerra, which being translated signifies "leap to war."

The poet looked at the ancient stone with great interest and attention, and on the way back to Venice he seemed lost in thought. Though he said but little, I could follow through that the current of his thought. He was repassing in his mind that complicated bit of medieval Italian history so strongly treated in his own great poem. While he took a vivid and ever-present interest in all he had written, he very rarely spoke on the subject, even to his most intimate friends. In a letter of thanks for a manuscript collection of dramatic episodes taken from Venetian archives, he said:

> The extracts are all very characteristic and valuable. If I do not immediately turn them to use, it is because of an old peculiarity in my mental digestion—a long and obscure process. There comes up unexpectedly some subject for poetry, which has been dormant, and apparently dead, for perhaps dozens of years. A month since I wrote a poem of some two hundred lines about a story I heard more than forty years ago, and never dreamed of trying to repeat, wondering how it had so long escaped me; and so it has been with my best things. These *petits faits vrais* are precious.

The poem he spoke of is "Donald." I always fancied that in Venice the poet was more ready to be pleased than elsewhere; everything charmed him. He found grace and beauty in the *popolo*, whom he paints so well in the Goldoni sonnet. The poorest street children were pretty in his eyes. He would admire a carpenter or a painter who chanced to be at work in the house, and say to me: "See the fine poise of the head, the movement of the torso, those well-cut features. You might fancy that man in the crimson robe of a senator, as you see them on Tintoret's canvas."

I would occasionally translate his compliment to the man in question, in milder terms: "The signore says you look like the people in the old pictures"; and it amused him to see the workman change color at words of praise from the one he well knew as the *sommo poeta*. Professor Molmenti wrote to him one day with the request that he would write something for a pamphlet published at the time of the unveiling of Goldoni's statue in Venice. He acquiesced without hesitation, and the very next day the sonnet was ready for print. It was written very rapidly; probably it was thought out carefully before he put pen to paper, as I observed there were but two or three trifling alterations in the original copy. He seemed pleased that the committee should have asked him to write, and pleased to accede to the wish. The subject appealed to his taste, and he seemed most happy to show his sympathy with Venice and Venetians.

The saying that "no man is a hero to his valet de chambre" was disproved in the case of Robert Browning. He was so gracious and yet so dignified with servants that he was as profoundly revered by them as he was beloved. An exact account of his gentle geniality in this regard might read like exaggeration. He appeared to dread giving his inferiors trouble; it was as though he would fain spare them the sense of servitude, which his own independent spirit caused him to imagine a painful burden. It seemed as if he were ever striving to place a cushion under a galling yoke, and in vain one sought to convince him that service rendered to such as he could only be a source of pride and pleasure to the server. He would always resist the hand of a friend or menial that tried to assist him, even in so small a matter as the adjustment or removal of his great-coat or his hat.

"Nothing that I can do for myself should be done for me," he would say, and brave was the servant who dared hold an umbrella over his head as he stepped into or out of the gondola. "What do you take me for," he would exclaim—"an infant or a man?"

In Venice his memory will live in many a humble heart until its pulse has ceased to beat. "There'll never be another like him,"[1] is still the common saying whenever his name is mentioned to those who served him.

In his immense humanity he refused to make distinctions of manner among those of his own class of life who approached him, always excepting the rare cases where base qualities had been proved beyond a doubt to his mind. The thing he most abhorred was untruthfulness; even insincerity in its most conventional form was detestable to an upright mind which loved and sought for truth in all its phases. His first impulse was to think well of people, to like them, to respect them; they were human souls, and therefore to him of the greatest earthly interest. He conversed affably with all. Lover of beauty as he was, he would talk as pleasantly with dull old ladies as with young and pretty ones. He made himself delightful at a dinner-party; whether the guests chanced to be of mediocre intelligence or of superior brains, his fund of sparkling anecdote for all was never exhausted. In this, as in many other ways, one learned from him the lesson of self-forgetfulness. He never asked, "Do these people amuse me? Do I find them agreeable?" His only thought was, "Let me try to make their time pass pleasantly."[2]

He wrote a few words some years ago in the album of Lia, a daughter of Princess Mélanie Metternich, a lovely little creature, just ten years of age, who died some months later of scarlet fever. Among her books the mother found one containing original verses, some most pathetic lines, bidding her brother farewell, and prophetic of her approaching death. The child had never shown them to any one, not even to her governess. I copied and sent them to Mr. Browning, and he thus wrote in answer:

> I want to say how much touched I was by those dear innocencies of the poor sweet child a week before the end. The mother's discovery of that book, those unsuspected yearnings in verse, one cannot venture to try and realize that. I like to think that when the kind little creature asked me so prettily to write my name in her birthday book there went

some sort of true sympathy (in the asking) with a person she had heard was a "poet," not merely a stranger with a name other people told her they had heard of. Perhaps she was meaning to be herself a "poet." Well, she is passed into poetry, for all who knew her even so slightly as I.

Some years ago an overflow of rivers, and consequent inundation of a part of the Venetian territory, interrupted for a time all communication between Venice and northern Italy. In a letter written at this fateful time, soon after his return to London, he said:

As for the failure to get to Venice, we, my sister and I, have only regretted it once, that is, uninterruptedly ever since. You must know that, besides the adverse floods and bridge-breakings, I was, for the first time in my life, literally lamed by what I took for an attack of rheumatism, which I caught just before leaving St. Pierre de Chartreuse, through my stupid inadvertence in sitting with a window open at my back,—reading the Iliad, all my excuse!—while clad in a thin summer suit, and snow on the hills and bitterness everywhere; ... but this was no such slight matter at Bologna, and I fancied I might be absolutely crippled at Venice if I even managed to overcome all obstacles and get there. Of course now that what is done is done, I am tantalized with fancies of what might have been done otherwise. But, if I live and do well, be sure that I will go as early to Venice next year, and stay as late, as circumstances will allow.

A gifted friend of mine, who met Mr. Browning in my house, thus writes of him:

It was evident to me that he always strove to excuse the faults of others and overlook their weaknesses, gathering all, with his large charity, into the great brotherhood of humanity. But his indignation at anything low, base, or untrue was like a flash of fire. His whole face would change and glow as he denounced those who used their talents to corrupt the world, as he thought some of the modern French novelists do. No word was too scathing, no scorn too intense, for that great sin consciously committed.

In this connection I recollect that a certain lady, whom he had known slightly years ago in Rome, met him one day in the street and greeted him with, "Oh, Mr. Browning, you are the very person I wished to see!" This was somewhat embarrassing, as he did not recognize his former acquaintance in the least; so she hurriedly explained to him who she once had been—the wife of an English banker in Rome—and who she then was—the wife of an Italian counselor of prefecture.

"And what, pray, can I do for you?" asked Mr. Browning.

"I have written a poem," was her answer, "and I want you to read it and tell me what you think of it"; so there and then she brought forth a manuscript from her pocket, and was about to read it aloud in the street when he stopped her, saying:

"Not here, not here! Had we not better go into a shop?"

So, as they chanced to be near the library on the Piazza, they stepped into a book-shop,[3] and the title and dedication of the poem were read. It was addressed to a French novelist,[4] whom the author called "the Jenner of literature." Mr. Browning was displeased, but, as he said, he managed to conceal his real sentiments, only saying:

"I think I should be an unfair critic on such a subject. I should rather not hear the poem."

Surprised, the lady asked his reason. "Do you not think," she inquired, "that the portrayal of the evil existing in the world has the effect of making people fear and avoid it?"

"Not in the very least," he explained; "the exact contrary is the case. It tends to make people who sin occasionally consider themselves admirably virtuous as compared with those who commit sins every day and hour." So saying, he took leave of the poetess.[5]

One of his great pleasures was to walk with my daughter through the little Venetian *calli*. He liked to find himself suddenly in one so narrow as to force him to close his umbrella, whether in sun or rain.

"Edith is the best *cicerone* in the world," he said; "she knows everything and teaches me all she knows. There never was such a guide."

In past years he had known little of the tortuous inner streets of Venice, so all was new to him. He sometimes fancied that he and his young companion had discovered a hitherto unknown bit of stone carving or bas-relief. I remember hearing him give a description of the tablet which marks the visit of Pope Alexander to Venice, which the two explorers had found in a dim, out-of-the-way corner, and he seemed so pleased that I dared not disappoint him by saying that its existence is mentioned in various guide-books. One of his favorite walks was to SS. Giovanni e Paolo to see the Colleoni, which he considered the finest equestrian statue in the world. He remarked that the artist was well named Verocchio, or "true eye," and related to us one day, in his own inimitable terse manner, the story of the checkered life of the great *condottiere*, and why his statue had been erected in Venice. He never passed a day without taking one or more long walks; indeed, his panacea for most ills was exercise, and the exercise he chiefly advocated was walking. He wrote:

> I get as nearly angry as it is in me to become with people I love when they trifle with their health,—that is, with their life,—like children playing with jewels over a bridge-side, jewels which, once in the water, how can we, the poor lookers-on, hope to recover? You don't know how absolutely well I am after my walking, not on the mountains merely, but on the beloved Lido. Go there, if only to stand and be blown about by the sea-wind.

His long walks on the Lido were among his greatest pleasures. At one time he went there daily with his congenial friends Mr. and Mrs. Sargent Curtis. He would return full of color and health, talk of the light and life and fresh air with enthusiasm, combined with a sort of pity for those who had remained at home. "It is like coming into a room from the outer air," he said, "to reënter Venice after walking on the sea-shore."

When storms kept him by force in the house all day, he never complained; but one could see that it troubled him to find himself a prisoner. He would stand at the window and watch the sea-gulls as they sailed to and fro, their presence a sure sign of heavy storms in the Adriatic. He remarked upon their strength of wing and grace of flight, as they swept down to the wreaths and long lines of dark-green seaweed floating on the surface of the canal between the house and the Church of the Salute. One day he observed: "I do not know why I never see in descriptions of Venice any mention of the sea-gulls; to me they are even more interesting than the doves of St. Mark."

Indeed, the white-winged creatures so charmed him that I often thought the world would see a poem from his pen to immortalize the birds. He admired the Salute, the sometimes adversely criticized Church of Our Lady of Health.

"Is it possible," he said, "that wise men disapprove[6] of those quaint buttresses? To me they rise out of the sea like gigantic shells; but then I am not an architect, and only know what is beautiful to my own eyes."

One of his most charming traits was the readiness with which he always acquiesced when asked to read aloud his own poems. He accepted no thanks, saying in a genial manner: "It is very kind of you to wish to hear them; when shall it be?"

He liked especially to read for his friends the Curtises at the Palazzo Barbaro, where he felt at home, feeling certain that hosts and guests were sympathetic. The day and hour fixed, he allowed nothing to interfere with his intention. The sense of honor which showed itelf in the smallest matters made it impossible for him to frame even a conventional excuse when his absence might disappoint others. Rather than break a promise he would brave a storm, or force himself to keep his word even when he justly complained that his throat was not quite as it should be. That word, once given, must be held to, despite all obstacles. Let me quote again from my friend's letter:

> His reading of his own poems was a never-to-be-forgotten delight— simple, direct, and virile as was the nature of the man. The graver portions he read in a quiet, almost introspective way, as if he were thinking it all out again. I remember once that in finishing the grand profession of faith at the end of "Saul" his voice failed him a very little, and when it was ended he turned his back to us, who were gathered about him in reverent silence, and laying the book quietly on the table, stood so for a moment. . . . He seemed as full of dramatic interest in reading "In a Balcony" as if he had just written it for our benefit. One who sat near him said that it was a natural sequence that the step of the guard should be heard coming to take Norbert to his doom, as, with a nature like the queen's, who had known only one hour of joy in her sterile life, vengeance swift and terrible would follow on the sudden destruction of her happiness.
>
> "Now, I don't quite think that," answered Browning, as if he were following out the play as a spectator. "The queen had a large and passionate temperament, which had only once been touched and

PALAZZO MANZONI. THE PALACE BROWNING WANTED TO BUY.

brought into intense life. She would have died, as by a knife in her heart. The guard would have come to carry away her dead body."

"But I imagine that most people interpret it as I do," was the reply.

"Then," said Browning, with quick interest, "don't you think it would be well to put it in the stage directions, and have it seen that they were carrying her across the back of the stage?"

Whether this was ever done I do not know; but it was wonderful to me, as showing the personal interest he took in his own creations.

He had a fund of simple playfulness which often comes with genius. One evening, after dinner at the Casa Alvisi, he was talking on the subject of certain music with the lady whose letter I have quoted, when he said suddenly:

"Come, I will play to you on the spinet in the anteroom."

So they went together, and found the place but partly lighted by one dim lamp. The spinet had no chair, so he knelt on the carpet before it, the light falling on his bent head, its snow-white hair, and on his small, eloquent hands.

He played a little fugue of Bach, and finding that one or two of the ancient keys refused to do their work,—for the spinet was a curiosity, and not meant for use,—he said:

"Raise the wooden bar over the hammers; let us see if it will do better."

The lady obeyed, and all going well, he was threading some of the intricacies of the great maestro, when she, thinking still to improve the tone, lifted the bar higher, then all at once the little hammers, tipped with bits of crow-quill, freed from captivity, leaped into the air and fell lifeless on the strings. Then all was lost, and in the midst of suppressed laughter he said:

"Now you have ruined the instrument! Let us cover it quickly and go back."

So they covered over the destruction, and, like naughty children, lifted the portière and went back demurely to the drawing-room, making no confession of the crime. He would refer to this escapade with boyish amusement.

He was on friendly terms with one of the foreign residents in Venice, an old Russian prince, a man of intelligence and varied experience. Born in Rome in the beginning of the nineteenth century and educated in Russia, he afterward represented his country at the courts of Athens, Constantinople, and Turin. At the latter place he was the friend of Cavour and of good service in maintaining friendly diplomatic relations between St. Petersburg and newly formed United Italy. Between him and Browning, therefore, numerous subjects of common interest existed, and their long conversations were enjoyed equally on both sides.

"I like Gagarin, with his crusty old port flavor," the poet says in one of his letters.

On one never-to-be-forgotten evening the subject of music took the place of old-time politics. To the great surprise of the prince, the poet recalled to his memory, and sang in a low, sweet voice, a number of folk-songs and national airs he had caught by ear during his short stay in Russia, more than fifty years before. First one would sing and then the other; if one hesitated for a note or phrase, the other could generally supply the deficiency, and with great spirit and mutual delight they continued the curious tournament for quite an hour. It was evident that the old music took them both back to the days of their youth. The Russian expressed himself amazed at the poet's musical memory. "It is better than my own, on which I have hitherto piqued myself not a little," he said at the time, and he often referred to the experience of that evening as the most remarkable proof of memory he ever met with.

Browning never failed to read the London daily papers, but seldom found time to look at those published in Venice. When he did take up one of the latter he would smile and say:

"Now listen to the iniquities committed in this wicked city yesterday!"

Then he would read aloud the police reports, which never recorded anything more serious than a petty theft of oars or *forcole, cavalli di gondola,* or, at the worst, some household linen—by a bold thief abstracted from its drying-place—to the value of five francs. Comparison of these delinquencies with those of similar columns in other lands was really a source of delight to the poet.

"How pleasant it is to be in the midst of so guileless a community!" he would say, with a genial laugh. On reading the necrologies, which often recorded the demise of some one "morte nella ancora fresca età di sessanta-cinque anni" (dead at the still youthful age of sixty-five), "They consider sixty-five an early death apparently," he said, with a smile.

A modern book was brought to his notice during his last sojourn (but one) in Venice. It is Tassini's "Curiosità Veneziane," which gives a history in brief of the old palaces, together with their divers legends; also the origin of the names of the streets and bridges. He was interested in this, and even mentions the book in a letter written after his return to London: "Tassini tempts me to dip into him whenever I pass the bookcase."

He was impressed by a story in this volume, which he afterward told in verse. It is published in "Asolando," and is entitled "Ponte dell' Angelo." Not content with Tassini's version of the legend, the poet looked it up in the "Annals of the Cappucini, by Father Boverio." He said nothing of this to any one until a certain day, when to the question, "Where would you like to go?" he answered promptly:

"To see the house of the Devil and the Advocate."

We rowed quickly to the place where three waterways meet, and where the Ponte dell' Angelo spans one of the narrow canals. Opposite stands the old Soranzo palace, with an angel carved in stone on the façade.

"Stop," he said to the gondolier, "broad-backed Luigi," as he always called him. "Do you know the story of that angel?"

"Si, signore."

"Then relate it."

The boatman at once proceeded to repeat most volubly in the Venetian dialect the tale, familiar to him from childhood.

"Do you think it is true, Luigi?" said the poet.

"Yes, sir, it is really true; it has been printed." The man's faith in the veracity of print amused the poet immensely.

He was much pleased on one occasion when Professor Nencioni came from Rome expressly to see him. Nencioni is perhaps the only Italian who has thoroughly mastered the difficulties of Browning's poetry, certainly the only one who has translated and written essays upon it, and one need hardly say that he is an enthusiastic admirer. Browning was already aware of this through a series of articles in the "Fanfulla della Domenica," published at Rome. Italian recognition of his work was especially gratifying to him for various reasons, and he welcomed this distinguished exponent of it with genuine gratitude and pleasure. "I subscribed to the paper at once," he said, with his usual frank geniality, "after reading your first kind notice of me."

Together with his clever young friend and "fellow-pilgrim" Carlo Placci the professor dined with the poet at Casa Alvisi. Every one was in the best of spirits, but to recall such conversation is beyond my power. I only remember that in the evening Nencioni, speaking to me in an aside, said: "I have studied Browning since my early youth, when first I saw him in Siena. I consider that his work has qualities not to be found even in Shakespeare; in fact in some respects I regard him as the superior of the two." After the professor had gone I said to the poet: "Do you know what your admirer says of you?"

"No; what?"

So I made myself a base tattler and repeated his words. The poet frowned and shook his head impatiently.

"No, no, no; I won't hear that. No one in the world will ever approach Shakespeare; never."

So I repented my boldness, but fancied, nevertheless, he must have been somewhat pleased by what, in his modesty, he found an exaggerated expression of admiration. Indeed, this was but one of many instances which went to prove that, although he had a sincere consciousness of his own merit as a poet, he placed others far above himself. Nothing annoyed him more than comparisons so often made between himself and Tennyson, for whom he had a heartfelt appreciation. The slightest word of dispraise or faint praise of his friend and brother poet roused him to positive anger. His admirers frequently displeased him in this way, thinking to flatter him by some such expression of opinion, and his sharp, quick answer always punished their want of tact and discrimination.

In one of his later letters he says:

> Did you get a little book by Michael Field, "Long Ago," a number
> of poems written to *innestare* what fragmentary lines and words we
> have left of Sappho's poetry? . . . The author is a great genius, a friend
> we know. Do you like it?

In speaking afterward to me on the subject of this work, his praise was enthusiastic, and he added to his expressions of admiration for the author's genius his sorrow for the trouble and anxiety she had been lately called upon to bear.

In Venice, as elsewhere, Browning rose early, and after a light breakfast went with his sister to the Public Gardens. They never failed to carry with them a store of cakes and fruits for the prisoned elephant, whose lonely fate was often pityingly alluded to by the poet, in whom a love of animals amounted to a passion. A large baboon, confined in what had once been a greenhouse, was also an object of special interest to him. This beast fortunately excited no commiseration, being healthy and content, and taking equal pleasure with the givers in his daily present of dainty food. After saying "Good morning" and "Good appetite" to these animals, he gave a passing salutation to a pair of beautiful gazelles, presented to the gardens by one of his friends;[7] then a word of greeting to two merry marmosets, the gift of another friend; then a glance at the pelicans, the ostriches, and the quaint kangaroos: he had a word and a look for each, seeming to study them and almost to guess their thoughts. After this he made the tour of the gardens, three times round the inclosure with great exactness, and then returned to his temporary home in the Palazzo Giustiniani-Recanati.

On a certain day he met one of the servants, whose joy it was to wait upon him, carrying a rather heavy basket of grapes and other fruits on her arm.

"Oh, Giuseppina," he cried, "let me help you!" and seized the basket suddenly from her hand.

PALAZZO REZZONICO, BROWNING'S HOME AND THE PLACE OF HIS DEATH.

It is on the left side of the palace, at the corner above the little canal, that one may see the memorial tablet erected by the municipality of Venice:

A
ROBERTO BROWNING
MORTO IN QUESTO PALAZZO
IL 12 DICEMBRE 1889
VENEZIA
POSE

"Open my heart and you will see
Graved inside of it, 'Italy.'"

The woman, overwhelmed by such condescension, protested, "Troppo onore, signore."

"Nonsense!" said the poet. "You are always helping me; won't you allow me for once to help you?"

Still the woman resisted, saying, "It is not for such as you, O signore!"

This was more than he could bear.

"We are all made of the same clay, Giuseppina"; and gaining his point,—for who could withstand his will?—he held one handle of the basket until they reached the palace door.

This same worthy woman is fond of relating a story of her master which illustrates another side of his character. He had paid her weekly account, and there remained one centesimo as change. The woman showed the little coin, saying shyly, "I cannot offer this trifle to the signore."

"Yes, my good Giuseppina," he said, taking it from her hand; "it is one thing to be just and another to be generous; you do right to return it to me."

"And not long after this," continues the woman, "he made me such a grand present!"

The Giustiniani-Recanati palace was in some respects worthy of a poet's sojourn. It is one of the oldest in Venice, built in the fifteenth century, and has a fine façade, with Gothic windows looking out upon a court and garden, and a southern exposure. It belongs to a lineal descendant of one of the most ancient and historically interesting families in Italy, the one in which the well-known circumstance of the marriage of a monk, by order of the Pope, occurred many centuries ago. The aroma of antiquity—and we may add sanctity, since many members of the family lived and died in the odor thereof— was a source of pleasure to the poet. He said once, "I am glad to have written some of my verses in the house of the Giustiniani," for his soul rejoiced in the heroic deeds and romantic records of bygone days.

It was curious to see that, on each one of his arrivals in Venice, he took up his life precisely as he had left it. On Sunday morning he always went with his sister to the same Waldensian chapel, in which they seemed to take great interest, especially enjoying the preaching of a certain eloquent pastor, whose name, I regret to say, I have forgotten. On the return from the brisk morning walk he read his newspapers and letters, answering each day a few among the many received from friends and admirers. He was amused, but never impatient, with the innumerable requests for autographs, some of which were written in illiterate and inelegant handwriting, many of them from the Western States and far California. When his instinct told him these were genuinely asked for, and not from the idly curious, he would answer them, unless, indeed, the number of important private letters took up too much of his precious time. When people asked him *viva voce* for an autograph, he looked puzzled, and said:

"I don't like to write always the same verse, yet I can remember only one."

Of course the person addressed replied: "I am grateful for anything whatever that comes to your mind." Then he would take up his pen at once and write:

All that I know of a certain star, etc.

Sometimes, when in a merry mood, he wrote this verse in so fine a handwriting that only such extraordinary eyesight as his own could decipher it, and on one occasion, in the same microscopic calligraphy, he wrote Mrs. Barbauld's lines,

Life! we've been long together, etc.,

saying, after he had read it aloud, "If she had never written aught but that one verse she would deserve to be forever remembered."

I recollect an amusing incident apropos of autographs. A Venetian banker had asked, through me, an autograph for his daughter's album. Browning said, "I really cannot write always the same thing"; then, after a pause, he exclaimed, "Ah, now I have it," and seating himself at a table, he quickly wrote a verse which I had often heard him quote and laugh at, about pence and pounds, a variety of the well-known proverb. Edith said timidly:

"But will they not find that rather personal?"

The poet thought a moment, and laughing heartily, said: "I believe you are right, my dear; here, keep this for yourself, and I will write something else for the banker's daughter."

He could not possibly have managed to keep pace with his large correspondence but for the aid of his sister, his guardian angel, who helped him in this as in many other ways—not obtrusively, for she knew his strong spirit of independence, but with the fine tact that can be inspired by intense affection only, combined with a high order of intelligence. The most perfect understanding existed between the two, and the devotion of the sister to the supremely endowed brother was appreciated and admired by all who were privileged to observe it. At midday these two dear friends took their second breakfast together, ordering by preference Italian dishes, such as *risotto*, macaroni, and all fruits in their season, especially grapes and figs. They enjoyed their novel menus and tête-à-tête repasts, talking and laughing the while, and approving especially of the cook's manner of treating ortolans, of which "mouthfuls for cardinals" the poet writes so amusingly in the prologue to "Ferishtah's Fancies." About three o'clock they went out in a gondola. To the question, "Where shall we go?" the answer was:

"Anywhere. All is beautiful, but let it be toward the Lido."

They seldom wished to make formal visits, though they were scrupulously exact in returning those which, as he always said, people were "kind enough to make him."

Sometimes, though rarely, they wandered through the antiquity shops. The poet had a keen flair for good bric-à-brac, and had an especial liking for tapestry and old carved furniture. He seldom sought for them, but his eye seized quickly upon an object of interest or value. He never hesitated or changed his mind; his intuition was always correct. A purchase once made, he was as thoroughly delighted as if the particular object were the first bibelot he had ever had the good luck to acquire. Like a child with a new toy, he would carry it himself (size and weight permitting) into the gondola, rejoice over his chance in finding it, and descant eloquently upon its intrinsic merits. In this, as in every other phase of his character, he was entirely unspoiled. Then he would explain minutely where the object should be placed in the London house, and add significantly, "I never buy anything without knowing exactly what I wish to do with it," which was quite true, as his mind was unfailingly clear from great things to trifles. "You might take this lesson from me, if none other," he said to me playfully; for he disapproved of the habit of buying useless things in a vague manner only because they were old and pretty.

He never expressed a wish to "see sights" in the tourist manner, but would occasionally visit such churches as SS. Giovanni e Paolo or the Frari, and study the monuments with close attention. These seemed to interest him more than old pictures, and he examined carefully, on one occasion, the marble carvings of the Miracoli within and without, which he called a "jewel of a church." The ancient palaces with their strangely varied façades were always interesting and suggestive to him; we see how suggestive in that wonderful short poem called "In a Gondola," in which he pictures Venice, it seems to me, as no one else in prose or verse has ever depicted the sea-city.

About five o'clock, when we returned to the Alvisi for tea, the poet would sometimes say, "Excuse me for to-day," and retire to his own apartments in the Giustiniani. He never gave nor was asked his reason for doing so; it was enough that he wished it. At other times he would join us at the tea-table and talk with equal facility in English, French, or Italian with visitors who chanced to be present. Occasionally, to our great delight, he would say, "Edith dear, you may give me a cup of tea to-day"; but, as a rule, he abstained from what he considered a somewhat unhygienic beverage if taken before dinner. When it so pleased them the brother and sister went together to their own rooms, and punctually at half-past seven returned to dine at Casa Alvisi. The poet, unlike many men of letters, was always scrupulously careful in his dress, especially in his dinner-hour toilet. His sister wore beautiful gowns of rich and somber tints, and appeared each day in a different and most dainty French cap and quaint antique jewels. They were both so genial and content that, puzzle the brain as one might, it was impossible to know whether the quiet family dinner or the presence of guests was the more agreeable to them. In face of the doubt we decided on the latter; it seemed selfish to do otherwise, and we were rarely without common friends to share the pleasure of the poet's conversation. If the direct question were asked on this subject, the invariable answer was, "Do as you please; you know we are always perfectly happy."

Browning's strong dramatic instinct made him take intense pleasure in plays, whether written or acted. Though he was rarely seen at the theater in London, he greatly enjoyed a "short season" at the Goldoni, where he went every night to see Gallina's clever Venetian comedies. He had two boxes thrown into one, and seated in an arm-chair quite at his ease, he followed each play with the deepest interest, never taking his eyes off the stage until the fall of the curtain. Gallina was invited during an entr'acte to come into the box to be presented to the poet and hear from his own lips an expression of genuine admiration for his work. The Italian was pleased and flattered, as may be easily imagined, for Browning's art of praise was as distinguishing a characteristic as was his art of dedication, which caused some one to style him the "Prince of Dedicators." It was a combination of judgment and enthusiasm, so turned that each word should have its due "specific gravity," and of which there should be neither too many nor too few.

Each night after the play Gallina waited at the door of the theater to see the poet pass, and the latter invariably turned a few steps out of his way to exchange a hearty hand-shake with his "brother dramatist," as he liked to call him. Browning's large and genial nature made him always wish to express his thanks, either for favors received, the occasion for which happened rarely in his independent mode of life, or for pleasures procured to him by any one, author or actor; whoever it might be, he always longed to say the words, "I thank you." The following extract from one of his letters, written at Primiero, is an illustration of this:

> The little train from Montebelluna to Feltre was crowded; we could find no room except in a smoking-carriage, wherein I observed a good-natured elderly gentleman—an Italian, I took for granted. Presently he said, "Can I offer you an English paper?"
>
> "What, are you English?"
>
> "Oh, yes, and I know that you are going to see your son at Primiero."
>
> "Why, who can you be?"
>
> "One who has seen you often."
>
> "Not surely Mr. Malcolm?"
>
> "Well, nobody else."
>
> So ensued an affectionate greeting, he having been the guardian angel of Pen in all his chafferings about the purchase of the palazzo. He gave me abundance of information, and satisfied me on many points.

The time of year which Browning always gave to his sojourns in Venice was one which all the great Venetian families pass in their country homes, so that comparatively few among them had the pleasure of the illustrious stranger's acquaintance. Among these few the Countess Marcello was a favorite of his, and he accepted, for himself and his sister, her invitation to pass a day at her villa at Mogliano. The day was bright and beautiful, and he seemed to enjoy the short hour's journey by rail, and to admire the smiling country about him. The countess, with several of her children, met us at the little station, and we were quickly whirled away, the younger people with their ponies, the elders in a comfortable landau, through the country road and pretty park to a villa of simple yet imposing architecture. On one side of the house is a sun-dial with the familiar motto (in Latin), "I count only the hours of sunshine," and the lawns near the house bear English mottos in flowers and colored plants, together with the device of the countess, a trefoil joined by letters to form her name, Andriana. After luncheon we all repaired to the tennis-ground, past the deer-houses and through a stately avenue of ancient beech-trees whose great branches met and interlaced far above our heads, making a gigantic arbor. The young people gave up their usual games and seated themselves on rustic benches, listening attentively to every word from the poet's lips. A Venetian sculptor, who chanced to be one of the guests, hid himself behind a group of trees, and peeping through their trunks from his coign of vantage, drew in his album a fairly good portrait of Browning. The countess, who was Queen Margherita's favorite lady of honor, showed the poet a specimen of the handwriting of her royal mistress, which he greatly admired, as being at once forcible and graceful.

Before the hour of departure, the daughter of the house, a young and very lovely creature, asked the favor that Mr. Browning should write in her album.

"With the greatest pleasure," he said, "but I am ashamed to say I remember only one verse."

Every one smiled at this, and the poet, as usual, wrote "My Star." When the *contessina* looked at it, she exclaimed: "This is one of my favorites. See, I have copied it in my book of verses"; and turning over the pages, she showed the poem, neatly written out by her own hand, among many others by the same author. Browning was surprised to find his writings understood and admired by this fair young foreigner, and complimented her on her proficiency in so difficult a language, adding, with a smile: "Even English girls do not find my poems easy to read, you know." Then he said: "Let us compare the verses, the one you have copied and the one I have written; I am sure we shall find some mistake."

There were indeed a few errors, and as he corrected them he said: "See what a service you have rendered me. I should have left the verse full of faults if you had not been able to correct me."

The girl flushed with pleasure, which made her beauty still more apparent. In speaking afterward of this most agreeable visit, Browning gave a glowing description of the beautiful mother and her children. "It is like an English family," he said, which was the highest praise he could bestow.

At the railway-station, while we were awaiting the arrival of the train, a young Italian litterateur[8] asked to be presented to Browning. The countess introduced him as "one who has already distinguished himself in the world of letters," which was of course a passport to the poet's interest. They talked together until forced to part by the shrill whistle of warning, and then came cordial farewells to all who had accompanied us to the station.

"He seems a youth of promise," said Browning, as we sped Venice-ward; "I liked him. I hope he will do well and that I shall hear of him again."

Unluckily, when next his name was mentioned, it was in connection with a series of lectures announced in the papers as "twelve lectures on Zola," which, as may be supposed, the poet expressed no desire to attend.

All who strove to attain in art or literature interested him. Each one struck, with more or less force, his most responsive chord. He was pleased, on the occasion of one of his readings at the Palazzo Barbaro, to meet the novelist Castelnuovo, and mentioned an incident which had long before made the writer's name familiar to his ear. He related how, on his second visit to Asolo, whither he had taken his sister to bear witness to the wisdom of his early admiration for the place, they found themselves without a book of any sort, an unusual position for book-lovers such as they. The poet went out in search of something or anything readable in the little town, where book-shops are even now unknown. He found one volume only, in a paper-shop I think it was, containing a series of short stories by Castelnuovo, entitled "Alla Fenestra." The brother and sister were both delighted with the book, and ever after procured for themselves each work by the same author as soon as it was given to the public.

Browning's memory is still green in Asolo, where many of the citizens remember him well, where his son owns not only Pippa's Tower, erected after his father's death, but other houses with fine outlooks over the Venetian plain. The small museum in the town hall has the son's bust of his father in plaster, and other relics of the poet who so doted on Asolo. These rambling reminiscences of hours spent with him in Asolo and Venice may have the good fortune to bring him in spirit nearer to his admirers, for I have striven to give an exact report of the man and his character as they appeared to me during an unbroken friendship of many years.

The manuscript of "Browning in Venice" shows a number of alterations from the printed text. Significant changes and additions are listed below:

1. Ah! no ghe ne nasce attri.
2. ... Thus his every word and every act was a sermon, the text of which each might find for himself. It was easy "to mark and learn" such precious teaching, as children find profit and interest in object lessons.
3. Ongania's bookshop.
4. Zola.
5. ... and vented his indignation by giving a description of the interview at home, the humorous side of which made the hearers laugh heartily.
6. Ruskin disapproves.
7. His friend Alexander Malcolm.
8. Fradaletto.

APPENDIX C

Robert Browning 1879 to 1885

By Daniel Sargent Curtis

> "I too have noted that our whole conversation is little or nothing else but Biography or Auto-Biography; ever humano-anecdotical. (menschlich anekdotisch.)"　　　　　Sartor Resartus.[1]

THE FIRST TIME we met him was at the Lido, where he was with M^r & Mrs W.W. Story,[2] of Rome, and they introduced us to him. This must have been in 1880—or '79. M^r & Miss Browning were then living at Hôtel Universo,[3] the Palace next to the Iron Bridge and to the Accademia. We were at Barbier's,[4] opposite to the Prefettura or Palazzo Corner. The 'Universo' was kept by an old couple, Dalmatian, or other, with a title of Count and very poor. The husband was constantly away, sailing his boats on the lagunes, and could hardly be called a 'landlord.' His wife did what house-keeping and cooking she knew—which was little enough. The halls and rooms were spacious but bare, and guests few. The food was bad and the cold intense, but Mr Browning is not difficult and sometimes stays for months in mountain inns, where eggs and milk are the staple bill of fare. They dined with us at Barbier's, and later at Palazzo Barbaro, and we dined with them, at his old house in Warwick Crescent, on our several visits to London.

It became a habit with us to row over to the Giudecca, after breakfast, and landing at the Church of S. Biagio, now displaced by the Mill of Stücky, to walk as far as S. Giorgio and back, which took forty minutes. I regret not having earlier kept some note of his conversation, anecdotes and reminiscences, always so *abundant* and so interesting, and *illustrating* the extent of his knowledge, the many-sidedness of his mind, & the strength of his character. But I well remember that, one morning, as he looked over his letters just received, he handed one to me to read. It was the first proposition and programme for a 'Browning Society.'[5] He said, 'Il me semble que cela frise le ridicule?['] He received at the same time some doggrel [sic] verses from America, about his poetry. I afterwards knew that these were sent by Miss *Maria Potter* [sic] of New York.[6]

[167]

The earliest notes I find are dated Oct. 5. 1883—and are as follows–

Robert Browning arrived in Venice October 4, 1883. He has often said that, as long as he lived, he hoped and meant to pass a month or more in Venice every year. In 1882 he got as far as Verona, when the inundations[7] cut off all communications with Venice, and he returned to England. This year he passed some time in a spot inaccessible but to mules and pedestrians, near Aosta—by an ascent of seven or eight hours. In Venice this year M[r]. Browning is lodged in an appartment [*sic*] connected with Casa Alvisi, opposite to the Church of la Salute, his old hotel, 'Universo,' being discontinued.

October 6. at an evening reception at Pal[o] Barbaro, M[r]. Browning was present. He talked much of Carlyle.[8] Someone expressed sympathy with Mrs. Carlyle as a suffering wife. R.B. said [']'Not a bit of it! Carlyle spoke of her as if she had stepped down from the stars to marry him. What was she, after all? The daughter of a small Scotch doctor in an obscure country village.[9] She did no more work than was good for her. I have known plenty of Curates, gentlemen's sons, with wives and families living on as little as the Carlyles, and working as hard, and saying nothing about it! She would get servants from that barbarous place who knew nothing of their work—which in fact they came to learn. And the vermin she said so much about, it seems after all came from Scotland in her own mother's old bed. She encouraged all Carlyle's whims and fancies, adopted all his ideas and opinions and exaggerated them; but ridiculed them to other people. She showed her private journal to Miss Williams Wynn,[10] who advised her[11] to burn it; and she thought she had burned the whole of it, except ten pages. She would say, 'Carlyle talks of getting no sleep! that is, if he lies awake from a quarter past one to two o'clock—he has had no sleep!—' One day, D[r]. Quain[12] called. Mrs. Carlyle came down *en toilette*—for her—. Carlyle said, 'I thocht ye were ill.['] (as she had been two days in bed.) Whereupon she threw a cup of coffee at him.["]

Browning said that she had no beauty, except good eyes and hair—but her nose! and here he drew a line in the air to give its upward turn—'And her complexion! like nothing but pickled walnuts.[']

Carlyle had known Browning's father, and had always been kind to Browning when a young man– On B's return from Italy, he dined at M[r] Kenyon's,[13] where was Carlyle—and after dinner many more people, and among them Mrs. Carlyle. Those at table sat for some time before joining the others, at which Mrs. Carlyle was piqued, and when Browning spoke to her, affected to disbelieve it could be he, 'No! Ye're so changed!' However, she asked him to tea for the next evening. He had not seen a tea-table and service for so many years, that when she said, "Now, M[r]. Browning, be useful, and hand the tea-kettle from the hob," he obeyed, not knowing what to do with it. She chose to think he was putting on airs, and cried, 'Fill the tea-pot!['] which he did, left with the kettle in his hand. 'What am I to do with it now?'—'Put it down.' So down he put it, on the carpet at her feet. She was quite vexed, at what she believed his affectation of a fine travelled gentleman.

Browning always went to see Carlyle on his birthday.[14] "They had no real sorrows and cares. Now, if they had children, one ill or dead of scarlet fever, another of croup, they would have had something else to think about than of their own sweet selves. His arrogance excessive—his contempt for all which he did not know or think. As for Michel Angelo when Grimm's book[15] came out—his scorn! He accepted all attentions as simply due to his genius. Allingham (d. 1889) used to devote two hours daily to walking with him—the cream of the day, though a literary man writing for bread. Carlyle regarded him as a sort of faithful dog, who might be kicked.[16] (with a gesture.) Carlyle's power of description! You might be sure he had well looked up his subject. His account of Waterloo—the ground—the scenes—the Prussians coming up! You'd think you were there yourself!—Perhaps Froude[17] came across some things, in Mrs. Carlyle's Diary, not pleasing to himself, and did not care to *ménager* her.["] (Mr. B. repeated this in 1889.) At all events, he printed all, and got a good bit of money by it. R.B. saw Carlyle a week before his death.[18] He was lying comatose and took no notice of anything.— If you listened, without contradicting him, he talked wonderfully well,—better than he wrote– R.B. "never argued with him, but once, and then quite put him down." It was about Louis Napoleon, whom Carlyle was abusing roundly.– RB said, [']'You have, all your life, been preaching up *Force*—crying for a Man. Well, now you have him, and you call him upstart, usurper, &c. &c. Carlyle had nothing to answer"—

October 15. '83. Called for Mr Browning at 10.30, a warm, bright morning. He said that though he had lived so long in Italy, he was afraid of the sun. At the Dogana we hoisted the sail of my gondola, and with a light breeze we passed slowly down the Canal of Giudecca, towards the islet of San Giorgio in Alga, where stand the remains of an ancient convent, of which the tall tower has been taken down within a few years. An effective statue of the Madonna & Child, protected by an iron parasol, still remains. He spoke of the tendency, in Modern French Art, to extravagant and painful subjects—as the Prise de Troie, Astyanax thrown over the walls, women half-burned &c. Another of a Paysanne who recognizes her sister as a 'Cocotte' in a carriage—all life size. Of Critics, he said that where opinions are sustained or proved by extracts fairly made, there can be no objection. But the critic must *read* the book or *see* the picture, which are not to be condemned merely by Critic's dictum. He added that 'one Austin[']'[19] persistently printed extracts of his (B's) verse, which by alterations and omissions of words and punctuation, were made to seem to establish Austin's criticisms. B had sent them to Lord Carnarvon,[20] one of the promoters of the National Review of which Austin is the Editor. (He again repeated this Nov. '89.) Mrs. Story told us that when Austin was introduced to her, she asked him if he was the son of Miss Jane Austen, the Novelist?

Of French books on England, he said very few Frenchmen could get access to the upper classes in England, or see enough of them to enable them to describe them correctly—[']'as they carefully keep to themselves. I seem to know a good many—for some reason or other. Perhaps because I never had any occupation. My father wished me to do what I liked. I should not so bring up a son. My father and grandfather lived to great age.– Not long ago, one fee'd the servants where one dined. Hogarth[21] broke up those vails. A lord who left a Country-house without feeing the servants, received a letter from the butler with an old pair of breeches 'which they supposed must belong to him[']"–

He said Gladstone's Italian Version of Cowper's Hymn,[22] printed in XIX Century Review, was 'very bad, very bad.' Asked about Payne Collier[23]—Rascal.– Asked if the Poem of the Man and the Stag[24] was founded on fact? 'Exactly, the man told me his story forty years ago.' He described the death of the Elephant at Exeter 'Change which his father took him to see when a child.

Shelley—deserted his children, and Eldon[25] rightly refused to restore them to him. Shelley—the biggest liar (if lying is saying what is not true.) He cursed his father to his school-fellows. Nowadays, the boys would punch his head! He was coming out of it when he died. And had he lived, might have been—anything!

"Joaquin Miller,[26] an American poet—called on R.B. at Warwick Crescent, and supposed the whole Crescent to be M\[r] B's house, and the Canal his ornamental pièce d'eau. He said that in America a great writer was rich, and lived in a large house." B. said he was tempted to say that if *his* countrymen paid what they owed him, *he* could live in a large house.

Oct. 31/83. M\[r] Browning came to our garden, Villa Vendramin, at the Giudecca, with his sister, and walked for half an hour under the grape-trellises. He said they had arranged to go to Greece this week—and had so written to friends and servants in London– But, considering the sea-voyages and the lateness of the Season, they had decided to defer their plan to another year, when they could set out from Venice a month earlier—'for we are both bad sailors. But I am glad we have had this idea; that our thoughts have been turned to it—for now it will seem easier. To go to Greece has always seemed something too remote, impossible! Now it is no longer so, and next year we shall hope to go.['] (They did not go, and seem to have dropped the idea altogether. '89[.])

Nov. 2. 1883. Asked M\[r] Browning if there were any *sous-entendus* in his poem of Childe Roland?– 'Not the least. I wrote it on the 2\[d] of January, having begun the year with the intention of writing a lyric poem every day that year.' ["]The first I wrote was 'Women and Roses,' about a rose-tree which some American ladies sent to my wife as a New Year's gift. I wrote half of Childe Roland, and finished it the next day. Then somebody or something put it out of my head, and I relapsed into my old desultory way.'[']–

Speaking of Milton, ["]Tennyson said to me, lately, 'It stands about thus,— Byron ranks higher than he did; Milton hardly as high,—Shakespeare immense, and unapproachable.'["]

["]Mallock[27] I know very well. His uncle, M\[r] Spedding,[28] showed to me some of his writings, when he was quite a lad, and then brought him to see me. He then went to Balliol. Later, he said he owed his career to my encouragement, and to my advice to try to describe social scenes and character– As he says so I suppose it was so– His last books very objectionable—bad.["]

Miss Browning told this incident.

Mrs. Browning's Aunt had a tame monkey, with a very long prehensile tail, which one day he curled around Mrs. Browning's slender throat. She, almost lifeless, had the presence of mind to hold out her watch at arm's length, at which the monkey darted, uncoiling his tail, and she escaped suffocation.

Nov. 3. Being the anniversary of our wedding-day, M\[r] Browning brought as a gift to Mrs. Curtis a copy of 'The Inn Album,' with an autograph inscription on the fly-leaf.[29]

Nov. 27. '83. A dull damp day had not prevented M^r & Miss Browning's daily walk to the Public Garden, and he added, four turns around its circuit. Five! said Miss Browning. We all think her strength hardly equal to keeping up with his. For instance, she was seven hours on foot descending a road, impossible for carriages, or even for donkeys, from a mountain village where they stayed some time, and where there was no other food than eggs and milk with dry bread. She is, however, full of energy, mental and physical, at her brother's service, sitting erect in her chair, disdaining the support of its back. A great reader and a good rememberer of what she reads, and capable of excellent criticisms, though usually keeping subordinate to her brother's more emphasized personality, who likes to talk loud and long, full length in a low chair or sofa-corner, with legs thrust straight out and his hands either clasped behind his head, or plunged into his trousers' pockets. If anyone offer remark or rejoinder, he is apt to listen for a moment, and then raises his voice and over-talks the interruption. Yesterday afternoon he had in hand a Sonnet to Goldoni, composed in haste on the last day before the printing of an Album by the Committee for Goldoni's Statue. This sonnet he read aloud with his hearty manner and emphasis which are habitual and genuine—although quite in contravention of that undemonstrative nonchalance and affected indifference which is now *bien vu*. He read to us the note from Professor Molmenti,[30] of the Goldoni Committee, on receiving which, he at once sat down and wrote his Sonnet. The lines are in keeping with the subject—genial, affectionate and simple. I said 'there are no big words in it.' Browning said—[']I should think *not!'*–

Of Critics—he said he had never noticed them. That he was told that Editors always set their youngest hands to review Poetry, as on any other topic they would expose their insufficiency, while anyone could write of Poetry, 'this is wretched stuff!' or, 'this is truly poetical.' He had never thanked anyone for favourable notice, but Roden Noel,[31] who had before thought himself rudely treated by Browning, and had asked "if he were a kind man?" Proposed to pass Saturday evening with us, quietly.

28 Nov. 83—a superbly bright warm day. At ten o'clock we took gondola for the Lido. The post brought a letter for Browning, to my care. Passing the Public Garden, we saw his white felt hat and heard his voice, as he and his Sister were doing their four circuits. We rowed up to give him the letter, and proposed to them to go with us to Lido, which they did—and we asked them to dine on Saturday– ["]Oh,["] said he, ["]you'll make too much of us! If you will give us only your family dinner, we will come.["] At dinner he talked of Charles and Mary Lamb. Charles he never saw. But Mary, who was her brother[']s senior, he saw once, being taken to visit her by Lady Talfourd, who with some other ladies kindly took charge of her–

Lamb introduced Talfourd to Procter[32] 'my one admirer!' On one occasion Browning asked Procter, 'who, on the whole, was the best man he had ever known?'—'Oh, Lamb, of course.'– Lamb was admirably regular in all money matters, though so erratic in everything else. Browning said that Carlyle's remarks on Charles Lamb are most harsh; and agreed that Lamb's writings would survive Carlyle's.

Browning[']s earliest and best friends were Talfourd,[33] Procter and Kenyon. When he was but twenty-two years of age, and was quite unknown to the literary circles, Talfourd invited him to a dinner, at which were present Wordsworth, Landor, and many other men of letters– After dinner, Talfourd (who liked after-dinner speeches and kept them up, to the last) spoke in praise of the Elders, but added, 'We have here a younger poet, come among us, &c. &c.'—'an immense pride and encouragement to me at that time,' and added— 'for it is the April shower which developes the flower, not the later drenching rains.'

Talfourd married Miss Rutt,[34] one of the numerous daughters of a lawyer who lived freely and left nothing. A bar subscription was proposed, but Talfourd declined any aid, and himself supported his wife's family. He drank wine in old style, two or more bottles—after which, wet towels and his briefs—and next day early in his place. After one such effort he died in his robes in Court, and was carried home through the streets in his red gown.[35] He was mostly broken by his son's conduct, who got into debt and raised money on Post Obits, and became a mere scribbler of jokes and punning pieces. Another son, called Charles Lamb, died. Another was a clergyman.

["]Wordsworth did not strike me as vain. A vain man is smirking, and seeking your approbation. He was much indebted to his sister. Though none ever wrote fuller tribute than he did to her.["]

["]Dickens—in dress and manners was rather like a shop-keeper. His grand-mother was house-keeper to Lord Crewe, and told excellent tales to the children. The family got some place for her son, and tried to raise his condition. But he sponged on *his* son, drew bills &c. I saw him often and knew him well. Micawber[36] was easily recognizable. Once at Lord Crewe's, Charles Dickens was reminded, by Lord Houghton, of his grandmother. 'Yes, I know very well, she was house-keeper here.'["]

Crabbe Robinson[37] resolved to retire when he should have got £400 a year by the Law, and did so, with great content.

M.rs Browning's father had eight children, and never would hear of their marrying, nor would listen to her going to a milder climate as advised by the doctors. Browning, who had corresponded with her before they met, proposed at their first interview that they should be married, 'and I'll take you to a mild climate.' M.r Kenyon told M.r Barrett that he knew of no man to whom he would more readily give a daughter. M.r Barrett answered, 'I have no objection to him, but object to her marrying at all.' In later years though far from rich, the Brownings resolved to accept nothing of her father's property, but when he died he left her nothing. Another daughter was attached to a young officer. Her father said, 'give it up, or leave my house.' She left the house, and was married. When going to India with her husband, she wrote entreating him to allow her to take leave of him, which he refused, and ordered that his door should be shut in her face. Her emotion caused a miscarriage. He never saw her again, and left her nothing.[38] One of his sons fell in love with an adopted daughter, very lovely,[39] married her and they also were disinherited.

["]My first travel I made alone, from London to Trieste and Venice, whence to Asolo &c—on foot. My next journey was to Russia.[40] My second visit to Venice was made with my wife. None of her brothers and sisters had any especial talent. She was always quite devoid of self-esteem.["]

Oct. 10. '85 Mr Browning came to an evening reception at Palazzo Barbaro, where also came Professor Max Muller[41] and family of Oxford, a thoroughly Anglicised German, who said of English Etiquette and Conventionalities, that they *settled* questions for you, and that everyone understood what they had to do. He was surprised that in America 'precedence' is quite unknown.

Browning always interested in everyone and everything connected with Oxford, and especially with Balliol.

October 18. 1885, we went to Casa Alvisi, Canal Grande, to hear Browning read some of his own poems. About twenty-five persons were present. M^r and Mrs W.W. Story (the sculptor) of Rome, Mrs & Miss Bronson, Sir Henry and Lady Layard,[42] Sir W. & Lady Gregory,[43] Mr Hardinge,[44] the Misses Ker[r],[45] and others.

Browning read standing, as he always prefers to do, and without glasses. His reading is quite without effort at any elocution, or studied inflection of his voice, which is strong, and audible, but not melodious. The interest and attraction is in *his* interest—Ita si vis nec flere, flendum est tibi[46]—

When he reads his own poetry, he ceases to be the Browning of Society and puts off 'that side to show the world,'[47] and becoming Browning the Poet, is seen, as it were, under the afflatus by which he is inspired and carried away, and his voice, features, manner then reflect the great qualities of his verse and he is his greater Self,—and his own best interpreter. This evening he read many of his best pieces, as Hervé Riel, Andrea del Sarto, A Dialogue of Singer and Sculptor,[48] the Ride to Ghent, the Toccata of Galuppi, An Incident of the French Camp, Statue and Bust—repeatedly expressing the fear of tiring his hearers. After Hervé Riel, Sir H. Layard told an anecdote of a midshipman who asked for a box at the Adelphi for his reward. Before going away, Browning most kindly offered to read again, for Mrs. Curtis and any friends she might like to invite to our house, whenever she should desire it.

Oct. 20. '85. Mr Browning at an evening party at Sir H. Layard's house—He talked of the affair of his buying the Manzoni or Montecuculi[49] [sic] Palace, on Canal Grande, opposite to Palazzo Barbaro. As I had previously been in correspondence with the Marchese Montecuculi (who lives in Styria) to buy the Palace from his family for M^r. W. Story and myself, Browning requested me to reopen negotiations for his account, which I did, and the Montecuculi proposed to come to Venice on this business. He talked a long time of this affair, and took Mrs. Curtis in to supper. Miss Hammond played the zither quite well.

Nov. 4. '85 M^r & Miss Browning dined with us, and after dinner he read 'The Italian in England,' Home-thoughts—The Glove, Master Hugues of Saxe Gotha—Up in the Villa and Down in the City—The Patriot—The Twins Date and Dabitur—The Fugue,[50] which he said he wrote in the organ-loft of the Duomo at Florence. Of 'The Italian in England' he told us that Mazzini[51] read it to his friends to show them how an Englishman could sympathize with Italy.

Graf Rudolf Montecuculi left his card, and I went with M^r. Browning to call on him, at Albergo Europa, by appointment, to discuss the affair of the purchase of his family palace. On the next day, Browning visited the interior of the Palace for the first time, which had somewhat suffered from its having been occupied by Croats. There were doubts also as to the stability of the foundations, and there was a heavy *armatura* of beams placed to shore it up, since removed.

Looking at a clever but unfinished sketch, Browning said, [']'The finest line which I ever wrote is yet unpublished, and never has been printed. 'The Artist's greatest Curse—the incomplete'["] (or nearly thus.)[52] He said that he and Mrs. Browning had arranged to take the apartment on the upper floor of the Palazzo Barberini at Rome, in the opposite wing to that occupied so many years by our friends the Storys. They had applied for and obtained permission to put in a lift, for Mrs. Browning's convenience. Four days later she died. The anticipated change to this Roman house had been a source of great interest and delight to M.[rs] Browning, as all who know Casa Guidi and the Barberini Palace will well understand; to say nothing of the difference between the winter climates of Rome and Florence. She sat in her last days with the plans of the apartment before her, studying its disposition, and devising its improvements.[53]

Nov 11. '85 M.[r] & Miss Browning dined with us[,] he in great spirits at his probable purchase of Palazzo Manzoni, and discussed the question as to its restoration. His present intention is to hold on to London for some years, but ultimately to retire to Venice. Mr Hunt[54] came in the evening, the Architect employed to make the pedestal for the great statue of the Genius of Liberty and to set it up. Browning cited some of the rhymes of Hudibras,[55] 'which we of the *métier* think unequalled, as *medicines* and *dead since*.['] It is rarely that Browning does not know, and know well, about any book, person, matter worth knowing, past or present. He has been all his life a student blessed with a retentive memory, a close observer of Man and of Nature. He seems to know by heart the whole of English poetry, and of Music, Painting and Sculpture has practical experience. He read Hebrew, which he studied with a Jewish lady,[56] and had rather a liking for Jews, whom he and his sister always praised and defended. He had many Jewish traits, as cleverness, tenacity, courage. Intensity of purpose was his striking characteristic. Effort unrelaxed to the end, of whatever was undertaken, was the secret of the extent of his acquirement and performance. "Whatever book he began to read, it was his rule to finish," and what he once read he never forgot. Seventy years of such application account for much. Again, never was man with fewer artificial wants, more absolutely simple in habits, while at the same time he had no dislike to magnificence and luxury, though he hated waste or abuse of money.

Nov 12, 1885– M.[r] Browning came to Palazzo Barbaro with his son, to say that the affair of the purchase of the Manzoni Palace was agreed upon between himself and Montecuculi. I suggested that the agreement should be formally made and stated in writing, and[57]

Nov 14, '85 Browning came in the evening to say that he had taken Montecuculi to our lawyer Baschiera,[58] where they had made and signed the contract. Browning elated, and full of projects for buying and pulling down adjacent houses. He then read several poems, Lippi, Ratisbon, A. del Sarto, &c. He said of his father that "he lived to the age of 85—a man of vast knowledge, reading and memory—totally ignorant of the world." We saw at his house in London a portrait of his father, made by Miss Browning and an excellent piece of work.[59] His mother was a victim to tic-douloureux.[60] His sister might have married, but devoted her life to her parents and to her brother–

A distinguished Frenchman came to Balliol, and young Browning was sent for to interpret, as neither Mr Jowett nor any of the Dons could talk with him.

Nov. 18. 85 M^r & Miss Browning and Barrett Browning dined with us. The day previous they dined with Don Carlos,[61] who showed them his Indian curiosities, monkeys and dogs, and gave Browning his account of the Carlist War.

Browning told story of his acquaintance Lomonosoff of the Russian Legation at London, an irascible man who spoke English well. He went to order a visiting card, and was very long in choosing it—and the shop-keeper out of patience. 'Your name, Sir, I'll take, if you please,' pen in hand. [']L–o—lo. M–o—mo. N–o, no. S–o—so.' At which the man turned him out of the shop, for a farçeur. 'We'll have none of your humbug here!'–

Young Browning said that at one time his father had the habit of practising the pianoforte at 4 o'clock A.M. for two hours every day, *in the dark*.

Browning told us that his wife engaged a nurse who had attended the Duchess of Parma in her confinement a month previously– This nurse told them that when she informed the Duke that he had a son and heir he immediately went head over heels three times!

When the Duke was murdered, the Duchess placed his heart in a new silver sandwich box just arrived from Paris.

Nov. 21, '85 M^r & Miss Browning's last visit, as they start tomorrow for London. A rainy windy night—the rest of the company were the old Countess Thun-Hohenstein, Baroness Paffins, Capt. Avignone[62] of the Italian Navy, Horatio Brown,[63] Count Vai, Miss Ker, Mme de Pilat,[64] Princesse Iturbide.[65] Browning full of his palace, which many think too old, too cold, and on the wrong side of Grand Canal. The next day Sunday Nov. 22 he came to say good bye, and to leave with me certain directions as to the Palace purchase— which he is more delighted with than the rest of us are—though he ought to know. The façade is certainly noble and beautiful. I remember Browning being amusingly angry at the term 'goffagine,'[66] applied to it in an Italian description. But there is uncertainty as to the security of its foundations, which may involve great expense, and the internal decorations have entirely perished. Dec 3. he wrote from London. 'My buying a palace in Venice makes more talk than if I had written an Epic!' But the purchase fell through, to Browning's great annoyance, who was ready with his money[.] But the Montecuculi family, whether they could not give a title, or expected to get more money, failed to furnish their documents and threw over the affair– Browning was very vexed, and began a suit at law to compel performance, and would undoubtedly have succeeded, but finally became convinced of what was the general opinion in Venice—that the best thing he could do was to drop the suit and give up the palace. Which he did.

1. This quotation from Carlyle's satirical work was an afterthought, squeezed in the top margin of the page. Curtis also added a cover sheet to his manuscript which reads: "All the notes which I have recorded of M.ʳ Browning's remarks, reminiscences, and opinions were taken down at once, on the day on which he made them, and while his *exact words* were fresh in my memory." This appendix has been transcribed from the manuscript, now in the Armstrong Browning Library.

2. William Wetmore Story (1819–1895), American sculptor, and his wife, Emelyn, became close friends of Robert and Elizabeth Barrett Browning in Florence. The Storys made Rome their home in 1856 (*BAF*, p. 3).

3. See Letter 5, n. 7.

4. See Letter 2, n. 8.

5. See Letter 2, n. 4.

6. Actually Maria S. Porter of Boston. Curtis added her name to the text at a later time (see *Reconstruction*, E398 and E488).

7. See Letter 9, n. 1.

8. Thomas Carlyle (1795–1881), essayist and historian, was a friend of Browning's for over forty years. Although Carlyle found *Sordello* difficult to understand, by 1849 he considered Browning "one of the few from whom it was possible to expect something" (Griffin, p. 135). Browning lent Carlyle a book and letters when Carlyle was editing the letters of Oliver Cromwell (1845) and later accompanied him to Paris in 1851. After Elizabeth's death and his return to London, Browning saw Carlyle regularly at home in Cheyne Row. In 1877 he dedicated his translation of *Agamemnon* to him.

9. Jane Baillie Carlyle (1801–1866) was born at Haddington, Scotland, the daughter of a doctor, John Welsh. She married Carlyle at Templand on 17 October 1826. Mrs. Carlyle disliked Browning intensely and hadn't a good word to say about him. See Miller, pp. 55–57. The dislike was clearly mutual.

10. Jane Carlyle met Charlotte Williams Wynn at Addiscombe, and their friendship continued until Mrs. Carlyle's death.

11. At this point, Curtis has inserted: "Who is to read this? What is the use of it? You wouldn't print it? burn it."

12. Drs. Quain and Blakiston treated Mrs. Carlyle for neuralgia in 1863.

13. Browning returned from his first visit to Italy in July 1838; but according to Mrs. Orr, RB met John Kenyon in 1839 at a dinner given by Serjeant Talfourd. John Kenyon had long been a friend of the family and introduced Browning to Elizabeth Barrett.

14. 4 December.

15. Hermann Grimm's *Leben Michelangelos* published in Berlin in 1860–63 and translated into English by F.E. Bunnett in 1865. This was a pioneer biography of the painter, highly important in its day, but now superseded.

16. William Allingham (1824–1889), Irish poet, was editor of *Fraser's Magazine* from 1874–1879. In a letter to Mrs. Thomas FitzGerald dated 14 April 1883, Browning made a similar statement: "Allingham's name occurs neither in [Carlyle's] Will nor the Reminiscences,—if I remember as to the latter: yet for years he had been at C's beck & call—giving him two hours' daily companionship in his walk—and those out of a poor man's breadwinning time" (*LL*, p. 160).

17. James Anthony Froude (1818–1894), the English historian. As Carlyle's literary executor, he published *Reminiscences of Carlyle* (1881) and *Life of Thomas Carlyle* (1882–84). The letters and memoirs of Jane Carlyle were edited by Froude in 1883. He included "the Carlyles' biting judgments and wounding statements, offending many and causing acquaintances to look forward to future publications with apprehension" (*LL*, p. 161).

18. Carlyle died on 4 February 1881. On Browning's last visit: "He was lying on a sofa, wrapped in a shawl. I stooped over him and said a word or two, and he put an arm round my neck. That was all" (Miller, p. 58).

19. Alfred Austin (1835–1913), minor English poet, essayist and novelist, whose critical views on Browning were included in his *Poetry of the Period* (1870). Browning's *Of Pacchiarotto, and How He Worked in Distemper* was a long poem in Hudibrastic

rhymes which was an assault on contemporary critics and poets—especially Alfred Austin. In 1896 Austin succeeded Tennyson in the laureateship. See *LRB*, pp. 358–363.

20. Henry Howard Molyneux Herbert (1831–1890), statesman and fourth Earl of Carnarvon. See Letter 34.

21. Above the name of "Hogarth" (1697–1764), Curtis pencilled the name "Voltaire" (1694–1778).

22. William Cowper (1731–1800), English poet, collaborated with John Newton, a Calvinist preacher, in producing the Olney Hymns (1779). On 28 December 1883, Browning wrote to Mary Gladstone: "In common with everybody, I read while abroad Mr. Gladstone's translation of Cowper's Hymn, and noticed a prefatory remark that there existed few or no Hymns, original or translated, in Italian—so much, at least, was implied, if I remember rightly. In Venice, I attended the interesting Waldensian Service held there, and fancied Mr. Gladstone might come to look over the Hymnal in use—of which I venture to send a copy" (*NL*, pp. 295–296).

23. John Payne Collier (1789–1883), English journalist, lawyer and Shakespeare critic. His work on older English literature was brought under suspicion by a series of literary frauds.

24. The story of the man and the stag is in Browning's poem "Donald," the first long poem of the *Jocoseria* volume, 1883. (See Letter 5, n. 2.)

25. On 17 March 1817, the Lord Chancellor Eldon ruled that Percy Bysshe Shelley should not have custody of his two children (Ianthe and Charles) by Harriet Westbrook Shelley.

26. An American writer whose original name was Cincinnatus Hiner (or Heine) Miller, (1839–1913). He was led to adopt his pseudonym from having written in defense of Joaquin Murrietta, a Mexican brigand.

27. William Hurrell Mallock (1849–1923), author, nephew of J.A. Froude. He started his career as a poet by winning the Newdigate Prize at Oxford in 1871. Browning praised his early verse and enjoyed his most famous book, *The New Republic* (1877). This is a satiric country-house novel in the style of Thomas Love Peacock, in which a number of friends discuss problems of religion and society. Thanking Browning for his appreciation of *The New Republic*, Mallock wrote on 24 May 1877: "I am glad in a special way that it should have pleased you: because I attribute what success I may have attained, in a very great measure to the kind advice you gave me when you read my early poems; for it was your counsel that, as it were woke me up, from dreaming merely about seas & waves and flowers, and made me turn to men, and man's life" (*BBIS-8*, p. 72). Mallock's later books, philosophical and political treatises, such as *Social Equality* and *The Old Order Changes*, were not to Browning's taste, probably because of their Conservative bias. In his reminiscences Mallock recalls meeting Browning at a breakfast at Balliol given by Jowett: "He now held out both his hands to me with an almost boisterous cordiality. His eyes sparkled with laughter, his beard was carefully trimmed, and an air of fashion was exhaled from his dazzling white waistcoat. . . . When I quitted his presence and found myself once more in undergraduate circles I felt myself shining like Moses when he came down from the mount" (Mallock, p. 71).

28. James Spedding (1808–1881), contemporary and friend of Tennyson and Hallam at Cambridge, where he was a leading member of the "Apostles," a secret literary society and discussion group, to which Tennyson was elected in 1829. Spedding dedicated much of his life to a study of Francis Bacon, whose works he edited. He first met Browning in the 1860's, entertained him to dinner regularly and later introduced him to Mrs. FitzGerald. On 19 March 1869 Spedding sent the manuscript of Mallock's *Prometheus Vinctus* for Browning to read (*BBIS-8*, p. 44).

29. Untraced—location is not listed in *Reconstruction*.

30. See Letter 16, n. 8. Born in Venice, Pompeo Gherardo Molmenti (1852–1890) wrote, among other works, a history of Venice (see *Reconstruction*, A1628–30).

31. Roden Berkeley Wriothesley Noel (1834–1894), English poet and critic. On 17 November 1883, Noel wrote to Browning: "It gratified me to receive your kind letter of the 8th—for though I had freely expressed (in the "Contemporary") the strong

admiration I have always felt for a great deal of your work, I had also freely expressed certain drawbacks to the enjoyment of it, which I have felt too. That this frankness has not annoyed you I am extremely glad to know from yourself; but you will have recognized all through the genuine warmth of my appreciation, & *gratitude* to you" (ABL). Noel's essay on Browning was reprinted in his *Essays on Poetry and Poets*, London, 1886.

32. See Letter 38, n. 2.

33. An English judge and author, Thomas Noon Talfourd (1795–1854), wrote *Life and Letters of Lamb* (1837) and *Final Memorials of Charles Lamb* (1849–50), as well as a number of plays, including the popular *Ion* (1835).

34. Rachel Rutt, eldest daughter of John Towill Rutt, married Talfourd in 1822.

35. Talfourd died suddenly of apoplexy during the performance of his judicial duties on 13 March 1854.

36. Wilkins Micawber, one of the principal characters in Charles Dickens's *David Copperfield*, was suggested by Dickens's own father, who was often in and out of debt.

37. Henry Crabb Robinson (1775–1867), lawyer and man of letters. Called to the Bar in 1813, he retired in 1828 with £500 a year. He helped to found London University and was a leading nonconformist and Liberal thinker. Browning knew Robinson as early as 1836 (when they were both present at the famous dinner-party at Talfourd's to celebrate the first performance of *Ion*), and they met occasionally in the next thirty years. Robinson corresponded with Elizabeth Barrett in 1843 and was introduced to her later by John Kenyon.

38. Henrietta Barrett (1809–1860), third of the twelve Barrett children, married William Surtees Cook (later Altham) in 1850. In January 1855 the couple spent three weeks in London, prior to Surtees' reporting for duty at Plymouth—though they never left England.

39. Curtis inserted in pencil, "the original of 'A Portrait.'" This poem was written by Elizabeth Barrett Browning and was dedicated to Elizabeth Georgina (Lizzie) Barrett, a cousin, who married Alfred Barrett in 1855.

40. Curtis (or Browning) has the details the wrong way round. Browning went to Russia in 1834 and made his first visit to Italy in 1838.

41. Friedrich Max Müller (1823–1900), a German English Sanskrit scholar and comparative philologist, settled in Oxford in 1850. He was the curator of the Bodleian Library, 1856–63 and 1881–94.

42. See Letter 12, n. 1.

43. Sir William Henry Gregory (1817–1892), once Governor of Ceylon, was appointed as a trustee of the National Gallery in 1867. He retained this post until his death. He married Isabella Augusta Persse, the poet and dramatist, in 1880. The Gregorys were close friends of the Layards and the Curtises.

44. A friend of Mrs. Bronson's, William Money Hardinge.

45. See Letter 2, n. 3. The sisters were Olga, Magdalen and Judy Kerr.

46. "So if you want not to weep, you must weep."

47. An approximate quotation from "One Word More," line 185.

48. "Youth and Art," first published in *Dramatis Personae* in 1864.

49. See Letter 41, n. 1.

50. Curtis probably alludes to Browning's "Master Hugues of Saxe-Gotha," although it could as equally refer to "A Toccata of Galuppi's."

51. Giuseppe Mazzini (1805–1872), an Italian patriot and revolutionary, who was introduced to Robert and Elizabeth Barrett Browning by Mrs. Carlyle in 1852. He translated Browning's poem "The Italian in England" into Italian.

52. Curtis added in pencil, "It is in 2 of his poems." The exact line, "Artistry's haunting curse—the Incomplete," is found in *The Ring and the Book*, book XI (published in 1869) and "Beatrice Signorini," in *Asolando* (1889).

53. EBB's plan appears in *Reconstruction*, plate 4.

54. Richard Morris Hunt (1827–1895), American architect, is best known for his masterpiece, the William K. Vanderbilt house, begun in 1878. He was also responsible

for the main portion of the Metropolitan Museum of Art in New York, the National Observatory in Washington, and the base of the Statue of Liberty in New York Harbor (1886).

55. This satirical poem by Samuel Butler (1612–1680) was so called from the name of the hero and employed the mock-heroic metre.

56. The "Jewish lady" was Emily Marion Harris (d. 1900). Mrs. Thomas FitzGerald introduced Browning to Miss Harris and their correspondence and friendship continued from 1883 until his death.

57. Presumably interrupted here, Curtis did not complete the entry.

58. Antonio Baschiera, the lawyer in Venice who handled Browning's legal affairs pertaining to the purchase of the Manzoni Palace.

59. Untraced. Possibly the crayon portrait that sold in the *Browning Collections* as part of lot 95* (see *Reconstruction*, H59).

60. A tic of the facial muscles with severe neuralgic pains.

61. See Letter 15, n. 4. Don Carlos lived at Palazzo Loredan, opposite Palazzo Barbaro.

62. See Letter 15, n. 7.

63. Horatio Robert Forbes Brown (1854–1926) and his mother arrived in Venice in 1879 after a short stay in Florence. They took an apartment on the Grand Canal, in the Palazzo Balbi-Valier, but before long moved to the Zattere. After the death of Rawdon Brown in 1883, Horatio Brown (no relation) was appointed to carry on the task of completing the calendars of Venetian state papers. He published an important autobiography and wrote extensively on Venetian matters.

64. See Letter 2, n. 11.

65. Gisella, daughter of Augustin de Iturbide (1783–1824) who was Emperor Augustin I of Mexico from May 1822 to March 1823.

66. Clumsiness; dullness; awkwardness.

APPENDIX D

The 1842 text of "In a Gondola"

Browning first published "In a Gondola" in *Dramatic Lyrics* (1842). By 1849 he had revised the text, sophisticated the punctuation, and simplified the meaning by adding stage directions, thus converting the poem into a dramatic scene—the version we now know. The 1842 text, more intense and more confused, better conveys the impact Venice made on Browning in 1838 and, for that reason, is reprinted below.

IN A GONDOLA.
——

I.

I send my heart up to thee, all my heart
  In this my singing!
For the stars help me, and the sea bears part;
  The very night is clinging
Closer to Venice' streets to leave one space
  Above me, whence thy face
May light my joyous heart to thee its dwelling-
     place.

II.

Say after me, and try to say
My words as if each word
Came from you of your own accord,
In your own voice, in your own way:
*This woman's heart, and soul, and brain
Are mine as much as this gold chain
She bids me wear; which* (say again)
*I choose to make by cherishing
A precious thing, or choose to fling
Over the boat-side, ring by ring;*
And yet once more say ... no word more!
Since words are only words. Give o'er!
Unless you call me, all the same,
Familiarly by my pet-name
Which if the Three should hear you call
And me reply to, would proclaim
At once our secret to them all:
Ask of me, too, command me, blame—
Do break down the partition-wall
'Twixt us the daylight world beholds
Curtained in dusk and splendid folds.

III.

What's left but—all of me to take?
I am the Three's, prevent them, slake
Your thirst! 'Tis said the Arab sage
In practising with gems can loose
Their subtle spirit in his cruce
And leave but ashes: so, sweet mage,
Leave them my ashes when thy use
Sucks out my soul, thy heritage!

IV.
1.

Past we glide, and past, and past!
  What's that poor Agnese doing
Where they make the shutters fast?
  Grey Zanobi's just a-wooing
To his couch the purchased bride:
  Past we glide!
2.

Past we glide, and past, and past!
  Why's the Pucci Palace flaring
Like a beacon to the blast?
  Guests by hundreds—not one caring
If the dear host's neck were wried:
  Past we glide!

V.
1.

The Moth's kiss, first!
Kiss me as if you made believe
You were not sure this eve,
How my face, your flower, had pursed
Its petals up; so here and there
Brush it, till I grow aware
Who wants me, and wide ope I burst.

[181]

2.

The Bee's kiss, now!
Kiss me as if you entered gay
My heart at some noonday,
A bud that dares not disallow
The claim, so all is rendered up,
And passively its shattered cup
Over your head to sleep I bow.

VI.
1.

What are we two?
I am a Jew,
And carry thee, farther than friends can pursue,
To a feast of our tribe,
Where they need thee to bribe
The devil that blasts them unless he imbibe
Thy . . . Shatter the vision for ever! And now,
As of old, I am I, Thou art Thou!

2.

But again, what we are?
The sprite of a star,
I lure thee above where the Destinies bar
My plumes their full play
Till a ruddier ray
Than my pale one announce there is withering
      away
Some . . . Scatter the vision for ever! And now,
As of old, I am I, Thou art Thou!

VII.

Oh, which were best, to roam or rest?
The land's lap or the water's breast?
To sleep on yellow millet-sheaves,
Or swim in lucid shallows, just
Eluding water-lily leaves,
An inch from Death's black fingers, thrust
To lock you, whom release he must;
Which life were best on Summer eves?

VIII.

Lie back; could I improve you?
From this shoulder let there spring
A wing; from this, another wing;
Wings, not legs and feet, shall move you!
Snow-white must they spring, to blend
With your flesh, but I intend
They shall deepen to the end,
Broader, into burning gold,
Till both wings crescent-wise enfold
Your perfect self, from 'neath your feet
To o'er your head, where, lo, they meet
As if a million sword-blades hurled
Defiance from you to the world!

Rescue me thou, the only real!
And scare away this mad Ideal

That came, nor motions to depart!
Thanks! Now, stay ever as thou art!

IX.
1.

He and the Couple catch at last
Thy serenader; while there's cast
Paul's cloak about my head, and fast
Gian pinions me, Himself has past
His stylet thro' my back; I reel;
And . . . is it Thee I feel?

2.

They trail me, do these godless knaves,
Past every church that sains and saves,
Nor stop till, where the cold sea raves
By Lido's wet accursed graves,
They scoop mine, roll me to its brink,
And . . . on Thy breast I sink!

X.

Dip your arm o'er the boat-side elbow-deep
As I do: thus: were Death so unlike Sleep
Caught this way? Death's to fear from flame or
      steel
Or poison doubtless, but from water—feel!

Go find the bottom! Would you stay me? There!
Now pluck a great blade of that ribbon-grass
To plait in where the foolish jewel was,
I flung away: since you have praised my hair
'Tis proper to be choice in what I wear.

XI.

Must we, must we Home? Too surely
Know I where its front's demurely
Over the Giudecca piled;
Window just with window mating,
Door on door exactly waiting,
All's the set face of a child:
But behind it, where's a trace
Of the staidness and reserve,
Formal lines without a curve,
In the same child's playing-face?
No two windows look one way
O'er the small sea-water thread
Below them. Ah, the autumn day
I, passing, saw you overhead!
First out a cloud of curtain blew,
Then, a sweet cry, and last came you—
To catch your loory that must needs
Escape just then, of all times then,
To peck a tall plant's fleecy seeds,
And make me happiest of men.
I scarce could breathe to see you reach
So far back o'er the balcony,
To catch him ere he climbed too high
Above you in the Smyrna peach,
That quick the round smooth cord of gold,

This coiled hair on your head, unrolled,
Fell down you like a gorgeous snake
The Roman girls were wont, of old
When Rome there was, for coolness' sake
To place within their bosoms.
Dear loory, may his beak retain
Ever its delicate rose stain
As if the wounded lotus-blossoms
Marked their thief to know again!

XII.

Stay longer yet, for others' sake
Than mine! what should your chamber do?
—With all its rarities that ache
In silence while day lasts, but wake
At night-time and their life renew,
Suspended just to pleasure you
That brought reluctantly together
These objects and, while day lasts, weave
Round them such a magic tether
That dumb they look: your harp, believe,
With all the sensitive tight strings
That dare not speak, now to itself
Breathes slumbrously as if some elf
Went in and out tall chords his wings
Get murmurs from whene'er they graze,
As may an angel thro' the maze
Of pillars on God's quest have gone
At guilty glorious Babylon.
And while such murmurs flow, the nymph
Bends o'er the harp-top from her shell,
As the dry limpet for the lymph
Come with a tune he knows so well.
And how the statues' hearts must swell!
And how the pictures must descend
To see each other, friend with friend!
Oh, could you take them by surprise,
You'd find Schidone's eager Duke
Doing the quaintest courtesies
To that prim Saint by Haste-thee-Luke:
And deeper into her rock den
Bold Castelfranco's Magdalen
You'd find retreated from the ken
Of that robed counsel-keeping Ser—
As if the Tizian thinks of her!
As if he is not rather bent
On trying for himself what toys
Are these his progeny invent,

What litter now the board employs
Whereon he signed a document
That got him murdered! Each enjoys
Its night so well, you cannot break
The sport up, so, for others' sake
Than mine, your stay must longer make!

XIII.
1.

To-morrow, if a harp-string, say,
Is used to tie the jasmine back
That overfloods my room with sweets,
Be sure that Zorzi somehow meets
My Zanze: if the ribbon's black
I use, they're watching; keep away.

2.

Your gondola—let Zorzi wreathe
A mesh of water-weeds about
Its prow, as if he unaware
Had struck some quay or bridge-foot stair;
That I may throw a paper out
As you and he go underneath.

XIV.

There's Zanze's vigilant taper; safe are we!
Only one minute more to-night with me!
Resume your past self of a month ago!
Be you the bashful gallant, I will be
The lady with the colder breast than snow:
Now bow you, as becomes, nor touch my hand
More than I touch yours when I step to land,
And say, All thanks, Siora . . .
                            Heart to heart,
And lips to lips! Once, ere we part,
Make me thine as mine thou art!

XV.

It was to be so, Sweet, and best
Comes 'neath thine eyes, and on thy breast.
Still kiss me! Care not for the cowards! Care
Only to put aside thy beauteous hair
My blood will hurt. The Three I do not scorn
To death, because they never lived: but I
Have lived indeed, and so—(yet one more
kiss)—
        can die.
        ____

Index

Index